The World in a Selfie

The World in a Selfie

An Inquiry into the Tourist Age

Marco D'Eramo

VERSO

London • New York

This English-language edition first published by Verso 2021
First published as *Il selfie del mondo*
© Feltrinelli 2017
Translation © Bethan Bowett-Jones and David Broder 2021
An earlier version of Chapter 8 appeared as 'UNESCOcide',
in *New Left Review*, no. 88, July–August 2014.

1 3 5 7 9 10 8 6 4 2

Verso
UK: 6 Meard Street, London W1F 0EG
US: 20 Jay Street, Suite 1010, Brooklyn, NY 11201
versobooks.com

Verso is the imprint of New Left Books

ISBN-13: 978-1-78873-107-2
ISBN-13: 978-1-78873-110-2 (US EBK)
ISBN-13: 978-1-78873-109-6 (UK EBK)

British Library Cataloguing in Publication Data
A catalogue record for this book is available from the British Library

Library of Congress Cataloging-in-Publication Data

Names: D'Eramo, Marco, 1947– author.
Title: The world in a selfie : an inquiry into the tourist age / Marco
  D'Eramo ; translated by Bethan Bowett-Jones and David Broder.
Other titles: Il selfie del mondo. English
Description: First English-language Edition Hardback. | Brooklyn : Verso is
  the imprint of New Left Books, 2021. | Series: Campi del sapere | First
  published: Milano : Feltrinelli, 2017, under title Il selfie del mondo.
  | Includes bibliographical references and index. | Summary: 'The World
  in a Selfie offers a spirited critique of the cultural politics of a
  tourist age. Tourism is not just the most important industry of our
  century, generating huge waves of people and capital, calling forth a
  dedicated infrastructure, and upsetting and repurposing the architecture
  and topography of our cities. It also encapsulates the problem of
  modernity: the search for authenticity in a world of ersatz pleasures' –
  Provided by publisher.
Identifiers: LCCN 2020045101 (print) | LCCN 2020045102 (ebook) | ISBN
  9781788731072 (Hardback) | ISBN 9781788731102 (eBook)
Subjects: LCSH: Tourism – Social aspects. | Tourism.
Classification: LCC G156.5.S63 D4713 2021 (print) | LCC G156.5.S63
  (ebook) | DDC 306.4/819 – dc23
LC record available at https://lccn.loc.gov/2020045101
LC ebook record available at https://lccn.loc.gov/2020045102

Typeset in Sabon by MJ & N Gavan, Truro, Cornwall
Printed and bound by CPI Group (UK) Ltd, Croydon, CR0 4YY

Contents

1

Tourism in a Time of Cholera

April 2020, a metropolis of your choice: Paris, New York, London, Barcelona, Berlin, San Francisco, Rome, Moscow. Your city is a metaphysical painting by de Chirico. It is deserted, streets empty, monuments and skyscrapers petrified, stripped naked by the absence of traffic, buses, pedestrians. We, the inhabitants, locked up in our homes, visit it on TV screens, on monitors, on mobile phones. How much would we give to experience it in person! To walk it in solitude, to feel it, to imbibe it in silence.

But we can't. We are confined to our homes by the coronavirus pandemic, all of us longing for the city out there, a city finally 'restored', 'like we've never seen it before'.

This was the common experience of urban residents over much of the planet. It was a fleeting experience, soon to be forgotten. But in those months it seemed irreversible to the citizens of half the world.

Even locked in our homes, the gaze we turned on our own cities was touristic, for the city that flashed onto our screens in our confinement fulfilled the dream of every tourist – a place without other tourists, which is to say: without ourselves. The cities emptied by the virus were analogous to the pristine Caribbean beaches of the travel brochures. And yet, they are unreachable, because the moment we the confined are able to dive into the city again, it will immediately be degraded by traffic jams, crowds and our very presence.

Until then, the vast conurbations emptied by the virus are dead cities, non-cities. The shutters are closed, the meeting rooms silent, all interactions cancelled. Only the homeless occupy the sidewalks, sleeping even during the day. There is a sense of abandonment, as if some Pied Piper had taken all the residents with him.

The virus has emptied the city in the exact same way tourism usually does, when in summer the streets are abandoned by native residents fleeing to distant shores. There is an uncanny similarity between the emptiness of the tourist city and the city the virus has emptied of tourists. It shows how deeply touristic our very idea of the city is, how deeply rooted it is in our very core, how inseparable it is from our experience of urbanity.

No previous civilisation, from any century or any part of the globe, has ever known anything that could be described as a 'tourist city'. It is a novelty peculiar to modernity – or should that be, postmodernity?

Tourism belongs to that category of social phenomena, like sport or advertising, that are omnipresent, familiar, yet seldom truly explored in depth. And as with the study of sport or advertising, the bibliography of tourism studies is endless, yet finding new ideas is like looking for a needle in a haystack. Original contributions to the field can be counted on the fingers of one hand.

But tourism is even more important than sport or advertising – so much so that we could quite plausibly term the current era 'the Age of Tourism', in the same way that we used to speak of the Age of Steel or the Age of Imperialism. Here we come to a paradox. Tourism trades in an intangible commodity; it belongs to the experience economy. The tourist is awestruck by the immensity of the Grand Canyon, by Machu Picchu at first light, by the Acropolis of Athens. But to retail such wish-fulfilments, tourism sets in motion a very prosaic infrastructure: airports and planes, railway stations and trains, hotels and food wholesalers, telecommunications and IT networks.

We are used to thinking of 'real industry' as mining, steel manufacturing, ship and car building – in short, in terms of coal, electricity and steel – and so we view tourism as a kind of postmodern frill, as superstructural rather than foundational. But the truth is that tourism is the most important industry of the century.

When I presented this thesis three years ago in the first Italian edition of the book you have in your hands, I was looked at indulgently, as one who likes to exaggerate, who has a weakness for catchphrases. It is depressing that the most compelling evidence of this thesis had to be provided by a tiny virus, when the proof was already right there in front of our eyes.

Why hadn't tourism's importance fully registered before the Covid-19 pandemic and the lockdowns? Because tourists themselves are hard to take seriously. They are often comically dressed, literally out of place, walking in mountain boots in the middle of the city, wearing ridiculous baseball caps alongside businesspeople in suits. It's hard to take tourists seriously.

And yet the tourism industry was worth 8,800 billion US dollars in 2018 (10.4 per cent of global GDP, or one and a half times the GDP of Japan, the third largest economy on the planet) and supported 319 million jobs (10 per cent of global employment).[1]

Within these overall figures, international tourism actually counts for less than its domestic counterpart. In 2016, New York had 13 million visitors from abroad, while 48 million arrived from within the United States.[2] France makes more than twice as much from domestic tourism (108 billion euros) as from foreign tourism (51 billion euros in 2016), despite being the world's top destination for foreign tourism (there were 83 million foreign visitors to France in 2016 compared to 76 million to the USA, 75 million to Spain, 59 million to China and 52 million to Italy).[3]

It would be difficult to overestimate tourism's impact on individual national economies. In Spain, it accounts for 14.9 per cent of GDP and 15.1 per cent of total employment, while in Italy the figures are 13 per cent and 14.7 per cent respectively. London, the financial capital of the world, didn't suffer as much as it might have in the global financial crisis of 2008–9. That's because the fall in the British pound attracted a rise in tourism from abroad, making up for the losses of jobs and revenue in the City's financial sector.

Then we have the souvenir industry, the postcard industry, the tourist guide industry, the maps industry, and so on – not to mention other, less respectable industries that survive purely thanks to tourism. There exists a galaxy of institutions and businesses (travel agencies, hotel chains, publishers of tourist guides, *pro loco* agencies or local tourist information offices, advertising agencies, specialist banking services that flog loans to finance holidays, estate agents, the mock Gladiators who charge for photos in front of the Colosseum – the list goes on and on), which Stephen Britton has referred to as the 'tourism production system'.[4]

In fact, as well as these direct earnings from tourism, we also have to take into account the secondary beneficiaries – further up and further downstream. As well as the hotel industry and almost all of the restaurant industry, we also need to count the earnings for tourist transport. For example, in 2015 the turnover for international air travel amounted to 727 billion US dollars.[5] To this sum, which can quite comfortably be filed under the title of 'tourism', we also must add others such as the aircraft and airport industries, which mainly operate for the benefit of tourists, as well as the cruise ship and yacht-building industries. The pandemic has proved the centrality of tourism through tourism's omission. Once this industry ceased, not only airlines and shipping companies but aircraft manufacturers and shipyards found themselves on the verge of bankruptcy.

Tourism also feeds a large chunk of the car industry, the construction industry (through second homes, hotels and tourist villages) as well as road construction (and consequently cement production, steelworks and other metal manufacturing).

Of course, construction did not emerge as an industry in order to serve tourism (it predates it by some thousands of years), but it would be interesting to know how many fewer buildings would be built if it were not for tourism. To get a sense of the vast dimensions of real estate speculation related to tourism, we need only visit the Andalusian coast, with its horrendous series of concrete apartment blocks, or wander Aegean Turkey's endless succession of squalid and mostly empty developments awaiting buyers, usually Turkish emigrants from Germany. And as we have seen, the aircraft industry is conceptually independent of tourism, but we should then ask ourselves how many fewer flights there would be were it not for tourism. It would be interesting, in other words, to draw up tourism's Leontief matrix of input versus output.

Once again, the proof that tourism is the *sine qua non* of all other sectors was provided when we had to close it down, shutting ports, airports, hotels, restaurants: the whole world economy stopped. And when governments wanted to restart the economy, the first measure they took was to revive tourism, even at the cost of reinvigorating the pandemic, of 'trading human lives for the Dow Jones', so much was at stake.[6]

Precisely because it involves such considerable infrastructure, tourism is the planet's single most polluting industry. According to the World Tourism Organization, air travel for tourism produces 8 per cent of total carbon dioxide emissions.[7] The gravity of the problem is such that there is ever more discussion of the concept of 'sustainable tourism', a term as oxymoronic as 'sustainable development'.

Take, for example, the case of winter tourism: to ski down a snow-covered mountain is to partake in one of the most graceful sports, and all it requires is the pure force of gravity and the use of the planet's contours. Yet in order to achieve this almost immaterial elegance, it is also necessary to build imposing ski lifts, chairlifts and cable cars. Snow cannons are needed because, even with constant snowfall, skiing erodes the snow on the slopes – 'natural' snow on its own would never suffice, and that's even before we consider the effects of climate change. Then there are the roads that cut across valleys to reach the ski resorts, and the buildings that spread like weeds across the countryside. Land that would once have lain deserted and silent over the winter is transformed into a metropolitan hive inhabited by thousands of people who use electricity, public services, water and other supplies, leaving their mark on the local climate and landscape. Walking through the mountains in summer, one can see for oneself the devastation produced by these winter pursuits.

We have been living through the Age of Tourism, and not only because of its economic importance. There are political connotations, too. It was during this age that, for the first time in human history, the demand for tourism triggered the collapse of a great empire. Few remember it now, but the chain of events that led to the fall of the Berlin Wall was sparked in August 1989 by the Hungarian authorities' decision to open the border to Austria, allowing 13,000 East German tourists to cross. The East German government reacted by closing its border with Hungary, at which point thousands of tourist visa applications were immediately presented to the Polish and Czechoslovak embassies, as people tried to bypass the restrictions by reaching Budapest via Prague or Warsaw. Eventually, on 9 November, the government, faced with hundreds of thousands of citizens waiting in front of the Wall, granted them permission to travel to the West. This rendered irreversible the process that less than two years later would result in the fall of the Soviet Union. Only fifty years earlier it would have been unthinkable for an empire endowed with nuclear weapons and an enormous military apparatus to be forced into humiliating surrender by a demand for visas.

The very real connection between tourism and political upheaval is also evident in the contemporary phenomenon of terrorism aimed specifically at tourism. This takes two guises. Firstly, it targets tourists themselves. Such was the case in Luxor, Egypt, on 17 November 1997, when sixty-two people, including fifty-eight tourists, were killed close to the tomb of Hatshepsut; in Bali, Indonesia, on 12 October 2002, when 202 people (164 of them tourists) were killed by a bomb in Paddy's Pub; in the Bardo National Museum, Tunisia, on 18 March 2015, when an attack killed twenty-four people, twenty-one of whom were tourists; in the Egyptian resort of Sharm el-Sheikh on 31 October 2015, when a Russian air charter was blown up, killing 224 tourists and crew members; in Sultanahmet, Istanbul, close to the Blue Mosque, on 12 January 2016, when a suicide attack in the heart of the main tourist district killed ten people, all of them tourists; or in the Barcelona attacks of 17 August 2017 that left 16 dead and 130 injured.*

---

* Nothing better illustrates the global and planetary dimension of contemporary tourism as the sheer number of nationalities among those killed and injured

Tourist terrorism also destroys visitor attractions, such as monuments, temples, ruins and castles. For example, the two Bamiyan Buddhas of Afghanistan, blown up by the Taliban in 2001; the minaret of the Great Mosque of Samarra, Iraq, flattened in 2005; the necropolis at Cyrene in Libya, destroyed in 2011; the ancient houses and shrine of Timbuktu in Mali, reduced to rubble in 2012; and then a series of incidents in 2015, representing a decisive acceleration, with the damaging of the Roman Amphitheatre of Bosra and the ancient city of Palmyra in Syria, the castle at Baraqish in Yemen, and the splendid Assyrian ruins of Nimrud and Hatra in Iraq. In January 2017, yet another case occurred in Palmyra when an amphitheatre was blown up. Tourist attractions are seen as an enemy because they have symbolic value: they are emblematic of the values being fought against. But they are also attacked as a means of depriving the enemy of economic resources, representing as they do ever more important sources of income.

It is a common belief that there is nothing more apolitical than tourism, perhaps because we confuse tourism with tourists. But just as any industry is determined by an industrial policy, so tourism is conditioned by the tourism policy of a particular country. Not only that, but the survival of a political regime may depend on tourism, or on its absence. Tourism is the (apparently apolitical) form that protest can take against a regime until it collapses; tourism can be both the object, the stakes and the target of political struggle, even armed struggle. In short, it has a sly, hidden, but persistent and ultimately cumbersome political dimension.

---

in the Barcelona attacks: Algerian, American, Argentinian, Australian, Austrian, Belgian, British, Canadian, Chinese, Colombian, Dominican, Dutch, Ecuadorian, Egyptian, Filipino, French, German, Greek, Honduran, Hungarian, Irish, Italian, Kuwaiti, Macedonian, Mauritanian, Moroccan, Pakistani, Peruvian, Romanian, Spanish, Taiwanese, Turkish and Venezuelan.

2

The Leisure Revolution

Tourism, in the modern sense of the term, was an invention of the nineteenth century and boomed in the century that followed. It owed its birth to two revolutions, one technical and one social. A revolution in transport and communications (railways, steam navigation and the telegraph) made *travel* possible and relatively inexpensive, while paid holidays and the pensions of retirees led to a boom in leisure pursuits, thus creating *travellers*. Only when both of these revolutions reached their climax in the second half of the twentieth century did ours become a true tourist civilisation.

The nineteenth century saw the appearance of the first travel agency, Thomas Cook. The eponymous founder, a temperance campaigner and Baptist missionary, put together the first organised excursion (1841), the first group trip (1845) and the first organised trip around the world (1872), which lasted 222 days and cost 200 guineas; he also invented what would become the traveller's cheque.[1] The tourist guide industry was born during the same period, with the names of well-known publishers like the German Karl Baedeker becoming synonymous with 'guidebooks'. Other travel companions, like those produced by the Englishman John Murray III (whose father, John Murray II, coined the term 'handbook' for his son's publications and notably published Lord Byron), were also widely celebrated. The Murray guides were the first to introduce the asterisk to indicate sites of particular interest.[2]

From the outset, new means of transport offered ever wider sections of the population the opportunity to travel. This, however, began to give rise to fears that travelling as a pastime would be spoilt. In the August 1848 issue of *Blackwood's Edinburgh Magazine*, an article titled 'Modern Tourism' opens with the following statement:

> The merits of the railroad and the steam-boat have been prodigiously vaunted, and we have no desire to depreciate the advantages of either. No doubt they carry us from town to town with greater rapidity than our fathers ever dreamt of … No doubt they are convenient for the visitor who desires to reach America in a fortnight … But, they have afflicted our generation with one desperate evil; they have covered Europe with Tourists.[3]

Rail travel, wrote John Ruskin in 1849, 'transmutes a man from a traveller into a living parcel', as the passenger 'hardly knows the names of the principal cities through which he passes, and only recognises them, if at all, by the steeples of the best-known cathedrals which appear like trees by some faraway road.' The metaphor of the tourist as parcel came to have great currency in the years that followed.[4]

And, indeed, the distinction between the 'traveller' and the 'tourist' – with the first characterised by positive connotations and the second negative – dates back to this period. In 1871, the Reverend Robert Kilvert wrote in his diary: 'if there is one thing more hateful than another it is being told what to admire and having objects pointed out to one with a stick. Of all noxious animals too the most noxious is a tourist.'[5] It is a characterisation so successful that we still speak today of 'herds of tourists'. And indeed, in France the expression was coined, not unsurprisingly, by the same Arthur de Gobineau whose *Essai sur l'inégalité des races humaines* is considered the primogenitor of race theory: '[A]board the ship … were to be found a big herd of those excellent animals that fashion expels from their sties every spring, driving them, as they say, to voyage in the Orient'.[6] But as Daniel Boorstin points out, the metaphor had already been used in 1865 by an Englishman who described the tourists that thronged the Italian cities as 'droves, herds, flocks' and compared the guide to a sheepdog.[7] Disdain of this sort was commonplace in the ersatz aristocratic posture of the English middle classes. This was neatly portrayed by Evelyn Waugh in 1930 when he wrote, 'Every Englishman abroad, until it is proved to the contrary, likes to consider himself a traveller and not a tourist.'[8]

The root of this stigmatisation lies in a social mechanism that Pierre Bourdieu frequently referred to in his sociology seminars. According to Bourdieu, the class struggle often manifests itself in the form of one class catching up with another (*rattrapage*) over time. So where, for example, secondary and then higher education was initially only available to the ruling class, over time it was extended to the comfortably off and finally became 'compulsory' for all, and its duration continues to increase. Another case is car buying; reserved at first for only a select minority, then extended to almost the entire population. And the same goes for holidays. However, in the passage from the privileges of the few to a majority social practice, each of these social 'conquests', each of these *rattrapages*, changes in sign and value. In the Italian case, a diploma from a *liceo classico* (classical grammar school) once represented the ticket for entry into the ruling class (for instance, in the conscript army only those Italians who had a diploma in classics could take the training course to be an officer), but with the advent of mass education, not even a university degree can offer this guarantee. This catching up provokes what Pierre Bourdieu called the devaluation of school certificates (as a result of inflation).[9] Indeed the same rule applies to every social practice: as it spreads among the 'masses' it becomes progressively devalued in terms of how it is generally considered. As Bourdieu wrote:

The dialectic of downclassing and upclassing which underlies a
whole set of social processes presupposes and entails that all the
groups concerned run in the same direction, toward the same
objectives, the same properties, those which are designated by
the leading group and which, by definition, are unavailable to the
groups following, since, whatever these properties may be intrinsically, they are modified and qualified by their distinctive rarity and
will no longer be what they are once they are multiplied and made
available to groups lower down. [10]

Thus, according to this dynamic, 'summering' becomes 'annual
leave'. The stages of the traveller's growing contempt for the tourist
correspond to the spread of the practice of leisure travel from the
aristocracy to the bourgeoisie (nineteenth century), and then from
the bourgeoisie to the proletariat (twentieth century). As early as
1903, Alexander Innes Shand wrote in his *Old-Time Travel: Personal Reminiscences of the Continent Forty Years Ago Compared
with Experiences of the Present Day*, of his memories of travels
some half a century past: 'in those days tourists were compara-
tively rare, and there were no cheap trippers'. And he reserved
an even harsher judgement for the present state of the famous
Swiss resorts: 'The Playground of Europe has been swamped with
sightseers and the sanctuaries where Chaos and Old Night once
reigned supreme have been desecrated and vulgarised'.[11]

It was, though, at the end of the sixteenth century that travel
for the purposes of 'pleasure and education' first began to be
prescribed (and reserved) to the new generations of the nobility.
This trip abroad, which came to be known as the Grand Tour,
required that the young man in question learn the languages of
the countries he was to visit and that he be accompanied by a
tutor, already familiar with the intended destinations, who would
oversee his progress. Francis Bacon tells us this much in his two-
page essay 'Of Travel' (1625). Reading Bacon's suggestions to
Grand Tour–goers, we have no trouble discerning the social class
of his intended reader:

The things to be seen and observed are: the courts of princes, especially when they give audience to ambassadors; the courts of justice, while they sit and hear causes; and so of consistories ecclesiastic; the churches and monasteries, with the monuments which are therein extant; the walls and fortifications of cities, and towns, and so the heavens and harbours; antiquities and ruins; libraries; colleges, disputations, and lectures, where any are; shipping and navies; houses and gardens of state and pleasure, near great cities; armouries; arsenals; magazines; exchanges; burses; warehouses; exercises of horsemanship, fencing, training of soldiers, and the like; comedies, such whereunto the better sort of persons do resort; treasuries of jewels and robes; cabinets and rarities; and, to conclude, whatsoever is memorable, in the places where they go. After all which, the tutors, or servants, ought to make diligent inquiry. As for triumphs, masks, feasts, weddings, funerals, capital executions, and such shows, men need not to be put in mind of them; yet are they not to be neglected.[12]

By the eighteenth century the Grand Tour had become something like a duty for the noble classes. For a Piedmontese aristocrat like Count Vittorio Alfieri (1749–1803), it involved visits to Milan, Florence, Rome, then Paris, London, St. Petersburg, Spain, Portugal, Germany and Holland.[13] It had become so commonplace as to prompt jibes from Adam Smith (1723–90) in his *Wealth of Nations*:

In England it becomes every day more and more the custom to send young people to travel in foreign countries immediately upon their leaving school, and without sending them to any university. Our young people, it is said, generally return home much improved by their travels. A young man who goes abroad at seventeen or eighteen, and returns home at one and twenty, returns three or four years older than he was when he went abroad; and at that age it is very difficult not to improve a good deal in three or four years. In the course of his travels he generally acquires some knowledge of one or two foreign languages; a knowledge, however, which is seldom sufficient to enable him either to speak or write them with propriety. In other respects he commonly returns home more conceited, more unprincipled, more dissipated, and more incapable of any serious application either to study or to business than he could well have become in so short a time had he lived at home. By travelling so very young, by spending in the most frivolous dissipation the most precious years of his life, at a distance from the inspection and control of his parents and relations, every useful habit which the earlier parts of his education might have had some tendency to form in him, instead of being riveted and confirmed, is almost necessarily either weakened or effaced. Nothing but the discredit into which the universities are allowing themselves to fall could ever have brought into repute so very absurd a practice as that of travelling at this early period of life. By sending his son abroad, a father delivers himself at least for some time, from so disagreeable an object as that of a son unemployed, neglected, and going to ruin before his eyes.[14]

As harsh as this judgement may seem, Adam Smith was only the first in a long series of stern critics who damned in words a practice they themselves indulged in. Smith had in fact accepted a tutoring post with the immensely wealthy Duke of Buccleuch, purely to have the chance of accompanying his heir Henry Scott on his Grand Tour in January 1764. This opportunity allowed him to spend thirty-two months travelling the Continent and meeting the greatest economists of the time.

However, in his scathing criticism of the Grand Tour, Smith neglected one key element. When playing the society game, the player's capital (their 'stake') is not purely economic but also symbolic and social. These two forms of capital are also essential trump cards. It is for them that the ruling classes are willing to spend even without the prospect of immediate economic returns, if this represents a genuine investment in terms of transforming economic into symbolic capital. One man who understood the importance of these kinds of investments was a contemporary of Adam Smith, Samuel ('Doctor') Johnson (1709–84). This much is apparent in his statement that 'a man who has not been in Italy, is always conscious of an inferiority, from his not having seen what it is expected a man *should* see. The grand object of travelling is to see the shores of the Mediterranean.'[15]

To use Bourdieu's terminology, what Dr Johnson noted was that in the eighteenth century a visit to Italy was an indispensable component of a person's symbolic capital *comme il faut*. For whoever did not have that experience would always be in a state of 'inferiority'. Yet in turn, even making the trip would require that the traveller already have the resources (economic capital) and connections (social capital) that only a distinguished gentleman could possess.

One piece of advice repeated ad nauseam to the young scions of the aristocracy as they prepared for departure was the need to keep a sketchbook at all times, so that they could capture the sights and landscapes (whether in tempera or watercolour). Thus, travellers ended up making 'paintable-ness' a priority in deciding what to see. These are in fact the origins of the term 'picturesque', which went on to become a fundamental criterion for the tourism of the future. It is perhaps useful to note that in the almost three centuries in which the ritual of the Grand Tour took form the European publishing houses turned out copious amounts of material that could be described as tourist guides *avant la lettre*. However, there is one substantial difference between these early travel companions and the nineteenth-century Murray and Baedeker pocketbooks and the Michelin and Lonely Planet guides of the twentieth: while the guides published from the mid-eighteenth century onward (that is, after the transport revolution) described destinations (such as places to visit or monuments), those of the previous centuries provided advice on method. They were, as can be inferred from their titles, educational 'instruction' manuals for acculturation rather than guidebooks.

Such titles included *A booke called the treasure of travellers* (William Bourne, 1578), *A direction for travellers* (Justus Lipsius, 1592), *Instructions for forreine Travell* (James Howell, 1642), *Directions for Seamen bound for Voyages* (Laurence Rooke, 1665), *De L'Utilité des Voyages et l'avantage que la recherche des Antiquités procure aux savants* (Baudelot de Dairval, 1686*), General heads for the natural history of a country great or small, drawn out for the use of travellers and navigators* (Robert Boyle, 1692), *Brief Instructions for Making Observations in All Parts of the World* (John Woodward, 1696), *The Method of Inquiry into the State of Any Country* (William Petty, Marquis of Lansdowne, 1737–1805), *Essai d'instructions pour voyager utilement* (Jean Frédéric Bernard, 1715) and *Instructions for Travellers* (Josiah Tucker, 1757).[16]

This difference between the 'manuals' for the Grand Tour and the modern 'guides' gives us a clear idea of the image the authors had of their readers. The first was aimed at directing the prospective traveller's gaze toward certain objects and events, as the particular destinations were taken for granted; they explained *how* and not *where* to travel and look. In the case of the more modern guide, however, the reader is told where to go, how to get there and at what cost (for the eighteenth-century travellers that last topic would have been beyond the pale of decency, as it was supposed that the traveller was ignorant of such things). Between the manuals and the guides we see the difference between the aristocracy, who were the intended readership of the first, and the bourgeoisie, that of the second.

Here we can see first-hand the extent to which the practices of the class that led the way change in meaning and connotation when they are adopted by the classes that seek to emulate them. When, at the beginning of the nineteenth century, the emerging bourgeoisie followed the nobility in pursuing the Grand Tour, as it sought to appropriate for itself the cultural capital that this offered, the Tour was transformed, and the advice and instruction manuals for young gentlemen turned into tourist guides.

The practice is constantly adopted anew, and takes on a new guise every time. A form of the Grand Tour is still pursued in the English-speaking world: in the UK it takes the form of the gap year, the year dedicated to travelling the world between completing school and beginning university, while in New Zealand there is the Big Overseas Experience, which is longer and more often connected to post-university work experience.[17]

This dynamic of emulation, as the bourgeoisie follow the lead of the nobility, is reproduced or replicated within the bourgeoisie among its various layers. From its very origins the bourgeoisie's pursuit of noble pastimes prompted the kind of snobbery that became characteristic of subsequent centuries. In 1820, Stendhal (though not aristocratic himself) turned his nose up at the foreigners in Florence who thronged the avenues of the Cascine Park, 'blocked up with six hundred Russians or Englishmen, *Florence is nothing but a museum full of foreigners who transfer their own customs and habits there.*'*

Stendhal's attitude was one that would be replicated by countless writers and commentators. It was an attitude that consisted of the attempt to distance oneself from one's own class origins by enhancing one's own cultural capital (that is by knowing how to view and understand the objects of observation) and devaluing the cultural capital of others (on account of their incapacity to see what is in front of them, or to at least to see with understanding).

The same procedure took place again when the summer retreat and pensioned retirements, privileges for the few, gave birth to a widespread social practice with a new name and significance: the 'vacation'. In this case, however, the transformation took place only when, following fierce social conflict, paid holiday leave eventually became an almost universal right. The extension of

---

* Stendhal, *Rome, Naples et Florence* (1826), Gallimard (Folio), Paris 1987, p. 284 (emphasis added). Incidentally, as far as I am aware, Stendhal was the first author to use the term 'tourist' in the title of a book: *Mémoires d'un touriste* (1838).

paid annual leave and pensioned retirement went hand in hand with the advent of tourism. The first workers to obtain paid leave in France were army officers, followed in 1858 by civil servants (fifteen days a year, on full pay). In Germany, by as early as 1908, 66 per cent of private-sector employees had paid leave.[18] The real turning point, however, was the law approved in 1936 by the Popular Front government in France that guaranteed four weeks paid holiday to all workers and, as such, extended the practice of 'vacation' to the entire working class. Only when everyone could enjoy paid holidays did travelling become a possibility for the masses.

Gobineau's old stigmas became even more entrenched as tourism became truly a mass pastime, because the tourist remained subject to two inexorable restraints: money and time. These restraints make it impossible for the tourist to ever really relax, as the trip must be experienced *to the full*. Hence when we think of modern tourism we inevitably think of the rush, of what might be called 'hit and run' tourism. If financial constraints are obviously the biggest limits for the working class on vacation (and economic constraints also create time constraints, as every day on holiday costs money), a lack of time also affects the new ruling classes. For in contrast to the old elites, they work tirelessly. 'We scarcely realise what a unique and astonishing phenomenon a "working" upper class is' wrote Norbert Elias in *The Civilising Process*, further reflecting, 'Why submit itself to this compulsion even though it is the "ruling" class and is therefore not commanded by a superior to do so?'[19] If a busy statesman like Otto von Bismarck could spend three months of the year at his villa, today's oligarchs are proud to work fifteen hours a day, seven days a week. As a result, however, they are unable to experience the comforts of the 'traveller' and must succumb to the proletarian destiny of becoming a 'tourist'.

Nowhere are the economic constraints on tourism more visible, ostentatious and internalised than they are in the case of the camping holiday. It was with the dawn of working-class tourism that camping became a mass pastime. The first organised camp-site on record was opened in Howstrake on the Isle of Man in 1894 – only ten years later it had 1,500 tents. In 2014, 366.5 million nights were spent at the 28,806 campsites in the European Union.[20] The camper occupies the lowest rung in the scale of contempt that indelibly stains tourism in the era of its prole-tarianisation. When even industrial and factory workers become tourists, tourism itself becomes an 'industry' (the tourist industry) and falls under the category of 'mass consumption', a constitu-tive element of 'mass culture'. It is thus capable of attracting the scornful gaze of the Frankfurt School, as an instance of 'alienated consumption'.

However, tourism could never have become a really mass prac-tice were it not for two concurrent 'massifications', namely, the spread of car and air travel. Europe in the 1960s and '70s saw the arrival of 'economy cars' (and again here, we see the social stigmatisation), followed by the arrival of low-cost airlines, estab-lished definitively in the 1990s. It was at this point that tourism – and international tourism in particular – became truly a mass pastime. In this sense, the global tourist revolution is a postwar phenomenon. Between 1950 and 1992 international tourism, measured in number of arrivals, grew at an annual rate of 7.2 per cent. In the decade from 1980 to 1990, tourism grew at an annual rate of 9.2 per cent, much higher than the growth rate in world trade as a whole.[21] 'In 1951 a mere fifty thousand tourists went [to Greece], ten years later they were half a million and in 1981 five and a half million,'[22] and in 2018, one could add, they numbered 28.7 million.

Across all countries, the number of international travellers stood at 25.3 million in 1950; 69.3 million in 1960; 158.7 million in 1970; 204 million in 1980; 425 million in 1990; 753 million in 2000; 946 million in 2010 and 1.4 billion in 2018.[23] As we can see, in the first twenty years, the number more than doubled each decade, and over the last sixty-eight years the number of travel-lers has multiplied by a factor of fifty-five. In the decade between

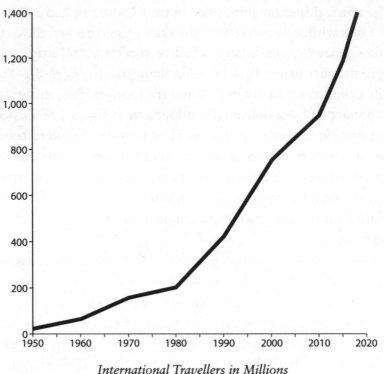

International Travellers in Millions
Source: UN World Tourism Organization

2000 and 2010, the rate of increase fell slightly to 25 per cent as a result of the September 11, 2001, terrorist attacks and then the financial crisis of 2007–2008.

With the rise of low-cost airlines, tourism was globalised. While in 1950, the top fifteen destinations accounted for 98 per cent of international arrivals, in 1970 this proportion had fallen to 75 per cent, dropping even further to 57 per cent in 2007. There can be no doubt that tourism is now global. In every normal year, one out of every seven people on the planet takes an international trip, a monstrous tide that we are all part of at some point. Put another way, there are now 1.4 billion arrivals every year. If we also include the trips made for internal tourism (the number of domestic tourists usually amounts to four times that of international tourists), we get the image of the whole of humanity in perennial, tireless flux.

In 2020, this exponential rise in travel was blocked by Covid-19. For a while tourism spared the skies a good part of the carbon emissions and chemtrails that had been released into the atmosphere the year before by 69 million flights (an average of 188,901 flights per day).[24] Many hoped that the moratorium permitted by the pandemic would push us to adopt a new way of life and grant our tormented earth a reprieve. They may have underestimated one fact: tourism is an essential component and aspect of globalisation. Taking it apart will be an even more titanic undertaking than setting it up. It took two revolutions to bring it into being; it would take at least one more to make it disappear.

3

The World's Finest Sewer

When tourism was invented in the nineteenth century, it looked nothing like the phenomenon we know today. However, the *attitude* of early tourists was not so different from that of their modern counterparts. There are, then, both differences and similarities between the two. These become clear when we look at what were considered in the nineteenth century to be worthy focuses of tourism – activities considered useful, pleasant or instructive – but are today overlooked or even deliberately shunned.

The sewers of Paris provide one such example, particularly in the period following the 1867 International Exposition, when they became a must-see attraction. An article from an 1870 edition of the *Illustrated London News* described the Parisian sewers as follows: 'Among the sights of Paris, which provincials and foreigners are most anxious to see, are the gigantic collecting-sewers beneath the city.'[1] The tours were so popular that participants were warned to watch out for pickpockets; the illustrations accompanying the article show boats crammed full of female visitors navigating the canals by gaslight as if in search of an underground escape.

This fascination for the underworld, in both a literal and metaphorical sense (the French word is *demimonde*), was in vogue. Dostoyevsky's *Notes From Underground*, published three years before the 1867 Paris Exposition, was very much of its time. In *Les odeurs de Paris*, published the same year as the Paris Exposition, Louis Veillot wrote, 'People who have seen everything say that the sewers are perhaps the finest sight in the world: the light glimmers through them, the sludge maintains a mild temperature, people take the boat to tour around them, hunting for rats down there, organising meetings there – several engagements have been celebrated.'[2]

Today what most strikes us, with our more delicate nostrils, is the fact that these swarms of elegant ladies in their smart hats riding boats through the sewers of Paris were not overwhelmed by the stench. This leads us to consider another major process that, as with all phenomena distinguishing the modern era, began in the nineteenth century and reached full maturity in the twentieth: the 'deodorisation' of both urban and personal spaces. At the end of the nineteenth century the poor (or the 'great unwashed') had already been branded with the social stigma of the 'stench', but our noses were still not fussy enough for us to worry about the smell of the sewers.

The idea that a sewer can be 'the most beautiful sight in the world' is bizarre enough in itself, so I decided to try the trip for myself. The tour of the Paris sewers is strongly promoted by the city council, though it does not appear in the Paris tourist guides. It was, however, a great disappointment. The entrance is close to the Pont de l'Alma, but once you get underground all you can really see are panels of photographs describing the sewers; you do a little tour on foot of less than a hundred metres but there is no boat trip on an underground river.

In addition to the Paris sewers, prisons also once ranked as tourist destinations, and looking back at Bacon's travel suggestions, it is worth noting that he considered an execution on foreign soil a compelling attraction. In 1781, twelve years before he was guillotined during the Terror for being a Girondin, Jacques-Pierre Brissot suggested: 'I propose that, from time to time, after preparing people's minds with a reasoned discourse on the preservation of the social order, on the utility of punishment, men as well as boys should be taken to the mines and to [forced] work camps and contemplate the frightful fate of these outlaws. Such pilgrimages would be more useful than the pilgrimages made by the Turks to Mecca.'[3] To which Michel Foucault added the commentary: 'Once one made charitable visits to prisoners to share in their sufferings (the seventeenth century had invented or revived this practice); now it was being suggested that children should come and learn how the benefits of the law are applied to crime – a living lesson in the museum of order.'

How things have changed! In our day and age, we can visit only those prisons that are long decommissioned, such as Alcatraz – an essential destination for any tourist who goes to San Francisco. Visiting a functioning prison today is practically impossible, and the only people allowed beyond the visitors' rooms into the inmates' quarters are members of parliament. Even if we were to be allowed in, however, it would feel too much like voyeurism. Similarly, it is practically impossible to visit a working factory unless you have a reason to be there, bringing to mind Foucault's observations that 'the prison is like a rather disciplined barracks, a strict school, a dark workshop, but not qualitatively different'.[4]

And it gets worse. The nineteenth century was eager to discover the 'wild' and 'primitive' side of humanity. For centuries 'freshly discovered' indigenous peoples from faraway lands had been brought to Europe to be exhibited to the public. Michel de Montaigne referred to this in the memorable chapter thirty-one of the first book of his *Essais*, titled *Des cannibales*, expressing sentiments to which we can trace the foundations of modern cultural relativism: 'I find that there is nothing barbarous and savage in this nation [the Tupinambá people of Brazil], by anything that I can gather, excepting, that everyone gives the title of barbarism to everything that is not in use in his own country.'[5]

However, the spirit with which Montaigne observed the arrival of these human beings from distant lands was not the same spirit in which, at the beginning of the nineteenth century, the young African woman Saartjie Baartman (1789–1815) was paraded around Europe. Of Khoikhoi origins, she was dubbed the 'Hottentot Venus', and her buttocks and genitals were the object of obsessive curiosity even after her death. In fact it took until 2002 for her remains, which consisted of her skeleton and two jars of formalin containing her brain and genitalia, to finally be repatriated to South Africa. Her odyssey is recounted in striking detail by Stephen Jay Gould.[6]

It was during the heyday of colonialism that the 'zoo', an institution that has had a relatively short existence, first opened to the public. In 1828, in the Ménagerie of the Jardin des Plantes, a giraffe was displayed to the public for the first time. Regent's Park Zoo was opened in 1847, and in Paris in 1859 the Jardin d'Acclimatation was created on the edge of the Bois de Boulogne. However, the first person to systematically formulate the concept of the human zoo, or rather the 'human botanical garden' as he explicitly termed it, was Joseph-Marie de Gérando (1772–1842). In his *Considérations sur les diverses méthodes à suivre dans l'observation des peuples sauvages* (1800), he wrote of his hope that explorers would return to Europe to feed his curiosity with whole families brought from afar:

> It would be especially ideal if they could convince a whole family to follow them. In that case, the individuals making up [that family], less restrained in their habits, less saddened by privations, would better preserve their natural character. It would make them more easily able to establish themselves among us and the relations that would exist between them would make the spectacle of their life together more curious and more useful for us. We would have in miniature the image of the society from which they were taken. For the naturalist would not settle for bringing back a branch, a flower that soon dries out; he would try to transport the plant, the entire tree, to give it a second life on our own soil.

De Gérando's proposal was reiterated by the first director of the Jardin d'Acclimatation, Étienne Geoffroy Saint-Hilaire. Hilaire sought out attractions that would reinvigorate the Jardin's precarious finances, and so, in 1877, he organised a series of 'ethnological shows', exhibiting Nubians and Inuit for the enjoyment of inquisitive Parisians. 'It was a stunning success. The visitors to the Jardin doubled and that year paid entries surpassed one million … Between 1877 and 1912 thirty or so "ethnological" exhibitions of this kind were produced by the Jardin zoologique, with constant success.'[7]

What jumps to our attention is the way that the 'savages' are *part of the design* of the zoological gardens, as much as any object, plant or animal. At the Paris Universal Exposition of 1878 and 1889 (the highlight of the latter one was the erection of the Eiffel Tower), a 'negro village' with 400 'indigenous inhabitants' was one of the main attractions. Such villages were replicated at the 1900 Exposition, visited by 50 million people, which hosted a 'living diorama' of Madagascar, and at the Colonial Expositions of Marseille in 1906 and 1922 and Paris in 1907 and 1931. In Italy, the first modern human zoo took place during the Turin exhibition of 1884.[8] As late as 1958 a 'Congolese village' was exhibited at the Brussels World's Fair.

One last example of a nineteenth-century tourist attraction that has since become something to avoid is provided by Samuel Clemens, better known by his pen name, Mark Twain, who in 1869 wrote *Innocents Abroad,* the seminal text for anyone interested in the study of tourism. Of all Twain's published works, it was *Innocents Abroad* that gained the most popularity during his lifetime: it sold 100,000 copies, and 70,000 in the first year alone. Today we generally remember Twain for his novels, but his contemporaries were in fact far more interested in his travel books. *The Adventures of Tom Sawyer*, for example, sold 24,000 copies in its first year, and *The Prince and the Pauper* a mere 18,000.[9]

Innocents Abroad is an account of Twain's 1867 trip aboard the cruise ship *Quaker City*, the first organised cruise taking visitors from the United States around the Old Continent.* The boat stopped off in Marseilles, allowing passengers to take a trip to Paris and Lyons, then Genoa, from whence they went on to visit Milan, Lake Como, Padua, Verona and Venice. The boat then

---

* The full title is: *Innocents Abroad, or The New Pilgrims' Progress; Being some account of the Steamship Quaker City's pleasure excursion to Europe and the Holy Land; with descriptions of countries, nations, incidents and adventures as they appeared to the Author*, by Mark Twain (Samuel L. Clemens).

moved down to Livorno, allowing a visit to Florence and Pisa, then Civitavecchia so that they could see Rome, and so on. There were also stops in Athens, Constantinople (Istanbul), Smyrna (İzmir), the Holy Land, Egypt for the pyramids, and elsewhere, before the boat finally returned to the United States.

Upon boarding the *Quaker City*, Twain was thirty-two years old and an experienced traveller. In the previous year he 'had gone to the Sandwich Islands, travelled extensively there before returning to San Francisco in August, 1866; had taken to the lecture platform, touring his way to Virginia City, Carson City, and back to San Francisco; had sailed to New York via the Isthmus after a harrowing voyage on a cholera-swept ship; had taken a two month trip from New York to Saint Louis, Hannibal, and Keokuk'.[10]

Mark Twain stood, therefore, at 'the beginnings of what can be termed the *Tourist Age*'.[11] In fact, 'the *age of tourism* was here to stay. As Hawthorne left Rome in 1860, something like a thousand American tourists a year visited to inspect its sites ... forty years on the numbers would be thirty thousand, and Americans were now replacing the British as Italy's typical tourists.'[12] With *Innocents Abroad*, Mark Twain 'provided us a report on the birth of the Tourist Age, of which he was simultaneously a creator, a characteriser and a prototype' – offering us both a testimony and satirical analysis of the revolution in organised tourism in its early days. As Bruce Michelson writes,

> When Mark Twain called the voyage 'the New Pilgrim's Progress' he was not being wry about the historical importance. With or without his company, the excursion was a memorable event. The first invasion of the old world by the American 'guided tour' was so unprecedented an act that the steamship and its passengers were objects of wonder – and suspicion. At Livorno, local authorities detained the ship in the harbour for several days, having never seen the like and fearing some dark ulterior purpose. They were right to be uneasy. The *Quaker City* contained the vanguard of the largest and richest invasion of wandering pleasure-seekers in history. The

Americans were coming to turn Europe into one vast amusement park, to transform every gallery, palace, cathedral, and house of state into a hometown sideshow.[13]

Yet among the sights they saw were not only palaces, museums and cathedrals. Twain provides an account of a visit made during his stay in Paris that no one would dream of making today:

> Next we went to visit the Morgue, that horrible receptacle for the dead who die mysteriously and leave the manner of their taking off a dismal secret. We stood before a grating and looked through into a room which was hung all about with the clothing of dead men; coarse blouses, water-soaked; the delicate garments of women and children; patrician vestments, hacked and stabbed and stained with red; a hat that was crushed and bloody.
>
> On a slanting stone lay a drowned man, naked, swollen, purple; clasping the fragment of a broken bush with a grip which death had so petrified that human strength could not unloose it – mute witness of the last despairing effort to save the life that was doomed beyond all help. A stream of water trickled ceaselessly over the hideous face. We knew that the body and the clothing were there for identification by friends, but still we wondered if anybody could love that repulsive object or grieve for its loss. We grew meditative and wondered if, some forty years ago, when the mother of that ghastly thing was dandling it upon her knee, and kissing it and petting it and displaying it with satisfied pride to the passers-by, a prophetic vision of this dread ending ever flitted through her brain. I half feared that the mother, or the wife or a brother of the dead man might come while we stood there, but nothing of the kind occurred. Men and women came, and some looked eagerly in and pressed their faces against the bars; others glanced carelessly at the body and turned away with a disappointed look – people, I thought, who live upon strong excitements and who attend the exhibitions of the Morgue regularly, just as other people go to see theatrical spectacles every night.[14]

And here we have it: at a certain point in history there were people who went to visit the morgue every evening in the same way that we might go to the cinema or head out for a pizza. And similarly there were people who went to visit human zoos, sewers and prisons. 'In Paris, at the turn of the present century, sightseers were given tours of the sewers, the morgue, a slaughterhouse, a tobacco factory, the government printing office, a tapestry works, the mint, the stock exchange, and the supreme court in session' (MacCannell).[15] At least a few of Bacon's precepts for travellers were still being observed. Why, then, have these destinations come to be neglected or even consciously avoided? In part because at that time tourism was still in its infancy: it was still in a sense untamed, or yet to be sterilised.

The (human or animal) zoo was eventually stripped of its status as a tourist attraction as a result of the effects of tourism itself. Once it became easy to travel to Kenya to visit a Masai reserve and see lions and elephants in their natural habitat, the zoos of Europe were consigned to the status of bland day out for the kids. The zoos, like the Universal Exposition, were designed as a means of visiting faraway lands and exotic animals (and peoples) without having to travel. Even today, the idea of travelling without moving is not totally extinct. Since 1993, the 115-acre Beijing World Park (which has since been copied) has offered 1.5 million visitors a year the chance to visit miniature (but not tiny) versions of 109 famous monuments. Some on offer are the Taj Mahal, the Eiffel Tower, the Tower of London, Piazza San Marco, Red Square, the Leaning Tower of Pisa, the Imperial Palace of Katsura and, eerily, the World Trade Center as well as almost 100 of the world's most well-known statues from the *Venus de Milo* to Michelangelo's *David*. The park was made famous by the 2004 film *The World*, directed by Jia Zhangke, which tells the stories of the park's service staff, all immigrants from rural areas of China.

Just as safaris rendered obsolete the tourism *sur place* of displays of exotic animals, the same went for 'savages'. Though we no longer brought them to our zoos, the attraction of seeing 'primitives' in the wild proved persistent. Evidence of this desire could still be found, for example, in this 1952 article by Bernice M. Goetz for *National Geographic*: 'Working in Bogota for an oil firm and planning once again a wilderness vacation ... Except for a crew of Indians I go alone; primitive peoples are a hobby of mine.'[16] I have seen for myself the reality of this phenomenon much more recently, in Pevas, a Peruvian village on the Amazon River, east of Iquitos. On encountering a group of indigenous activists in the process of taking off their jeans and T-shirts and painting their skin, I asked them why they were doing so. Their response rather took me aback: 'On Wednesday the tourist boat arrives.' Some years before, I had been to the village of Yaapsie on the Sepik (the Papua New Guinean equivalent of the Amazon) and here again – thousands of miles away – I saw that all the indigenous people were wearing Western clothes. When I asked them if the traditional hairstyle we see in anthropology books was ever worn for ritual occasions the response I received was even blunter: 'We put them on only when the *National Geographic* people come.' The few 'savages' remaining today are sought after in their own homes – there is no need to construct them a fake habitat in an anthropological zoo. What all this goes to show is that tourism is a nonlinear phenomenon; it sparks feedback processes, erasing, creating and modifying tourist destinations.

But human zoos, sewers, prisons and morgues have fallen out of favour with tourists for another, less obvious reason. In one of the final considerations of the book *Human Zoos* – one hinted at in the subtitle of the original French version, *De la Vénus hottentote aux reality shows* – the authors set the human zoo in relation to the reality show. If human zoos created a setting where the 'abnormal' Other could be displayed in a 'normal' location, reality shows do the very opposite: they exhibit a 'normal' Other in an abnormal or even exotic context, as in shows like the *Survivor* franchise, or *I'm a Celebrity Get Me Out of Here*. Furthermore, in both cases the exhibits are placed in a contained space. And in both cases the element of voyeurism is decisive.[17]

This observation leads us to another more general conclusion: it is false to say that we no longer go to visit the morgue every evening. As a matter of fact, we are always attracted to corpses or to staring death in the face (the death of others, that is). It is just that our attraction is more aesthetic than that of our predecessors. When we go to visit the *Body Worlds* exhibition (along with 40 million others worldwide), are we not essentially doing the same thing as ogling corpses in a morgue? *Body Worlds* is a display of real but chemically preserved or 'plastinated' corpses provided by 'willing donors' – some of them allegedly prisoners executed in China – with the skin removed to reveal the muscles, tendons and organs. The difference between this and a morgue being that these bodies are all placed in 'everyday' poses and are lithe and energetic looking, even in their *post mortem* state.[18]

But we also visit what we could call 'virtual' morgues when we watch TV series like *CSI*, whose central characters are basically the dissected corpses, displayed frequently in the made-for-TV forensic pathology labs. If it is true that we no longer visit morgues and sewers as tourists, is it because we constantly come across them in films and television series? Indeed, TV and cinema have greatly influenced tourism, not only in terms of encouraging tourism to specific places (like Monument Valley in Arizona, whose fame as a tourist destination was boosted tenfold by its setting for many a Western), but also in terms of *freeing us from the burden* of having to visit certain destinations. TV and cinema exert an indirect but decisive influence over trends in tourist destinations, taking 'attractions' off the map and out of the guidebooks while adding or even creating new ones.

Moreover, film and TV, like tourism, are essentially *visual* experiences. The sociologist John Urry has dedicated an entire book to the theme of how sight came to take precedence over smell, touch, taste and hearing,[19] demonstrating the ways in which the formation of the 'tourist gaze' is a nonlinear and collective process.[20] Over time the focus has been increasingly on sight to the exclusion of other senses. Tourists now tend to find experiences that involve the other senses perturbing. Noise has become deafening, smells nauseating and human beings unkempt and dirty. So they travel 'in closed starship buses above the crowd, sealed into their space capsules, watching out from the windows like a movie on a screen, the city reduced to a short film, isolated from odours and people' (Urry).[21] And while tourism becomes ever more 'visual', cinema becomes ever more realistic by means of CGI and 3D technology, surround-screen projections and surround-sound. The experience of the tourist and the spectator converge. For instance, those tourists who would never dare raft down the Grand Canyon's Colorado River are able to partake in the experience nonetheless – with the aid of a 525-seat IMAX cinema in Tusayan, a town at the canyon entrance. There, visitors can watch one of 'thirteen daily showings of *Grand Canyon – The Hidden Secrets*, a thirty-four–minute film projected on a seventy-foot-high screen with six-track Dolby stereo sound', which allows viewers to go 'up in a plane' and 'down through the canyon on the river in a raft'.[22]

4

Mark Twain's TripAdvisor

Mark Twain's *Innocents Abroad* tells us not only about the past but also about the present. From the pages of this book emerge a tentative response to the question of what motivates the tourist. What compels tourists to exhaust themselves travelling at such expense? To use the little free time at their disposal wearing themselves out like this? What's the point?

These are some of the implicit questions Mark Twain answers when he writes that 'in a little while we were speeding through the streets of Paris and delightfully recognizing certain names and places with which books had long ago made us familiar. It was like meeting an old friend when we read Rue de Rivoli on the street corner; we knew the genuine vast palace of the Louvre as well as we knew its picture.'[1] And along the same lines: 'We went to see the Cathedral of Notre Dame. We had heard of it before. It surprises me sometimes to think how much we do know and how intelligent we are. We recognized the brown old Gothic pile in a moment; *it was like the pictures.*'[2]

As a tourist in Paris, Twain seeks confirmation of what he has read and proof that the images he has seen in newspapers and book illustrations are real. As Dr Johnson observed in a 1773 letter, 'The use of travelling is to regulate imagination by reality, and instead of thinking how things may be, to see them as they are.'[3] The utility of travel is that one can compare what one sees with what one had previously imagined, and so calibrate, correct and modify it.

Put this way, the answer seems simple. Yet there is still something missing. Implicit in Twain's travelogues from Paris and, as we shall see, those from Milan and Palestine as well, is a further question, boring away like woodworm: is the need to compare reality to imagination sufficient justification to warrant the investment required to become a tourist?

As the number of tourists increased over the many decades following the voyage of the 'innocents', this question became ever more compelling. What had seemed at the moment of its onset to be an extravagance (or, for the aristocracy, a vulgarity), turned into a mass social phenomenon, all the more difficult to fathom the larger the numbers of people it involved.

To begin with, the tourist question was brushed aside, as we have seen, by a condescension that rendered any question of motives superfluous. If the tourists are merely a herd, there is no reason to explain why these bipedal bovines migrate. This was, after all, the golden age for theories of crowd psychology.

Yet in the 1950s and '60s, the flow of humanity that is tourism reached such gigantic proportions that the problem became impossible to ignore. The question was thus posed: what is it that really attracts the tourist? Or, to make a slight but significant semantic adjustment, what does the tourist *attraction* consist of?

Olivier Burgelin attempted to reply to this question in a somewhat pompous 1967 survey of 'the theory of sightseeing' for the review *Communications*, founded by Roland Barthes and Edgar Morin.[4] The neologism 'sightseeing' had been coined in 1847,[5] only two years after the first trip organised by Thomas Cook. The term is defined by Webster's dictionary as 'the act of visiting and seeing places and objects of interest'.

In its early, less hypocritical formulations, the so-called theory of sightseeing was hardly a theory. Rather, it was a repackaging of that age-old contempt for the *parvenus,* the plebeian masses, now poorly disguised as a discourse on the inauthenticity of mass culture. The University of Chicago social historian Daniel Boorstin thus answered the question of 'what attracts the tourist' in the following terms: 'The tourist looks for caricature; travel agents at home and national tourist bureaus abroad are quick to oblige. The tourist seldom likes the authentic (to him often unintelligible) product of the foreign culture; he prefers his own provincial expectations. The French chanteuse singing in English with a French accent seems more charmingly French than one who simply sings in French.'[6]

In the tourist's preference for their 'provincial expectations' we hear echoes of Samuel Johnson's 'regulating imagination by reality', only now with a derisory tone. Boorstin, predictably, takes the trite distinction between the traveller and the tourist and transfers it to the term 'sightseeing' itself: 'The traveller was active … The tourist is passive: he expects interesting things to happen to him. He goes "sight-seeing".'* Boorstin, born in the US in 1914 (died in 2004), was an ex-communist who became (as is often the case) fiercely conservative. He transformed himself into a herald of the true American identity, to be defended against a fake and duplicitous world dominated by advertising and 'pseudo-events', as the title of his book anticipates. The decisive adjective for Boorstin was 'authentic', a term which would come to play a central role in almost all theories of tourism.

There is an irony in the fact that the 'pseudo-ness' or inauthenticity of the modern world was in fact most often attributed to US influence. The first person to identify this sham quality was the German poet Rainer Maria Rilke, who wrote in a 1925 letter, 'Now, from America, empty indifferent things are pouring across, sham things, dummy life.'[7]

Someone who did partly succeed in rising above bourgeois snobbery was the German critic Hans Magnus Enzensberger, in his 1962 paper 'A Theory of Tourism'. Beginning his thesis with an attack on tourism's denigrators he states, 'There are few things in our civilisation that have been so thoroughly mocked and so diligently criticised as tourism.'[8] However, Enzensberger continues,

---

* Ibid., p. 114. A variation of the term 'sightseeing', which came into being around the same time though without much success, was 'sight-hunting'. 'Professional sight-hunters … go sight-hunting to the ends of the earth', as Harriet Martineau wrote in an article in *Blackwood's Edinburgh Magazine* of August 1848, already quoted.

what poses as criticism turns out to be a reaction in two senses of the word. In social terms, these voices [two previously cited authors] are reactions to a threat to their privileged positions. Implicitly, they both demand that travel be exclusive, reserved for them and their like. They never say exactly what it is that distinguishes them from "sight-seeing squirrels" or from the "cheap trippers" ... This criticism, however, is a reaction not only in sociological terms but also in psychological ones. It is no coincidence that this critique is part of tourism itself from its inception, without having substantially changed its arguments; nor is it a coincidence that its counter-images read like an ad in a travel brochure.

Enzensberger also works within the frame of sightseeing theory – 'the sight is not merely worth visiting; it authoritatively demands it. A sight is something that one is *expected to see*' (emphasis added) – with the difference being that here sightseeing is inserted into an idea of tourism as a desire to escape daily life, an impulse to liberate oneself, if only for the brief holiday period, from societal constraints: 'Fulfilling this duty delivers the tourist from the guilt that is implicitly recognised in taking flight from society.' He continues: 'The flood of tourism is, in fact, nothing but a gigantic escape from the kind of reality with which our society surrounds us. This escape, no matter how inane or helpless it may be, criticises that from which it withdraws. The desire that informs this stubborn, fierce, and futile critique cannot be repressed ... To mock tourism neither explains nor impedes this phenomenon. Tourism is based on the desire for the pursuit of happiness.'

Enzensberger does not use the term 'escapism'. Yet his reasoning is very much within the same conceptual horizon defined by Max Horkheimer and Theodor Adorno in 1947, when they developed their theory of 'the culture industry'. Before Horkheimer and Adorno coined this term, culture and industry had generally been seen to be mutually exclusive concepts. For the two founders of the Frankfurt School, the culture industry was brought into being not by technological development but by the needs of capitalism and by the alienation that capitalism produces in society, with the consequence that even our free or leisure time and our forms of amusement are moulded to fit the 'coercive nature of society alienated from itself'.[9] That coercive nature, for Enzensberger, can also be attributed to tourism, where – inevitably – the yearning for liberty takes the form of the organised tour: 'The pristine is "developed" by capitalism and "subordinated" by totalitarian means … Tourism is a parody of total mobilisation.'[10]

In many ways, tourism is also a culture industry, since what the consumer buys is purely an excess supplement of symbolic capital. And, inasmuch as it is a culture industry, it is defined by its mystifying character. After all, 'Enlightenment as Mass Deception' was the title Horkheimer and Adorno chose for the chapter on the culture industry. They wrote, 'An industry has been established to manufacture deliverance from the industrial world; travel beyond the world of commodities has itself become a commodity.'[11]

There is, however, an even more decisive commonality between culture industry and tourism: both are pursuits of an unattainable objective. 'The culture industry endlessly cheats its consumers out of what it endlessly promises. The promissory note of pleasure issued by plot and packaging is indefinitely prolonged.'[12] Horkheimer and Adorno go on to add: 'Originally conceived as something that redeemed its followers from society, tourism now brought society along. On the trip, the participants were able to read in the faces of their neighbours what they had intended to forget.'[13]

Like the culture industry, tourism defrauds its adepts; its promise is never honoured but perpetually put off. And tourists, for their part, are forever chasing the unattainable, as has been very often noted. The crux of the matter, then, is that escape from an alienated society can only be itself alienated. And in this way snobbery toward the masses leaves by the door but re-enters through the window, in both Adorno and in Enzensberger: 'The consumers are the workers and employees, the farmers and lower middle class. Capitalist production so confines them, body and soul, that they fall helpless victims to what is offered them … Immovably, [the enslaved masses] insist on the very ideology which enslaves them' (Horkheimer and Adorno).[14] Boorstin's arrogant disdain for the gormless hordes has been replaced with a compassion for the mental imprisonment of the masses; it is an understanding – a sympathetic one, even – of the self-deception that the dominated are led into. We could even say it is the modern version of the well-meaning Enlightenment pity for popular superstition. And it is not surprising that when discussing the culture industry, we are inevitably led back to Marx's concept of fetishism, the term he used to indicate the relation that capitalist exchange establishes with the commodity.

To put it in more basic terms, though Enzensberger rails against the reactionary nature of those who distinguish between the traveller and the tourist, and against those who seek to keep the privilege of travelling to themselves, he reasons within the framework of the Frankfurt School. And this, in fact, reproduces the same class division when it distinguishes between pre-industrial culture on the one hand (*practised* by elites) and the culture industry on the other (*consumed* by the masses). The tautology of alienation, that an escape from an alienated society is itself alienated, thus traps us in a logical feedback loop.

An important inroad toward a better understanding of tourism was made by Roland Barthes, who wrote a memorable chapter on the *Guide Bleu* in his *Mythologies* (1957). On the surface it could appear that Barthes was working the same terrain as Boorstin, making such statements as 'the American tourist in Japan looks less for what is Japanese than for what is Japanesey',[15] or describing the *Guide Bleu* on Spain as transmitting a certain idea of 'Spanishness' and of the 'picturesque'. Yet in contrast to Boorstin, Barthes was concerned with investigating what exactly this Spanishness, or the picturesque, consisted of. He sought to discover the underlying myth and demonstrated that this myth was a historical construction aimed at a very specific social class.[16] Barthes introduced, therefore, a semiotic analysis of 'sights', understood not only in terms of their authenticity or inauthenticity, but as signs and connotations of a constellation of social myths: 'Once society exists, every function is automatically transformed into a sign of that function.'[17]

It was Dean MacCannell who developed the semiotics of the tourist attraction with his 1976 *The Tourist*. For the sightseer to be able to not merely look but to look while visiting – and for these monuments, paintings, exhibits, natural wonders to become 'tourist attractions' – it is necessary that they be designated as such by a *marker*, a term which covers 'any information about a sight, including that found in travel books, museum guides, stories told by persons who have visited it, art history texts and lectures, "dissertations" and so forth'.[18] A marker is that invisible arrow which indicates something and tells us that that thing *must* be visited. Some markers are official certifications, like, for example, the 2,600 National Historic Landmarks chosen by the US Secretary of the Interior. Others are hyper-explicit, like the star rating system, directly based on the Murray guides of the nineteenth century, and used by the Michelin guides (*interesting, **worth a detour, ***worth a special journey), or by the Blue guides (*interesting, **very interesting, ***exceptional, with the addition of the sign ° to designate something of curiosity). As is well known, a star rating system is also used to rate the quality of restaurants in Michelin guides.

Once something has been 'marked', a sight becomes an attraction, and, in turn, the attraction itself becomes a marker. Thus, for a non-European travelling in Europe, Paris becomes a marker for Europe (one cannot see Europe without having visited Paris), the Eiffel Tower and the Louvre become markers for Paris, and the *Mona Lisa* becomes the marker for the Louvre. And, as we saw at the Beijing World Park, visitors will even swarm to visit replicas of these markers. Dean MacCannell writes,

Sightseers do not, in any empirical sense, *see* San Francisco. They see Fisherman's Wharf, a cable car, the Golden Gate Bridge, Union Square, Coit Tower, the Presidio, City Lights Bookstore, Chinatown, and, perhaps, the Haight Ashbury or a nude go-go dancer in a North Beach–Barbary Coast club. As elements in a set called "San Francisco", each of these items is a symbolic marker. Individually, each item is a sight requiring a marker of its own. There are, then, two frameworks which give meaning to these attractions. The sightseer may visit the Golden Gate Bridge, seeing it as a piece of information about San Francisco which he must possess if he is to make his being in San Francisco real, substantial or complete; or, the sightseer visits a large suspension bridge, an object which might be considered worthy of attention in its own right. The act of sightseeing can set in motion a little dialectic wherein these frames are successively exchanged, one for the other, to the benefit of both: that is, both San Francisco and the Golden Gate Bridge are felt to have gained a little weight in the act of looking at the bridge – or they are held to have been, at least to some extent, *meaningfully experienced*.[19]

The attraction, therefore, is socially created by the arrows that society points toward it, indicating that it is something that *must* be seen. The tourists themselves, who have seen the attraction thus marked out, produce new markers with the postcards they send, the photos they take and, as of twenty years ago, the reviews and 'bubbles' that they leave on TripAdvisor.

It is this semiological mechanism connecting the marker (signifier) and the attraction (signified) that generates the tourists' relationship with their cameras, which have now become objects of such intense obsession that the act of taking a photo very often takes over from the act of looking. This mania has been infinitely intensified by digitalisation and the invention of the smartphone as happy-snappers are no longer inhibited by the cost of film and developing. Photography, which John Frow defines as 'the most platonic of art forms', 'descendent both of the sketch pad and of the apparatus of scientific observation, unites in a dramatic way the disparate forms of knowledge – detached witnessing and aesthetic appreciation – that had made up [tourism's] history.' It is also a central element in the 'process of authentication, the establishment of a verified relay between the origin and trace'.[20]

The selfie, however, merits separate consideration. The ubiquity of selfie-taking has reached a point where selfie-sticks have now been banned in many places such as in the Uffizi gallery in Florence and at Wimbledon. Aside from reiterating the marking process, the selfie expresses an irrepressible need to confirm one's existence, to leave behind documentation of oneself, a trace of one's Heideggerian being-in-the-world, whether that be at the Great Pyramid of Giza or at the Taj Mahal. It expresses, in other words, a yearning to reassure oneself that our existence is not a hoax, that we are not mere ghosts being blown about by the wind, but that we *really* exist. The selfie captures such an insecurity that, just from looking at it, we are left with a knot in the stomach.

TripAdvisor reviews (with photos included) have achieved a step forward in the production of markers via other markers. They have altered the existing equilibrium and democratised the star or asterisk rating system, previously the exclusive pre-rogative of Michelin, Bleu or Lonely Planet guides. In 2019, 702 million enthusiastic TripAdvisor users had reviewed more than 8 million restaurants, hotels and attractions: 'The reviews demonstrate the abiding urge to share and the faith that sharing – even for that one-more-grain-of-sand 13,786th reviewer of the Bellagio Las Vegas – will make someone else's experience, or quite possibly *everyone's* experience, that much better.'[21] Horkheimer and Adorno had already made the observation that 'culture is a paradoxical commodity' because 'it eventually coincides with publicity, which it needs because it cannot be enjoyed'.[22] To this, reiterating the association between tourism and the culture industry, Enzensberger added: 'Tourism is that industry whose production is identical to its advertisement: its consumers are at the same time its employees. The colourful pictures taken by the tourists differ only in their arrangement from the picture post-cards that they purchase and send. These postcards are the travel itself on which the tourists set out. The world they encounter is the familiar world known beforehand from *reproductions*. They only consume the second-hand, confirming the advertisement poster that enticed them in the first place.'[23] At times the process of collecting markers becomes the dominating factor and thus the primary objective of travelling.[24]

Mark Twain makes explicit reference to markers when he 'rec-ognises' what he is seeing for the first time, the Rue de Rivoli or the cathedral of Notre-Dame, for example. To use a concept close to Walter Benjamin's heart, the marker is that which confers on the tourist attraction the seal of authenticity, or rather its *aura*. 'The unique value of the "authentic" work of art has its basis in ritual, the location of its original use value,' Benjamin suggested. It is possible, however, to turn Benjamin's reasoning on its head: whereas for Benjamin the aura surrounding the original work of art was stripped away in the process of mechanical reproduction, for MacCannell 'the work becomes "authentic" only after the first copy of it is produced.

> The reproductions *are* the aura, and the ritual, far from being a point of origin, *derives* from the relationship between the origi-nal object and its socially constructed importance ... this is the structure of the attraction in modern society, including the artis-tic attractions, and the reason the Grand Canyon has a touristic "aura" about it even though it did not originate in ritual.'[25]

Jonathan Culler observed that 'the distinction between the authentic and the inauthentic, the natural and the touristy, is a powerful semiotic operator within tourism. The idea of seeing the real Spain, the real Jamaica, something unspoiled, how the natives really work or live, is a major touristic *topos*, essential to the structure of tourism.'[26]

Authenticity is always relative, however. As MacCannell wrote, if the United States makes the rest of the world seem authentic, and Los Angeles makes the rest of California seem authentic,[27] the opposite is also true: the proliferation of markers turns the inauthentic into something authentic, and, thus, once its 'inau-thenticities' have been reproduced an infinite number of times in various media, Los Angeles acquires its aura. The European version of this 'acquired authenticity' is Neuschwanstein Castle near Füssen in Germany. Finished in 1886, the castle is a folly con-structed on the cliffs overlooking an Alpine creek by King Ludwig

II of Bavaria. An example of the Romanesque revival, complete with pointed turrets in faux-Gothic style, it was designed to be the archetypal fairy-tale castle, yet over time it has acquired its own undeniable 'aura'. Indeed, it is the same process that takes place in Disneyland, where everything is more real than reality, the castle is more medieval than any medieval ruin and the Indian village more 'Indian' than any built by Native Americans.

The marker marking the 'authentic', however, brings us once more within the realm of the unkept promise, of the IOU forever put off, of the pursuit of the unattainable. More precisely, the pursuit of something that once attained reveals itself to be different to what we thought we had been chasing after: 'The paradox, the dilemma of authenticity, is that to be experienced as authentic it must be marked as authentic, but when it is marked as authentic it is mediated, a sign of itself, and hence lacks the authenticity of what is truly unspoiled, untouched by mediating cultural codes … The authentic sight requires markers, but our notion of the authentic is the unmarked' (Johnathan Culler).[28]

It is in fact the marker that can leave the tourist disillusioned. Or rather, it is the marker that makes it difficult for tourists to admit their sense of disappointment, as Mark Twain's travel companions discovered when they went to see Leonardo's *Last Supper*:

> The Last Supper is painted on the dilapidated wall of what was a little chapel attached to the main church in ancient times, I suppose. It is battered and scarred in every direction, and stained and discoloured by time, and Napoleon's horses kicked the legs off most the disciples when they (the horses, not the disciples,) were stabled there more than half a century ago … The colours are dimmed with age; the countenances are scaled and marred, and nearly all expression is gone from them; the hair is a dead blur upon the wall, and there is no life in the eyes. Only the attitudes are certain. People come here from all parts of the world and glorify this masterpiece. They stand entranced before it with bated breath and parted lips, and when they speak, it is only in the catchy ejaculations of rapture:

"Oh, wonderful!" "Such expression!" "Such grace of attitude!" "Such dignity!" "Such faultless drawing!" "Such matchless colouring!" "Such feeling!" "What delicacy of touch!" "What sublimity of conception!" "A vision! A vision!"[29]

The experience described by Mark Twain is the forebear of those endless expressions of disappointment we find on Trip-Advisor. For example, a visitor to Cambodia's Angkor Wat left the following one-star review: 'BORING!!! Just a load of stupid rocks in a sweaty jungle.' The disappointment is unrelated to the actual object of the visit, it is an emotional state, which can be invoked as much by a Nazi concentration camp as by some Roman ruins. Indeed, one 'disappointed' reviewer left the following review of the world's most famous concentration camp: 'How can you not give the highest rating to Auschwitz? This is how …' And among the 145,882 reviews (as of 15 March 2020) left for the Colosseum in Rome, we also find this: 'You basically pay to see nothing. The Arena where the Romans used to have their shows costs about 12 euros but all you see are old stones.'

Tourists are disappointed because what they go to see are not actual places but rather the guidebooks themselves, in the sense that their experience of sightseeing consists of making a constant navigation between an experience ready-made by markers and the reality of the trip. Mark Twain, for example, made this comparison between the anticipation of an experience in the Palestinian desert, and the reality:

Picturesque Arabs sat upon the ground, in groups, and solemnly smoked their long-stemmed chibouks. Other Arabs were filling black hog-skins with water – skins which, well filled, and distended with water till the short legs projected painfully out of the proper line, looked like the corpses of hogs bloated by drowning. *Here was a grand Oriental picture which I had worshiped a thousand times in soft, rich steel engravings! But in the engraving there was no desolation; no dirt; no rags; no fleas; no ugly features; no sore eyes; no feasting flies; no besotted ignorance in the countenances;*

no raw places on the donkeys' backs; no disagreeable jabbering in unknown tongues; no stench of camels; no suggestion that a couple of tons of powder placed under the party and touched off would heighten the effect and give to the scene a genuine interest and a charm which it would always be pleasant to recall, even though a man lived a thousand years.

Oriental scenes look best in steel engravings. I cannot be imposed upon any more by that picture of the Queen of Sheba visiting Solomon. I shall say to myself, You look fine, Madam but your feet are not clean and you smell like a camel.[30]

In 1869 we begin to see signs that the senses unrelated to sight, for instance those that can feel dirt, heat and flies, hear irritating noises and notice odours, are becoming unwelcome. It is curious, however, that Twain was so struck by the noise and smell of the Bedouins yet did not report on what we would imagine to be the stench of the Paris morgue. Of course, in this case the marker that brought these 'innocents' to that desert pool consists of the 'fabled land of the Arabian nights', the modern equivalent of which are the kind of images conjured up by the 1990 Bernardo Bertolucci film *The Sheltering Sky*. To put it in more scholarly terms, the marker in this case is the invention of the 'Orient' as posited by Edward Said in his seminal book *Orientalism*. Whenever we see a crowd gathering on the street we instinctively want to know what summoned it. The crowd itself becomes a marker. But it does not stop here, because the marker in turn becomes a tourist attraction. As Mark Twain recalled of his stay in the French capital:

Of course we visited the renowned International Exposition [of 1867]. All the world did that. We went there on our third day in Paris – and we stayed there nearly *two hours*. That was our first and last visit. To tell the truth, we saw at a glance that one would have to spend weeks – yea, even months – in that monstrous establishment to get an intelligible idea of it. *It was a wonderful show, but the moving masses of people of all nations we saw there were a still more wonderful show.* I discovered that if I were to stay there a month, I should still find myself looking at the people instead of the inanimate objects on exhibition.[31]

In the words of John Urry: 'Other people give atmosphere to a place. They indicate that this is the place to be and that one should not be elsewhere ... It is the presence of other tourists, people just like oneself, that is actually necessary for the success of such places which depend on the collective tourist gaze.'[32]

In 2003 while in San Antonio, I witnessed for myself the phenomenon of tourists watching tourists taken to the extremes. The pride and joy of this south Texas city, and the envy of all Texas, is the River Walk, the promenade along its eponymous river. The San Antonio River has always been of great importance to the inhabitants of this arid climate, but it was polluted by oil spills and dammed after serious flooding in 1921 killed more than fifty people. In the 1930s, however, the Works Progress Administration (one of the agencies created by Franklin D. Roosevelt's New Deal) saved it from becoming a covered storm sewer, entrusting the new urban design to the architect Robert Hugman. So far, nothing particularly exceptional. However, none of this prepares you for the sight of the river as it is now. At street level you must go down a set of stairs around six metres (or around two storeys) deep. At the bottom of the stairs is the river, only a few metres wide and more of a stream than a river, which (at the time I visited) twists and turns for the length of twenty-one blocks. In 2011, it was extended for another ten kilometres into the suburbs, with cycle paths and jogging routes. The river is crossed by more than twenty bridges, while pedalos and motorboat taxis clutter its small surface. Along the banks are two quays, each one larger than the river itself, decorated with tropical flowers and crowded with visitors. The quays are packed with al fresco bars and restaurants, full of tourists drinking margaritas as if they were already in Mexico. (And to an extent they are not wrong, seeing as Laredo, at the Mexican border, lies only 250 kilometres to the south and 57.3 per cent of San Antonio's population is of Hispanic origin.) Aside from this, however, tourists on the River Walk can do nothing more than

48

stroll across a confined space continuously watching one another. They are essentially trapped there in an open-air underground canal surrounded by the sound of cars rumbling along the motorways above.*

The key word here is 'stroll', as it reminds us that the archetypical figure of the modern tourist, the Ur-tourist if you like, is the flâneur, made famous by Baudelaire in the nineteenth century and re-elaborated in the twentieth by Walter Benjamin. A flâneur is someone who ambles idly along the boulevard, glancing about or gazing distractedly at the crowds, the other strollers or the buildings, allowing themselves to be swept away by the sounds, lights and movement. As Urry writes, Paris

> was the city of the flâneur or stroller. The anonymity of the crowd provided an asylum for those on the margins of society who were able to move about unnoticed, observing and being observed, but never really interacting with those encountered. The flâneur was the modern hero, able to travel, to arrive, to gaze, to move on, to be anonymous, to be in a liminal zone. The flâneur was invariably male … The strolling flâneur was a forerunner of the twentieth-century tourist and in particular of the activity which has in a way become emblematic of the tourist: the democratised taking of photographs – of being seen and recorded, and of seeing others and recording them.[33]

Susan Sontag hammered home this connection when she wrote: 'The photographer is an armed version of the solitary walker reconnoitring, stalking, cruising the urban inferno, the voyeuristic stroller who discovers the city as a landscape of voluptuous extremes. Adept of the joys of watching, connoisseur of empathy, the flâneur finds the world "picturesque." '[34]

---

* Many other cities have created their own imitations of San Antonio's River Walk, even some megacities like Seoul, which has directly copied the River Walk's urban design for a 10.4 km stretch of the Cheonggyecheon river. A more detailed description of San Antonio can be found in my book *Via dal vento. Viaggio nel profondo sud degli Stati Uniti*, Rome: manifestolibri, 2004, in the chapter titled 'Lungo il fiume, sotterraneo'.

We have become, in short, tourists in our own cities, proof of how deeply rooted in the modern experience this way of perceiving the world has become. If the object of the flâneur's gaze can be other flâneurs encountered along the way, the tourist on the River Walk may look at other tourists as if they themselves were a tourist attraction. And is in turn gazed upon by other tourists. The tour of the 'tourist' thus ends by turning in on itself.

5

Tourism à la Carte

It seems simple enough to talk about 'tourism'. Yet like any expanding sector of the economy, it is articulated and segmented into differing specialised forms. Tourism can obviously be classified according to different typologies, such as summer and winter tourism, city breaks, tourism for art lovers, and so on. Or else the classification can be based on the different types of tourist. For example, recent decades have seen the notable spread of *tourism for the elderly*, fed by pension systems in developed countries. In some regions of Italy, the local authorities subsidise holidays for the elderly, getting them reduced fares using public funds. In the United States and Canada, such geriatric tourism takes on the dimensions of a seasonal migration, as uninterrupted lines of camper vans take elderly couples south to spend the winter in the Sun Belt. They are nicknamed 'snowbirds', in reference to migrating birds such as snow buntings, who like them head south in winter in search of warmer weather. This is the modern North American equivalent of the elderly English flocking to winter in the French Riviera in the nineteenth and early twentieth centuries.

However, of most interest to whoever wants to understand the tourism phenomenon are the different specialised markets targeted by tourist agencies.

First among these is *business tourism*. In a destination like Paris, the most visited city in the world, business tourism generated 39.9 per cent of all hotel bookings in 2014, a percentage that has remained stable over the years. In 1999 it was 40 per cent (12.6 out of 31.1 million overnight stays).[1] A city like Chicago, on the other hand, with little appeal for tourists, counted 53.7 million

US visitors and 1.5 million foreign visitors in 2017, but domestic business visitors were about a quarter of the overall total.[2] Domestic business tourism billed more than pleasure tourism. Overall, business travel in 2018 produced a turnover of more than 328 billion dollars in the United States alone.[3] In turn, an important part of business tourism is congress and convention tourism along with trade show and exhibition tourism. In 2016, 12.7 million visitors attended 3,872 events in Paris, including 413 trade fairs, 1,118 congresses and 1,895 business events, generating a turnover of 5.4 billion euros.[4] Even a city as inextricably linked to gambling as Las Vegas seeks to attract as many conventions as possible. In 2019, Las Vegas had 42.6 million visitors, of whom 6.6 million (16 per cent) had come for conventions.[5] What is more important, however, is that conventions generated one-sixth of the city's total tourism turnover (9.8 billion dollars out of 58.9 billion).

Of course, in 2020, with the Covid-19 pandemic, the collapse of business tourism was precipitous, and recovery will be even more difficult than with other forms of tourism; it will be years before we see it return to previous levels. In this case, the crisis of business tourism is multiplied by the crisis of the businesses for which it caters.

Business tourism is not always transparent. There are trips to Barbados, to the Cayman Islands, to Switzerland or Liechtenstein, indeed to any tax haven, for the purpose of opening bank accounts, evading taxes and recycling profits of an illegal or dubious nature. The very expression 'tax haven', or what is sometimes called a 'fiscal paradise', recalls the language of a travel agent's brochure. Yet even a respectable city like London was (and perhaps still is) 'the largest laundry in the world', to use the fraudsters' term. The implication here is that what is being 'laundered' is 'dirty money'.

Then there are various other specialised tourisms. Closely related to conference tourism is festival (or exhibition) tourism, in some cases part of a glorious tradition, as with the Salzburg music festival or the Avignon theatre festival. Over the last few decades, however, there has been an extraordinary proliferation of festivals. Social historian Guido Guerzoni writes that 'according to various estimates, more than 1,600 exhibitions and 1,200 festivals are organised in Italy each year.'[6] He has also surveyed some of the more bizarre festivals that take place in Italy:

> there are festivals of the labourer, the horse, the mongrel and the thoroughbred dog, theology, secularism, the sun, the moon, the wind, literature of the partisan war, longing, romance fiction, Ligurian crime fiction, tango on the beach, belly dancing, flamenco, contemporary Calabrian song for children, mandolin, bagpipes, sax, groove, fitness, walking, handball, lateen sailing, the sea, mountains, silence, short films, *brodetto* (Italian fish soup), stockfish, the golden courgette, the chilli pepper, fairly produced and traded food, growth, happy de-growth, bonsai, the flowering almond, sudoku, fundraising, and the 'city of business'.[7]

Even without encroaching on the more bizarre, we need only mention the festival of economics (Trento), and the festivals of sci-fi (Trieste), philosophy (Modena), journalism (Perugia), literature (Mantua), poetry (Genoa and Parma), mathematics (Rome), the mind (Sarzana), science (Bergamo), history (Gorizia), women's fiction (Matera), and so on.

Another tourism tied to events is *sports tourism*, which moves millions of people upon the staging of the Olympic Games, or for important finals like the Super Bowl in the US or the Champions League in Europe. Sport provides an occasion to visit a country, a city, or to travel to the great natural parks, as in South Africa, when in 2010 the football World Cup was held there. This tourism is so large in scale that it can alter daily life in the host city. In Italy, for example, when a city hosts a Champions League game attended by foreign fans, the sale of alcohol is prohibited for twenty-four hours not only in bars but also in shops and supermarkets.

Another tourism of great importance is *religious tourism*. We should not forget that the subtitle of *Innocents Abroad* was *The*

New Pilgrim's Progress, and that in the synopses of its sixty chapters, the terms 'pilgrims' and 'pilgrimizing' appear eighteen times. In 1867, the nexus between tourism and pilgrimage was already evident to a discerning eye like Twain's. In a certain sense, religious tourism is the archetype of all tourisms, ever since the ancient Greeks travelled to Delphi or to Aphrodite's sanctuary in Erice, Sicily. They were then followed by the countless medieval pilgrimages to Rome – of course – or to Santiago de Compostela or Jerusalem, not to mention the Hindu pilgrimages of oceanic proportions like the one along the river Ganges to Varanasi. And then there is perhaps the most important pilgrimage of all, the great ritual of the pilgrimage to Mecca, which confers the title of *haji* on the pilgrim who has made the journey there. We should remember that in one of the masterpieces of late-nineteenth-century European fiction, the steamer *Patna* – whose second in command is the character later nicknamed 'Lord Jim' – is transporting Muslim pilgrims from Asia to Mecca: here we see the transport revolution, with steam-powered navigation, used to serve a religious pilgrimage.

The transport revolution has changed the dimensions of pilgrimages, and – as Marx taught us – a quantitative leap also generates a qualitative one. According to the World Tourism Organization, between 300 million and 330 million people visit places of worship across the world every year. Since the first pilgrimage in 1858, more than 200 million pilgrims have come to Lourdes, but in the last decade there has been a sharp decline from 800,000 to 575,000 pilgrims a year, partly due to competition from Fatima and Santiago de Compostela, shrines where the influx has increased by 50 per cent thanks to more aggressive marketing.[8] An even more recent pilgrimage site is San Giovanni Rotondo, site of the shrine to Father (now Saint) Pius of Pietrelcina, more commonly known as Padre Pio. Designed by Renzo Piano, the shrine has transformed this small Apulian town into a crowded tourist hub.

A subtler nexus between pilgrimage and tourism was identified by Krzysztof Pomian, who saw a thread connecting the 'shrines, tombs, treasures of the temples' of antiquity to the 'galleries, museums and protected sites' of the last two centuries. This thread was our relationship with the *world of the invisible*. According to Pomian, every human society makes sacrifices to that world, each in its own way, withdrawing precious and useful objects from their human circulation and setting them aside for 'votive offerings', that are thus conserved and dedicated to this purpose. Yet while in the past, the invisible consisted of the afterlife and the sacred, in modern times the invisible to which sacrifices are made are not the gods or the dead, but future generations: we save artefacts from the past (paintings, monuments, works of art) to pass them down to our descendants. 'The museum is not a temple or a tomb, because the frontier between visible and invisible that it presupposes does not coincide with the one passing between this world and the afterlife … The frontier that it has to address is the divided and ever-moving one that separates the present from the past, but also from the future.'[9] Museum collections safeguard 'relics' of the past, which are handed down to the future. It is no coincidence that the relics acquired at great cost (or stolen) in places of pilgrimage made up the first kind of tourist souvenir as well as the first kind of tourist trap.

Indeed, as Victor and Edith Turner nicely put it, 'if a pilgrim is half a tourist, a tourist is half a pilgrim'.[10] This was in fact already the case in medieval times: in the first half of the thirteenth century the future cardinal Jacques de Vitry asserted that 'some light minded and inquisitive persons go on pilgrimages not out of devotion but out of mere curiosity and love of novelty. All they want to do is travel through unknown lands to investigate the absurd, exaggerated stories they have heard about the east.'[11] Pilgrims who come to Rome to see St Peter's Basilica rarely pass up the chance to see the Colosseum or the Piazza di Spagna. Nor does mass tourism simply replicate the forms of mass religiosity. Alongside tourist camps, faith camps are extremely popular in the US: see Heidi Ewing and Rachel Grady's extraordinary 2006 documentary *Jesus Camp*, about the training of children to become 'soldiers of Christ'.

If the tourist has become something of a pilgrim and the pilgrim something of a tourist, it is also because their ways of travelling have an underlying element in common. MacCannell remarks that in a sense tourism is the fulfilment of a modern ritual, because 'under conditions of high social integration, the ritual attitude may lose all appearance of coercive externality. It may, that is, permeate an individual's inmost being so he performs his ritual obligations zealously and without thought for himself or for social consequences.' As such, 'modern international sight-seeing possesses its own moral structure, a collective sense that certain sights must be seen.' In Greece one *has to* see Athens, in Athens one simply *must* see the Acropolis and at the Acropolis one *cannot* miss out on the Erechtheion: 'there are quite literally millions of tourists who have spent their savings to make the pilgrimage to see these sights.'[12]

In their study of pilgrimage the Turners show that in the modern world 'even when people bury themselves in anonymous crowds on beaches, they are seeking an almost sacred, often symbolic, mode of communitas, generally unavailable to them in the structured life of the office, the shop floor, or the mine.'[13] More broadly speaking, there exists today a pilgrimage that is not religious in form: 'Both for individuals and for groups, some form of deliberate travel to a far place intimately associated with the deepest, most cherished, axiomatic values of the traveller seems to be a "cultural universal" ... In the United States, for example, the bicentennial year 1976, celebrating the birth of the United States, was a sort of secular jubilee, with millions of travellers visiting the scenes of the liberation struggle against British rule.'[14] According to the Turners, even the millions of people who visit the national parks and forests every year, such as Yellowstone and Yosemite, do so not merely for the entertainment but as a way to 'renew love of land and country', a kind of pilgrimage as dictated by the religion of David Thoreau.

Indeed, would it be possible to call the tourism that brings countless legions of visitors to Graceland, Elvis Presley's mansion in Memphis, or to the tomb of Jim Morrison in the Père Lachaise cemetery in Paris, a 'pop culture pilgrimage' or *pop tourism?* However, if this is the case then how do we explain the fact that Frédéric Chopin's grave in this same cemetery has not once been without flowers for a century and a half? For cinema lovers the major film studios and the handprints of the stars on Sunset Boulevard in Los Angeles are certainly destinations of pilgrimage. No doubt, on this phenomenon, Theodor Adorno would be able to write unforgettable pages describing the passage from *follower* to *fan* (symmetrical to the passage from *glory* to *success*).

Naturally, pop pilgrimage destinations can also deteriorate very quickly. The most illuminating example is the tomb of Lady Di (Diana Spencer) at Althorp in Northamptonshire, which experienced a boom as a tourist destination in the years following her 1997 death, but then rapidly declined. Other 'temporary pilgrimage' destinations have included, for example, Metropolis in Illinois, purported to be the birthplace of Superman, or the monument to William Wallace in Scotland, which saw a 160,000-person rise in visitors after the 1995 release of *Braveheart*, the film about his life. Within the space of a few years, however, the William Wallace monument was considered so horrendous that when the local church tried to sell it at auction; it found no takers. As a result, they then tried to offload it onto the future president of the United States, Donald Trump, who, they hoped, could use it to adorn a golf course he had just opened in Scotland: *sic transit gloria mundi!*

In our survey of tourism's many varieties we must be sure not to shy away from mentioning the *sex tourism* that brings millions of European men – some paedophiles, some not – to Thailand or South East Asia more generally, hundreds of thousands of Western women to the Caribbean or to Gambia, and (uncounted) multitudes of gay men to the Maghreb. In Europe, Budapest and Prague are beginning to specialise in this type of tourism. As with religious tourism, it can happen that sex is an accessory to cultural or beach tourism in the same way that an excursion is an add-on to a cruise. The opposite can also be true: cultural tourism can be an accessory to the real, sexual motive for the trip. Again, this kind of tourism deeply alters the social structures of the host country. Paradigmatic of this is the case of Thailand, where the sex industry for foreigners is relatively recent and has its origins in the Vietnam War, from which Bangkok constituted a behind-the-lines retreat. For this reason Thailand began to specialise in the entertainment of American soldiers and marines on autho-rised leave. Estimates of the current situation speak of around 2.8 million sex workers, 800,000 of whom are minors.[15]

Another newly flourishing branch of tourism is *medical tourism*, which has distant roots in the pilgrimages to sites where mira-cles took place or which were known for their healing properties. Since antiquity, such sites have given rise to spas. Soon, however, these thermal baths became a mere pretext for whole resort complexes replete with social activities (it is from here that the term 'seaside resort' derives). Bath was a spa resort known for its healing waters even during the time of the Romans, though it was during the eighteenth century that it reached its apogee – so much so, in fact, that it became England's seventh most populous city. In the epistolary novel *The Expedition of Humphry Clinker* by Tobias Smollett, published in 1771, Bath, 'that famous center of polite amusement', reflects all the future commonplaces of the tourist resort – the first one being that, as would befall all tourist destinations of the following 250 years, the place *is no longer what it used to be*: 'I find nothing but disappointment at Bath; which is so altered, that I can scarce believe it is the same place that I frequented about thirty years ago.' Bath 'is become the very center of racket and dissipation'; 'Instead of that peace, tranquil-lity, and case, so necessary to those who labour under bad health, weak nerves, and irregular spirits; here we have nothing but noise, tumult, and hurry … A national hospital it may be, but one would imagine that none but lunatics are admitted.'

Even in 1771 (perhaps because the English bourgeois revolution had a half-century advantage over its European counterparts), the degradation of the resort was put down to the decline in the social status of those visiting it:

Every upstart of fortune, harnessed in the trappings of the mode, presents himself at Bath, as in the very focus of observation – Clerks and factors from the East Indies, loaded with the spoil of plundered provinces; planters, negro-drivers, and hucksters from our American plantations, enriched they know not how; agents, commissaries, and contractors, who have fattened, in two successive wars, on the blood of the nation; usurers, brokers, and jobbers of every kind; men of low birth, and no breeding, have found themselves suddenly translated into a state of affluence, unknown to former ages; and no wonder that their brains should be intoxicated with pride, vanity, and presumption ... Such is the composition of what is called the fashionable company at Bath; where a very inconsiderable proportion of genteel people are lost in a mob of impudent plebeians.[16]

In the second half of the nineteenth century, the trend for thermal baths had conquered continental Europe. It was in the German resort of Baden-Baden that Fyodor Dostoyevsky would meet Ivan Goncharov (author of *Oblomov*), argue with Ivan Turgenev (whose 1867 novel, *Smoke*, was set here), and gamble his meagre fortune right down to the last 'ten-gulden piece', as he recounts in *The Gambler* (1866). Even Leo Tolstoy often stayed in Baden-Baden, noting in his diary: 'Roulette until six in the evening. Lost everything.' Baden-Baden's literary heritage is so impressive that over the last twenty years, since the end of the Cold War, it has become a veritable pilgrimage site for Russian lovers of gambling and literature.[17]

The health benefits of visiting these spa resorts were evidently only a pretext, though in this same decade (the 1870s), a trend for medical resorts also took off. Sanitoriums, equipped with medical staff and physio-therapeutic facilities, arose in the fine clean air of the Alps or the warm, dry climate of places like Arizona. Clinics were built high up in the mountains, on the shores of the sea or in the middle of the desert, for treating diseases like tuberculosis, scrofula, hysteria and various other physical or mental pathologies it was thought could be alleviated by stays in such establishments. This trend peaked in 1928, when the architect Alvar Aalto designed the most celebrated of all sanatoriums, in Paimio, Finland.

Modern, perverse versions of this health tourism are the 'lung cleansing' trips organised by Chinese agencies, offering 'escape from the smog' excursions in places with pure air and blue skies – places that can only be reached by polluting means of transport. For those who cannot afford the trips to Outer Mongolia, Tibet, the island of Hainan in the South China Sea or the Zhoushan archipelago in the East China Sea, a cheaper solution is to buy pure air taken from these places, now available in canisters, like the bottles of Fijian 'mineral water' sold in US supermarkets.[18]

Modern medical tourism, however, has little to do with trips to the sanatorium, healing waters or pure air (not to mention roulette). It is a relatively new phenomenon, indeed an ever-growing one, and could be considered as the medical or health side of the globalisation of the economy. This kind of tourism has nothing to do either with the old 'journeys of hope', when a family would bleed itself dry to send an ailing member to be operated on by some illustrious surgeon in Dallas or Paris. Those trips were simply the secular or scientific form of the pilgrimage to Lourdes or Compostela, waiting – literally – on a miracle.

In fact the only truly serious antecedent of modern medical tourism (one that still flourishes in some countries) was the organised trips of the 1970s that took pregnant women and girls from Italy or France to London to abort unwanted pregnancies. The total price included the journey, the operation, a day's recovery and a night in the clinic. That particular medical tourism was caused by differences in the law, which was stricter in some countries than others. Until 2018 abortion was forbidden in Ireland unless the future mother's life was in danger, leading 7,000 women every year to cross the Irish Sea to terminate their pregnancies in England, where the procedure was legal.

These abortion trips already had the characteristics that today make travel for medical purposes a subcategory of mass tourism:

organised groups, agencies which function as tour operators and 'all inclusive' price packets.

Today there are many countries around the world that seek to attract tourist–patients. Adverts for medical centres and health companies resemble more and more the promotions of a tourist resort boasting of the lushness of its golf courses, the comfort of its five-star hotels, the quality of its cuisine and the attractiveness of its prices. Thus we see the emergence of medical travel agencies, selling organised trips to destinations like South Korea, most of whose plastic surgery tourists come from China.[19] In Texas the famous transplant clinics advertise themselves like seaside resorts, with brochures vaunting the quality of care and the training of their paramedic staff. Generally speaking, however, medical tourism is based on the same criteria as all other tourisms: if there is no difference in the quality of service, the tourists go wherever the cost is lowest. Dental tourists go to Prague, because not only is the orthodontist treatment high quality (the personnel were trained in East Germany), but it is five times less expensive than in Germany or Italy. Indeed, there are as many specialist sectors of medical tourism as there are different branches of medicine. Fertility tourism is particularly big at the moment, drawing tourists to destinations where artificial insemination is regulated by more elastic laws.

In general, the 'promotion' of medical tourism is left to private companies, to individual clinics or studios. Or it relies simply on road signs, as anyone will see who crosses the US–Mexico border over the Rio Grande (a river that is in fact rather measly, having been so depleted by human use). As soon as you enter Mexico you are confronted with gigantic billboards for medical and dental clinics, choice destinations for American visitors looking to get a better deal on their treatment.

There is, however, a country with its own genuinely official medical tourist agency. That country is Cuba and the agency is called Servimed, turismo de salud (Servimed, health tourism), whose promotional language is like that of a tourist brochure. Indeed, in Havana there is a hospital, the Clínica Central Cira

García, only for foreigners. Many Cuban emigrants to Miami come to get treatment here, because it is so expensive in the United States. So do Brazilians, Argentinians and Venezuelans, who can get treatment in Cuba of equal quality to that in the US but at much lower prices. There is even a Latin American congress on 'tourism and health' held at regular intervals in Havana.

Thus in Cuba today, there is a two-tracked or two-tiered medical system. But no one complains too much, for it is the tourist tier that supplies the dollars to pay for the free treatment of locals. 'For twenty-five years we treated all the foreigners who came here for free,' a Cuban doctor told me. 'Now we are going to make them pay for it.'

However, medical tourism does not always have such a sunny aspect. At times, behind the façade, lies the repugnant reality of human organ trafficking. According to the anthropologist Nancy Scheper-Hughes,[20] there are medical tour operators that offer all-inclusive packages in the field of organ transplants. In Tel Aviv, for example, operating in collaboration with one of Israel's most important transplant surgeons, a company has developed links with transplant surgeons in Turkey, Russia, Moldova, Estonia, Georgia, Romania and, more recently, New York City. The cost of the all-inclusive package has already risen from 150,000 dollars to 300,000 dollars and continues to increase.

Recently, an even stranger form of medical tourism has emerged: death tourism, a term coined in 1999 by the Zürich public prosecutor. With assisted suicide outlawed in most parts of the world, the Swiss organisation Dignitas has, since 1998, been filling this gap in the market for the cost of 10,000 Swiss francs, or 10,100 dollars. In a 2008 interview, its founder and director, Ludwig Minelli, explained: 'We have accompanied 868 people, 85 per cent of them foreigners. Of this percentage, more than half are German, with the English, the French and others following behind. In 2007, 141 people came and used our service to commit suicide. Of these only six were Swiss.'*

---

* From *Le Monde*, 25 May 2008. Assisted suicide has been legal in Switzerland since 1941. Although the phenomenon attracts heavy criticism, numbers remain

Delving into the euphemism 'accompanied' would take us off track, but Dignitas is not the first Swiss organisation to uphold 'the right to death'. A predecessor, Exit, was created in 1982, with 50,000 members, though it served only Swiss citizens. According to a 2015 study from the *Journal of Medical Ethics*, between 2008 and 2012 the number of 'suicide tourists' arriving in Switzerland has doubled: over those four years, 611 people made the trip to end their lives.[21]

On 15 May 2011, the residents of Zürich canton responded with a resounding No to two referendums – one proposing to ban euthanasia (rejected with 84 per cent of the vote), the other proposing to limit access to assisted suicide services to Swiss 'clients'. The two measures were put forward by the Evangelical People's Party and the Federal Democratic Union of Switzerland.

---

marginal, estimated to be around 1,400 people a year, 2.2 per cent of annual deaths. Polling of Swiss citizens shows that between 70 and 80 per cent remain supportive of the practice. Assisted suicide is a legal right in the Netherlands, Belgium, Luxembourg; while euthanasia, in which a doctor ends the life of a terminally ill patient, is legal in Sweden, Germany, Denmark and Spain.

6

A Brief Intrusion by an Earthologist Friend

Finally, there is compulsory tourism. Tourism is part of the school curriculum. School trips (four days in Paris or Rome or Athens) are effectively intensive courses in tourism. I remember my own first school trip abroad, to Munich, in my second year of middle school, which involved a long overnight trip on the train. It was not strictly compulsory but missing out would have resulted in my being marginalised (or downgraded) compared to my classmates. This is how the generations of the modern age learn to become a tourist. If Goethe were alive today, he would write *The Tourist's Apprenticeship* in place of Wilhelm Meister's theatrical equivalent.

But compulsory tourism does not end with school trips. In order to avoid gridlock in the Alps, the French school system is divided into three sections (A, B and C) of equal numbers of students so that the two-week winter break can be staggered. Often it is the schools themselves that take whole classes of kids to the mountains to ski. Then there is the obligatory August break.

Those in Spain or Italy who resist the summer exodus to the coast finds themselves forced to proffer explanations as to why they have chosen to stay in the city, like a teetotaller among drinkers. The emptiness of the Italian city in August is quite something. It was captured on film for the first time – at least as far as I am aware – in *Il sorpasso* (1962), directed by Dino Risi and starring Vittorio Gassman and Jean-Louis Trintignant. On this topic an extraterrestrial friend of mine had the following to say:

The Earthologists that study your world from space are unable to explain the mysterious mutation undergone by the hairless bipeds that are the planet's dominant animal species. Firstly, these bipeds are tending more and more to develop an external shell, a metallic exoskeleton in the shape of a little box – in actual fact they are made of metal sheets and plastic – in which the bipeds hide themselves away, alone or in groups, for long periods of their lives, usually moving but also very often stationary for many hours, all together with the little metal boxes lined up alongside one another, all emitting incredible amounts of carbon dioxide and infrared rays.

Secondly, the bipeds have taken to strange seasonal migrations, a trend that has left even the most veteran Earthologists completely flummoxed. Looking down from our satellites we see that the majority of the population lives spread across the continents, concentrated in agglomerations that light up at night, leaving in darkness only the vast obscure zones close to the equator that produce lots of oxygen, as well as other dark zones around to the poles.

But suddenly, in both hemispheres, around the time of their respective summer solstices, innumerable multitudes of bipeds begin lining up in their metal shells and concentrating themselves in a tight strip along the edges of the blue expanses – composed mainly of a solution of H_2O and sodium chloride – that cover the greatest part of planet earth. There they pass the time stripped of the layers of vegetable fibre in which they wrap themselves during the rest of the year. And there, with the dermis exposed to the light of their star, they continuously immerse themselves in the saline solution before lying down nearby. Some of them do this for two earthly rotations, some for seven (a number which has special significance within the rhythm of their seasonal migrations), others for one lunar rotation or even a little longer. Then they get back in their metallic exoskeletons and head back, in endless columns toward the places they reside in for the rest of the year. The migrations come to an end sometime just before the autumnal equinox.

66

Our Earthologists have not been able to interpret these migrations. We have observed other species that exhibit similar patterns; for example, the fish named salmon that on an annual basis make the same journey in reverse, from the saline solution to the origins of the long ribbons of H_2O that crisscross the planet's uncovered land. There are also species of anuran toad that have similar migratory patterns. Just like the bipeds, once a year swarms of toads jump from the earth to the sea. On an equatorial island called Sulawesi that has the shape of four fingers, there is a species of crab that does the same (and in this case is also equipped with exoskeletons). And just like the exoskeletal bipeds, during the seasonal migration many toads and crabs remain splattered along the way.

However, while these animal migrations are related to reproductive functions, our Earthologists have discovered, this is certainly not the case for the bipeds – who have named themselves humans. The peak in the birth rate of biped young takes place not, as we would expect, ten moons after the migration, but rather eleven or twelve moons after they return home. Some Earthologists have hypothesised religious motives. The migration to the edge of the saline solution could be a form of cult adoration for the primeval soup that gave birth to life on the planet. The great nocturnal dances close to the bank of the solution – banks made of a fine powder produced by erosion seem to be particularly favoured – could be sacrificial offerings. According to the theory, then, these pilgrimages represent an invocation of fertility.

I have to concede to my extraterrestrial friend that they have found a real head-scratcher. Human civilisations have traditionally had a sceptical relationship toward saltwater. We can gather as much from looking at the number of great cities built close to the sea yet set back from it, just inshore, such as Athens, Rome and London. When, during the course of our seasonal migrations (which go by the name of the seaside holiday), we begin to get close to the sea, we realise that the coastal agglomerations are all very new, all tied to the tourist industry, while the older city centres are all raised, up on a hill and standing some kilometres away from the beach. Indeed, there are numerous towns with two names, for instance, Pietrasanta, Silvi or Riace for the ancient town centres and Marina di Pietrasanta, Silvi Marina and Riace Marina (the Italian word *marina*, in this context, meaning something like the English 'on-sea') for the new urban areas built to accommodate the seasonal migrators and holidaymakers. Close to the sea, living conditions were bad due to malaria, household fixtures would fall to pieces because of the salt and inhabitants lived in constant fear of raids by pirates.

Aside from the present day, no other human civilisation has witnessed the mass practice of seawater immersion. In the past, if people went in the sea it was because they had no choice, as in the case of fishermen, or hunters of pearls, sponges or coral. At no point did it cross their minds that a dip in the sea could be *good* for health. No other civilisation has ever produced clothes specially made for the beach and going in the sea. When other cultures decide to get a taste of this Western peculiarity they enter into the water with their everyday clothes. Today you can still see many South Asian women at the seaside with their saris spread out around them in the water as they happily submerge themselves. There are also the more religious Muslim women who go swimming with not only the hijab but also two layers of clothes, to avoid their wet clothes sticking to their bodies and revealing their shape. The second layer of fabric is held at a distance from the first using special clips – all this to not miss out on a dip in the sea!

No other civilisation has ever considered exposure of the body to the sun to have curing effects, nor has it ever been thought that baking for hours under its rays in the hottest part of the year could be at all healthy. As they used to say in colonial India: 'Only mad dogs and Englishmen go out in the midday sun.' This, then, prompts the question: Why has something that has previously been considered pure madness, and still is in other parts of the globe, become practically an obligation? As Umberto Eco once wryly remarked, Chinese and African anthropologists are carrying out studies on this inexplicable Western passion for seaside nudity.

Aside from the mass expansion of the transport system and the institution of paid leave, two other factors have contributed to this revolution in customs and their related costumes:

1) The Industrial Revolution urbanised large swathes of the population, *drawing them away from the countryside* and increasing pollution in cities that became blackened from soot and engulfed in the stench of industrial and human waste;

2) Colonisation and imperialism brought Europeans into contact with equatorial and tropical populations that lived without clothes. An example of this is the myth of the happy Pacific Islanders, peddled from the outset by James Cook, the first European explorer to reach them. Writing in his diary, Cook said of the indigenous inhabitants of New Holland (Australia), 'they may appear to some to be the most wretched people upon earth, but in reality they are far more happier than we Europeans; being wholly unacquainted not only with the superfluous but the necessary conveniences so much sought after in Europe, they are happy in not knowing the use of them'.[1] And then there are the images of beautiful Tahiti with its courteous, poised and sensual Tahitians passed down to us by Louis Antoine de Bougainville in his account of his voyage around the world:

> I thought I was transported into the Garden of Eden ... [E]verywhere we found hospitality, ease, innocent joy, and every appearance of happiness amongst them ... [W]hat better proofs can we desire of the salubrity of the air, and the good regimen which the inhabitants observe, than the health and strength of these same islanders, who inhabit huts exposed to all the winds, and hardly cover the earth, which serves them as a bed, with a few leaves; the happy old age to which they attain without feeling any of its inconveniences; the acuteness of all their senses; and lastly, the singular beauty of their teeth, which they keep even in the most advanced age ... Thus accustomed to live continually immersed in pleasure, the people of Tahiti have acquired a witty and humorous temper, which is the offspring of ease and of joy.[2]

The myth of the happy savage was fed in large part by the words Denis Diderot put into the mouth of the old Tahitian in his *Supplement to Bougainville's Voyage,* which were anathema to the European invasion: 'And you, chief of the brigands who obey you, distance your vessel from our shore at once: we are innocent, we are happy, and you can only damage our happiness. We follow the pure instinct of nature, and you have tried to erase its character from our souls. Here, everything belongs to all; you have preached I-don't-know-what distinction between *yours* and *mine* ... We are free, and here we see you have planted the contract of our future slavery in our soil.'[3]

The myth of the noble savage derives from a combination of industrialisation and colonial ventures, and likewise the myth of the original state of nature. With the ascent of this myth came a re-evaluation of the savage's nudity, and even a highly significant re-evaluation of brown skin. It is impossible to say, however, to what extent primitivism or myth has played a role in the modern cult of tanned skin. In other civilisations and other times, tanned skin was a sign of the servant or the peasant and thus was shunned. People made sure to protect themselves from the sun and in some places still do. For instance, well-to-do women in Vietnam travel by moped in long sleeves and gloves with their faces covered by a veil. However, in many parts of the world, it is even possible to pay for artificial tanning treatments where you are exposed over a series of sessions to ultraviolet rays. The theme of the happy Tahitian takes us to some odd places.

Jean-Jacques Rousseau is at once product, formulator and propagandist of this new ideology, echoes of which could be seen in the naming of the months in the revolutionary calendar. Names like Floréal (flower), Brumaire (mist) and Thermidor (summer heat) give back to the calendar a sense of the year's natural cycle. The natural world lent itself to a symbolic universe capable of substituting religious values. It wasn't by chance that in 1778, only a few years before the Revolution, the term *naturism* was coined in Belgium by doctor Jean Baptiste Luc Planchon.[4] Meanwhile, in 1776, La Peyre and Lecomte presented to the royal academies of medicine and surgery a communication on *Principes du ray-onnement solaire intégral sur le sujet intégralement nu*, which translates as 'principles of full solar radiation on the fully naked body'. Even before this, in 1753, the doctor Richard Russell published *A Dissertation Concerning the Use of Sea Water in Diseases of the Glands,* in which he promoted the health benefits of marine water for the most diverse diseases. The book was taken very seriously by the Prince of Wales, who started the trend of spending the summer season in Brighton. Thus, solariums were born and the field of heliotherapy came into existence. Then in the bay of Lerici off the Ligurian coast in 1822, Percy Bysshe Shelley became the first poet in the world to die *sailing for pleasure.*

This new hygienic invention was the coming together of a range of different strands of thought. It was a doctrine concerning the body that then became a fascination with the mystique of sport. It was a natural philosophy, as it believed that maintaining good health required near-constant exposure to nature. And it was a social doctrine, as it sought to restore the *natural relationships* between human beings. It was, then, an ideology in the fullest sense of the term, which was sustained and formulated most of all by the middle and upper-middle classes. It was put into practice at an astonishing rate following the development of rail and steam travel (ironically through the development of industries *antithetical to the natural world*), and in conjunction with the 'invention of the holiday' and the birth of the first tourist agencies. The invention of rail transport meant the sea could be brought to the city, as we see in the metaphor Heinrich Heine used in 1831 when he described how 'by the railway space is annihilated ... In three hours and a half one can now go to Orleans ... I seem to see the mountains and forests of every country coming to Paris. I smell the perfume of German lime-trees; the billows of the North Sea are bounding and roaring before my door.'[5]

Modern naturism therefore assumed its definitive form, with its formal societies and founding principles, toward the end of the nineteenth century, once rail and steam had made travel commonplace and once travel agencies had begun springing up. One of its variants is alpinism, whose founder is usually identified as the Swiss geologist Horace-Bénédict de Saussure (1740–99) who, in 1787, was the first man to climb Mont Blanc. In 1857, the Englishman Edward Kennedy founded the first Alpine club, and others followed. The Club alpino italiano was founded in 1863, the Deutscher Alpenverein in 1869 and the Club alpin français in 1874. One gets an absurd sense of nostalgia from looking at the black-and-white photos of nineteenth-century ladies in long skirts, crinolines and wide-brimmed hats, all roped together and marching in single file along alpine glaciers. 'The key role of alpine endeavour consists in the fact that it symbolizes the very concept of the romantic ideology of tourism. It strives for the "elemental", the "pristine", the "adventure"' (Enzensberger).[6]

Indeed, it was Protestantism that provided the conditions for naturism. Instituting a direct relation between the individual and God unmediated by the Church, Protestantism allowed nature to become the sole intermediate with the divine. Hence, naturism found its following among North European protestants. In 1893, Heinrich Pudor, a publisher and hygienist, wrote the propaganda text *Nackenden Menschen: Jauchzen de Zukunft*, and in 1903 he coined the term *Nacktkultur* ('nudist civilisation'). That same year the first naturist centre in Europe was opened in Lubeck, the *Freilichtpark* ('free light park'), where noncompetitive gymnastics were compulsory, alcohol and tobacco were banned and the diet was strictly vegetarian. Nudism as a social movement is considered one of the founding elements of naturism. The International Naturist Federation provides the following definition on its website: 'Naturism is a way of life in harmony with nature characterised by the practice of communal nudity with the intention of encouraging self-respect, respect for others and for the environment.'

In 1896, the Wandervögel youth association was born. Its members included the writer Ernst Jünger and, less predictably, the great physicist Weiner Heisenberg.[7] The Wandervögel organised trips, did forest or mountain trekking and practised collective nudity, sometimes while singing in chorus. After 1933, the Wandervögel was absorbed into the Hitler Youth, and the Schutzstaffel's (SS) weekly, *Das Schwarze Korps* (The Black Corps), regularly published pictures of nude males. Yet Hitler himself proclaimed that 'naturism is one of the worst dangers for our culture'.[8] Nazism, therefore, had an ambiguous relationship with naturism, evidenced by Nazi propaganda film director Leni Riefenstahl's fascination for the naked African body.

Naturism and nudism represent a life philosophy, but they find their practical outlet in secluded places, outside of everyday life, in hidden communities in the woods or on the 'nudist beach'.

Nudism has thus lost its battle with daily routine. Today no one walks around the city naked (at least aside from the occasional guru in the Indian metropolises), nor do they sit in the office without clothes. However, thanks to the introduction of paid holidays by the French Popular Front government in 1936, nudism could win its battle at least within the window of time in which we are released from the ties of ordinary life, suspended in the bubble of the holiday. It is a partial victory, a compromise with society and the market. We are always clothed, yet nudity on the beach is acceptable (with some sub-compromises: sometimes the bikini, sometimes topless bathing, which for any other civilisation would be equivalent to full nudity). A market for nudity and semi-nudity has been created, a seaside ghetto of nudity. Seaside tourism is precisely this: the market segmentation of the naturist ideology, much as the car is industry's response to a demand for freedom of movement. When added together, the membership of all Italian naturist societies (the Italian Naturist Federation is made up of a number of smaller organisations like the Italian Union of Naturists and the Italian Naturist Association) consists of only around 6,000. Yet the number of people who strip off on the beach is in the millions. In other words, militant naturism has been killed off by mass consumerist naturism.

As with many other modern phenomena, this commodified naturism in fact destroys itself, by means of a mechanism that the US economist Fred Hirsch described as the 'social limits to growth' in his book of the same title, a ground-breaking but often overlooked work. Hirsch's theory was that growth is limited not because resources are limited but because the social ends growth can serve are limited. When everyone wants a chalet in the mountains, the mountains become nothing more than an urban periphery, thus the mountain escape that was originally sought after no longer exists. If everyone wants to go to the sea, there will be no seaside left to go to, as the current state of the Costa del Sol makes perfectly clear, cemented over to such an extent that there is nothing of the 'seaside' left about it. Hirsch himself illustrated the same point with this comment from a middle-class professional on the fact that the arrival of low-cost flights to places previously considered 'exotic' was destroying them: 'Now that I can afford to come here I know that it will be ruined.'[9] As Groucho Marx proclaimed he would never join a club that would want him as a member, so the tourist, upon arriving at their destination, complains because 'there are tourists here already'.

Thus we see Bourdieu's mechanism in action once again, sporting a new look each time it turns up. According to Simon Coleman and Mike Crang:

> The élite must always find new locations, uncontaminated by the mass – places which will thus still carry a high level of symbolic capital and which are guaranteed as different by the difficulty in getting there, hardships or cost. Modern tourism is therefore an inherently expansive economy, constantly appropriating and constructing new experiences and places. Yet such activity bears with it the ironic seeds of its own destruction, as the very presence of the tourists corrupts the idea of reaching an authentic and totally different culture. Paradoxically, a nostalgic semiotic economy is produced, one that is always mourning the loss of that which it itself has ruined. The really authentic unspoiled place is always displaced in space or time – it is spatially located over the next hill, or temporally existed just a generation ago.[10]

As we have remarked, tourism is a self-destructive practice, in both conceptual and material terms. In the same way that naturist ideology finds its ultimate triumph on the beach, the process of industrialisation that brought tourism into being is also the process that is making exposure to the sun more and more dangerous as holes in the ozone layer allow more cancerous ultraviolet rays to reach the earth. Never before have so many people had the habit of stripping off on the beach when the sun is most harmful, or of bathing in a polluted sea. The existence of pollution and the greenhouse effect is a result of those metallic exoskeletons that have become so indispensable for achieving the seaside naturist ideal. And this is one of the things that make it even more difficult for the Earthologists to understand the great summer migration that has become so fundamental for us hairless bipeds with our exoskeletons.

7

The Tourist City

There is an extraordinary symmetry to the way that the city, at the same time it empties of its inhabitants who head to the seaside, fills up with urban tourists.

Nowadays, as Lucy Lippard has observed, 'there appears to be a social mandate: everyone must go somewhere else and spend money in someone else's home, so that everyone living *there* will be able to go to someone else's home and spend money, and so on.'[1] The idea being that my city fills up with tourists while I myself go to be a tourist in another city.

This two-way flow – both coming and going – is of course particularly marked in the so-called 'tourist cities'. Moreover, the seasonal tourists in exodus from the tourist city create their own tourist cities on the coast. Though, it is interesting to note that these seaside cities in fact belong to another class of urban aggregation, one we ought to call *temporary cities*, or, in this case specifically, *seasonal cities*, given that 'out of season' they are literally dead.

Geographers have identified 'three types of tourist city: resort cities "built expressly for consumption by visitors" and tourist-historic cities that "lay claim to a historic and cultural identity". The third type consists of converted cities, places of production that have had to carve out a tourist space amidst an otherwise hostile environment for visitors.'[2]

In every city in the world you'll come across some tourists, even if only accidentally so. Thus, the term tourist city needs to be clarified. São Paulo, for example, has many visitors, but, as makes for a liberating discovery, its vast size means it can afford to ignore tourists to the point where it is impossible to buy a postcard. In general, then, any city with an annual number of visitors that supersedes the number of inhabitants is a tourist city, a definition that would include not only Kyoto, Dubrovnik, Bruges, Venice or Florence, but also larger cities like Rome, Barcelona and even Paris, London and New York.

However, the term could have a narrower definition. For some cities, tourism is becoming the single most important industry, thus transforming them into 'company towns' in the same way that Essen existed because of the Krupp steel plant, Clermont-Ferrand because of Michelin, and Detroit and Turin because of General Motors and Fiat.

If each physical substance has a temperature above which it changes its state from solid to liquid or from liquid to gas, called the phase transition threshold, we could describe in the following terms the threshold that separates a tourist city in the narrower sense from those cities where tourism is not the sole source of income:

While the number of visitors remains below the threshold, tourists use services and provisions designed for residents. Once this threshold is crossed, however, residents are forced to use services designed for tourists.

Going beyond this, the transition threshold has unforeseen and irreversible consequences. We see this with restaurants, for example. On this side of the threshold, tourists eat in restaurants catering to locals. But beyond that threshold, locals must eat in restaurants aimed at tourists. Thirty years ago, it was almost impossible to eat badly in Rome or Florence, whereas today it is incredibly difficult to eat well. If the main market is tourists, why would a restaurant break its back cooking for a customer that will probably never return? And even if the chef had the best of intentions, he or she would be forced to give in to demands for ketchup on truffles in Italy, oysters in France and other such culinary atrocities.

In the language of mainstream economics, the market created by demand from locals does not coincide with the market created by demand from tourists, though they overlap in terms of both time and space and can come into conflict or diverge from one another.[3] If a local resident needs to repair her shoes but the tourist is in search of a snack, and if tourists spend more than residents, then over time cobblers will disappear while fast-food restaurants will multiply.

And it does not stop there. In the tourist city it is not only the kind of services offered that changes drastically but sometimes even the function of the buildings themselves. Once upon a time, entering a church was not only free of charge but encouraged. After all, if the poor were supposed to be first in line for entry into heaven, why should they pay to get into a church? Nowadays, however, many churches, such as Santa Croce in Florence, charge entry while 'throughout the world, churches, cathedrals, mosques, and temples are being converted from religious to touristic functions'.[4] The temples of a religion that considers money to be the Devil (Mammon) are accessible only by means of that same cursed money.

And tourism subverts the human environment as well as the physical. The core of the tourist city 'tends to be dominated by retail and entertainment facilities rather than office uses, and centrally located working-class residential districts are a rarity. Consequently the city centre belongs to affluent visitors rather than to residents, resulting in the exclusion of working-class residents from the core.'[5]

Yet it is not only the working classes that get pushed out. In some cases, even the indigenous middle classes are at risk. I live in the centre of Rome, close to the Colosseum, in a building with seven floors and forty apartments. Until around fifteen years ago all the residents were Italian. Now, of the forty, seventeen have become holiday homes or bed and breakfasts, another three being inhabited by a large number of Bangladeshis, easy prey for unscrupulous landlords. Half of the original inhabitants have moved away, taking advantage of the building's prime position to extract income from it.

Because of this trend, the impact of Airbnb was devastating.

The company was founded in 2008, and after only ten years it offered 4 million units to 150 million users in 65,000 cities in 190 countries. In Italy's three most touristy cities, the number of apartments offered on the hosting site doubled in just three years from 2015 to 2017. In the historic centres, the number of apartments on offer went from 9,000 to just under 18,000 in Rome, or put it another way: from 7.2 to 12 per cent of units. In Venice the number went from 5.8 per cent to 11.8 per cent, and in Florence from 10.1 per cent to 21.4 per cent. Naturally, where 'tourism' started late, growth was more rapid: in Milan we see a rise from 1.7 per cent to 4.1 per cent and in Naples from 0.9 per cent to 4.4 per cent.[6]

These apartments offered by Airbnb have been abandoned by their indigenous owner–residents who go to live in the suburbs or in the countryside, where life is cheaper. So the economic impact of tourism extends beyond the historic centres, beyond the cities. This is how, during the pandemic, the tourism blockade and therefore the Airbnb crisis was felt even in places untouched by the tourist's shadow. It will take years to recover from this crisis.

Airbnb has prompted a great amount of hostility on the part of locals toward tourists, which we saw in Barcelona in 2017. Before the advent of Airbnb, visitors to the Spanish city had been largely confined to the tourist ghetto of Las Ramblas and its surroundings, but then they began sneaking into the local neighbourhoods.* The remaining natives feel like survivors, abandoned by their fellow human beings, surrounded by uncommunicative aliens.

The proliferation of businesses and infrastructure for tourism also goes hand in hand with the disappearance of productive and artisan activities, among others, though it is not clear which of the

---

* And in Barcelona there were 'only' 18,344 listings for room and apartment rentals on the Airbnb website, while there were 77,096 in London (as of 7 March 2019), the highest of any other major European city. Airbnb listings were also high in Paris (59,881), Rome (29,436), Copenhagen (26,026) and Berlin (22,252). Jennifer Luty, 'Number of Airbnb listings in European cities 2019', statista.com, 9 August 2019.

two phenomena is cause and which is effect. Often they are each effects of the other, and work to mutually reinforce each other.

In accordance with the 'postmodern' understanding of tourism, it is held that cities invest in tourism to compensate for the decline resulting from deindustrialisation. This was certainly the case in the UK in the 1970s, '80s and '90s, when the country's past started to become one of its industries. As Robert Hewison observed, of the 1,750 museums in the UK in 1987, more than half opened after 1970. In only sixteen years more museums had been opened than in all previous centuries put together! In his words: 'While future perspectives seem to shrink, the past is steadily growing.'[7] Even Manchester, chosen by Engels in the nineteenth century as the archetypal manufacturing town, has sought to reinvent itself as a tourist destination (focusing in particular on football tourism, for the fans who come from across the globe on pilgrimage to Old Trafford). In the centre of town, you could ride the Wheel of Manchester, a 52.7-metre Ferris wheel, despite there not being much to see from the top. The city's version of the London Eye, it was dismantled in 2015.

In fact, the compensatory function of tourism extends beyond making up for the loss of manufacturing. The importance of tourism for a city tends to grow in inverse proportion to the decline of any of the economic activities that used to produce its wealth. When Liverpool ceased to be a functioning port, for example, it reinvented itself as a tourist attraction. Liverpool's once rapidly rising fortunes were owed to the slave trade, and in the part of the city where slaves were bought and sold, there is now a 'slavery museum'.

Of course, the classic example of this is Venice. The Italian city began to cultivate its tourist industry in the seventeenth century, when its dominance as a great commercial power was fast becoming little more than a memory. It was during this period that the Carnival of Venice gained its Europe-wide fame as an attraction, reaching its peak in the eighteenth century when it could bring in tens of thousands of foreigners and all of Europe's nobility. If visitors came for the art and the beauty, they most certainly also came for the gambling, which at the time was spreading like wild-fire, as well as the debauchery, general lawlessness and freedom to transgress all social inhibitions (a bit like the Rio de Janeiro Carnival today). It was, however (as is also the case with the Rio Carnival), a channelled and carefully controlled lawlessness, as it took place under the watchful eye of the Most Serene Republic of Venice: 'An outright policy for pleasures was introduced. The Carnival became a weapon, designed to exorcise the anguish produced by the falling number of nobles and by the erosion of Venice's primacy on the European political and economic scene.'[8]

As early as the eighteenth century, Venice was displaying some of the characteristics that were to become ubiquitous in the twentieth. First and foremost was the 'invention of tradition'. While in previous centuries the Carnival had been celebrated between Epiphany and Lent, in the seventeenth century it was gradually extended until it eventually reached the point of covering half the year (winter, May and June, and then again in autumn), becoming essentially 'normality' for Venice. The remaining Carnival-free months became 'dead' months. Carnival thus became Venice's most important business, so much so that it shifted from being a private-sector matter to a truly 'state affair'. And then came the attempt to offer more variety to visitors. Of course, Carnival was the main attraction but there were also its artworks and even religious relics, of which it possessed perhaps more than any other city outside of Rome, fruit of the centuries of trade, theft and plunder of Venetian merchants. A 1740 inventory of Venice's relics and artworks, published under the rather cumbersome title *Forestiere Illuminato intorno le cose più rare, e curiose, antiche, e moderne della città di Venezia e dell'Isole circonvicine. Con la descrizione delle Chiese, Monasteri, Ospedali, Tesoro di San Marco, Fabbriche pubbliche, Pitture celebri e di quanto v'è di più ragguardevole*, numbered them well into the hundreds.[9]

Finally, we find in seventeenth-century Venice what was essentially a kind of tourism propaganda apparatus. After all, what are the paintings of Canaletto, Francesco Guardi, Giandomenico Tiepolo or Pietro Longhi (who painted numerous scenes of

Carnival) if not canvas versions of our modern tourist brochures, inviting visitors to the city?

If tourism is an industry, then tourists are the market the tourist cities must fight among one another to carve up.

> The three elements of urban tourism – the tourist, the tourism industry, and cities – interact to produce a complex ecological system. The tastes and desires of tourists are fickle; just like car buyers, they will yearn for next year's model even before it appears. With the entry of transnational corporations, plus the globalisation of credit, media and electronic communications, the tourist industry is in the midst of a revolution in which images, information, and money are transmitted at lightning speed. The object of the chase, the tourist, is a moving target. To appeal to tourists, cities must be consciously moulded to create a physical landscape that tourists wish to inhabit. No city can afford to stand still for a moment, no matter how much it has recently done or how much money it has spent doing it.[10]

The technologies for remodelling a tourist city have now been so tried, tested and perfected that they have become almost standardised. As such, we begin to see the same 'typical, characteristic, regional' urban design being introduced everywhere. The tourist industry has, according to Françoise Choay,

> developed the conditioning processes which allow the handing-over of historic centres and ancient districts already primed for cultural consumption … An arsenal of established mechanisms make it possible to attract the excited, keep them there, organise the economy of their time, and uproot them in a manner where they remain surrounded by familiarity and comfort: systems of signs and graphics to orient them; stereotypes of the urban picturesque; letterboxes, plaques, shelters, pedestrian passageways paved with cobblestones or in old-fashioned style, kitted out with standard and more or less retro industrial fittings (candelabras, benches, bins, public

telephones), livened up as space allows by fountains, rustic vases of flowers and international saplings; stereotypes of urban leisure: open-air cafés with the right furniture, artisan outlets, art galleries, second hand dealers and again, always, everywhere, in all forms, exotic, regional, industrial, the restaurant.[11]

To emphasise their uniqueness and attract tourists, tourist cities in fact end up rethinking and redesigning themselves – and they do so all in the same ways, as they compete among themselves for the same market. Consequently, it no longer makes sense to speak of the individual tourist city, but rather of a network or system of tourist cities.

The most visible change to the urban fabric of tourist cities, however, is the effect of what Dean MacCannell identified as one of tourism's specific characteristics. For MacCannell, authenticity is visible to a tourist only where it is 'marked' by something specific, 'overexpressed', or even 'staged'.[12] MacCannell therefore makes explicit reference to the theory formulated by Erving Goffman in *The Presentation of the Self in Everyday Life*, which in the French translation was rendered as 'the staging of the individual', and in German contained the bolder assertion that 'we are all acting in a play'. 'The perspective employed', Goffman tells us in his preface, 'is that of the theatrical performance; the principles derived are dramaturgical ones. I shall consider the way in which the individual in ordinary work situations presents himself and his activity to others, the ways in which he guides and controls the impression they form of him, and the kinds of things he may or may not do while sustaining his performance before them.'[13]

Goffman's idea is that in the interpersonal relationships found in modern society, the individual presents their self to others by constructing a representation of themselves that changes according to the context or interlocutor. The individual thus displays themselves on a 'frontstage' while at the same time reserving a 'backstage' for re-arranging the presentation, rehearsing, preparing the costumes, learning the lines or just charging his batteries.

It ought to be emphasised that for Goffman the theatrical dimension of the relationship of the self to others is not an accessory. In any interaction it will always be present; there is no opting out. We will see later how this point is of vital importance for criticism of current theories of tourism.

It is this staging that gives the tourist city its unmistakable theatricality. Every city must 'play' itself; Rome must act out its Rome-ness and Paris must perform the role of the American image of Paris. The bistro becomes a caricature of a bistro, just as Trastevere in Rome is a caricature of the Italian capital's old folk culture. And it is a process that reproduces itself right under our eyes, in all the cities of the globe, without us realising. Hence why Québec City looks like how an inventor of fairy tales would imagine a gloomy fortress on the St Lawrence River. Or why contemporary New Orleans looks just like the stereotype image of New Orleans – indeed, the first part of the city they rushed to reopen after Hurricane Katrina in 2005 was the famous French Quarter.

When the effects of staging are coupled with those of the elimination of other productive activities, the result is a comprehensive degeneration of the tourist city. I spent the best part of the 1970s in Paris's Latin Quarter and would describe it then as lively but nonchalant. Fifty years later, however, it is a dead neighbourhood, overrun with cheap squalor. The Latin Quarter is a good example of how tourism can kill a neighbourhood by supposedly bringing it to life. The whole of the fifth arrondissement has been emptied from the inside. All the useful shops like hardware and homeware stores, haberdasheries or electrical goods have closed, and every manifestation of local life has over time been supplanted by fake Chinese or Greek restaurants, or sandwich and ice cream bars, despite the fact that the neighbourhood is still home to the Sorbonne, the Collège de France and top-end grammar schools.

Not long ago I went back to San Gimignano for the first time in thirty years. There was not a single genuine butcher, greengrocer or baker within its walls. But in fact, once the bars, restaurants and souvenir shops had closed for the night, none of San Gimignano's inhabitants were to be found in the old city – they all live outside its walls, in modern apartment blocks close to shopping centres. Within the walls, everything has become a set for a medieval costume movie, with the inevitable products of 'invented tradition' on commercial display.

The 'inventions of tradition' continued to proliferate throughout the twentieth century. The medieval and Renaissance-style aspects of the Palio di Siena were introduced in 1904, while the victory parade was introduced only in 1919. A similar competition in historical costume, this time in the Umbrian town of Gubbio, the Palio della Balestera, dates back only to 1951. And the 'ancient' Palio Marinaro of Livorno (in this case a boat race) is actually no older than the postwar period. In Avellino, south of Naples, the Palio della Botte was rediscovered in 1998. And the list could go on. Interestingly, the book that opened this line of inquiry, *The Invention of Tradition* by Eric Hobsbawm and Terence Ranger, appeared in 1983. That is, it was published amid the rush to open new museums across Great Britain as a means of valorising its historical heritage, compensating for the loss of industry with the invention of the heritage industry. One of the starkest examples used by Hobsbawm and Ranger is the kilt, symbol of Scottish identity, which was invented by an English industrialist, Thomas Rawlinson, in 1727, twenty years after Scotland gave up its independence.[14]

But the invention of tradition, even in this case, is not simply a swindle or a rip-off (at least not in every case). Discussing one of the major paradoxes of the conservationist ideology of tradition, Richard Handler and Jocelyn Linnekin write that 'attempts at cultural preservation inevitably alter, reconstruct, or invent the traditions that they are intended to fix. Traditions are neither genuine nor spurious, for if genuine tradition refers to the pristine and immutable heritage of the past, then all genuine traditions would be spurious. But if, as we have argued, tradition is always defined in the present, then all spurious traditions are genuine.'[15] Even if originally the invented tradition was thought of as a fraud, it comes to acquire its own truth, its own reality, just as the kilt has become a *real* sign of Scottishness.

The concept of 'staged authenticity' opens up new perspectives. Especially when we take into account the fact that tourists are not (that is, *we* are not) completely stupid and know very well that what is being exhibited for their (*our*) benefit has been staged, engineered, put in the spotlight. So, they always want to look behind the scenes, like the food connoisseur who tries to get into the restaurant kitchen to find out the recipe. It is this dynamic, then, the progressive unveiling of the backstage offered to the tourist as a spectacle, that provides one of the motors of the tourist industry. Hence a *Lonely Planet* guide may recommend a residential neighbourhood of Madrid because here 'you can see how the locals really live, far from the madding crowds of tourists'. The 'traditional markets' are another example of the spectacle of the backstage because here the tourist searches not for the tourist bazaar but for the place where locals *actually* go to get their daily amenities. These markets initially serve merely as an object of the tourist's gaze, preserving their 'indigenous' character, but over time they begin to offer goods to the tourists, or simply to package the same foodstuffs as gifts or souvenirs, until eventually the market becomes a wholly tourist market, like Madrid's Mercado de San Miguel.

The pursuit of the backstage is a pursuit with no end, because once you turn the spotlight on the backstage it itself becomes a new show, and then it is the backstage of the new show that has to be found, and so it goes on. Like a modern version of Zeno's paradox of Achilles and the tortoise, the tourist never stops chasing that behind-the-scenes authenticity, yet by the time they get there the behind-the-scene has itself already been staged, 'marked' and, thus, rendered inauthentic.

However, the notion of staged authenticity is particularly fertile when applied to the relation between the 'native' or 'indigenous' locals of a tourist city and its 'visitors'. When theories of tourism discuss visitors, ninety-nine per cent of the time they don't mention the visited. In *The Tourist Gaze*, for example, John Urry discusses at length how our way of perceiving reality is changed when we view the world through the lens of the tourist, which in turn changes the reality we produce, something we do more and more frequently. But when Urry speaks of the tourist gaze it is always the gaze of the person doing the tour, not someone from the place being toured.

Tourism studies has always placed the relationship between visitors and locals within the category of 'hosts and guests', as reads the title of the first collection of anthropological studies of tourism. The book's editor expresses a cautious optimism about the future of tourism (despite the book including a chapter on 'Tourism as a Form of Imperialism').[16] The studies collected here focus in particular on cultural changes brought about by tourism within the two groups, the guests and the hosts, and make the argument that these changes are asymmetrical because tourists 'are less likely to borrow from their hosts than their hosts are from them, thus precipitating a chain of change in the host community'. What we see clearly here, however, is a conception of tourism based on an underlying assumption of visitors from an industrialised and wealthy West to third world or 'backward' countries.[17] But the real issue is that the relationship between local residents and tourists is anything but a relationship based on hospitality and invitation, or at least it would be were it not for the involvement of money.

Indeed, within the group of the hosts, it is necessary to distinguish between two categories: those who depend – directly or indirectly – on tourism for their survival and those whose economic fortunes are apparently independent of tourism. While a waiter in a restaurant depends directly on the flow of tourists, for a high school teacher or someone who works in a bank the connection is much more indirect: if the tourists stop arriving they will only see a change of fortune in the longer term, when the lack of hospitality workers and their families means there are not enough schoolchildren to justify a class or enough customers to keep a bank branch open.

Precisely because of the theatrical nature of tourism, the 'position of labour in the supply of many final demand tourism products is unusual in that workers are simultaneously providers of labour services and part of the consumed product' (Britton).[18] In other words, workers in tourist hospitality form part of the infrastructure of sightseeing, yet at the same time they are also themselves one of the sights to be seen. The quality of service, the 'friendliness and politeness' tourists find when they step into the 'local' bar or restaurant, are major assets for a tourist destination. Not only must waiters serve tables, they must also turn their waiting on tables into a performance. In Barthes's terms, a waiter's body language serves to connote not only his profession but also his 'Italianness' or 'Frenchness', his 'typical character' in the sense of 'typical products'. Even more so because hospitality workers are usually the people tourists most frequently come into contact with, and in some cases, the *only* people they come into contact with.

There were some who hoped that tourism would become a tool for improving mutual understanding between different cultures and peoples, bringing them closer together. This had also been the case with the advent of rail travel: the advocates of Saint-Simonianism thought believed that the railways ('the most perfect symbol of universal association') would allow all the world's nations to get to know one another, eradicating conflict and creating a 'fraternal bond' across all humanity. In fact, the creation of the railways merely facilitated the transportation of troops and arms in times of war. And we could say that tourism, far from bringing peoples together, has pushed them further apart because it brings out the worst in both tourists and locals. Locals reveal their greediest and most miserly selves, dollar signs (or euros or yuans) flashing in their eyes. For the local tour operators, tourists are less guests to be welcomed than lemons to be squeezed for every last drop, taking advantage of the tourist's complete (though perfectly justified) ignorance of the ways of the city.

And what about the locals who do not depend on tourism? We Italians understand very well that the 'tourist gaze' modifies those who are its target and not only the gazers themselves. The residents of a tourist city live forever in the tourist gaze; under the constant surveillance of a watch that is literally 'out of place'. It is like having your house full of unwanted guests, then having to step over unknown bodies lining the hallway to get to the bathroom at night. The metaphor is appropriate because, in Goffman's terms, the lavatory is behind the scenes, indeed it is the perfect example of the backstage to our daily lives:

> In our society, defecation involves an individual in activity which is defined as inconsistent with the cleanliness and purity standards expressed in many of our performances. Such activity also causes the individual to disarrange his clothing and to "go out of play", that is, to drop from his face the expressive mask that he employs in face-to-face interaction. At the same time it becomes difficult for him to reassemble his personal front should the need to enter into interaction suddenly occur. Perhaps that is a reason why toilet doors in our society have locks on them.[19]

If the progressive unveiling of the 'unstaged' backstage is a never-ending pursuit, and if the tourist is Achilles, then the local resident is the tortoise, forever running from the tourist's reach in search of unchanged places or situations. Locals are forced to become clandestine in their own cities, to pass on in hushed tones the coordinates for the last remaining tolerable pockets of the city, whispering, 'But don't let the tourists know!' They do so knowing full well that sooner or later even these will be uncovered, a spotlight thrown on them, and then the search for new provisional refuges will have to begin again. But as they are also well aware, the outcome has already been decided. The tourist city inevitably becomes unliveable as a city of residence as locals find it more and more difficult to survive economically and are more and more socially excluded. After all, tourism is an industry, and like any industry, it will make a city more and more unliveable, just as manufacturing brought slums, smog and stench to manufacturing towns.

And if tourism does not produce precisely the same effects of slums and smog, it is only because it kills a city in subtler ways, by hollowing it out from the inside and emptying it of life, just like the mummification of a corpse. It turns the city into a giant theme park, a vast historical Disneyland, through a kind of urban taxidermy. It fills it with museums and sandwich bars, antique ruins and luxury boutiques, the *son et lumière* of pizza-slice joints and Michelin triple-starred restaurants, pedestrian zones and expanses of smart middle-class accommodation. The modern pedestrian zones of Northern Europe all look the same (they are another example of Marc Augé's 'non-places'), and the town centres have all been transformed into 'entertainment districts' where no one actually enjoys themselves.

The visitor, on the other hand, even in the best of cases, carefully visits not so much the country itself but the country's *Lonely Planet* or *Guide Bleu*. In any case, visitors do not have the time, means or opportunity to be concerned with the local human beings; they only care for 'dead humanity' (as capital cares only for 'dead labour'), namely, monuments and museums. Archetypal of this is the tour of the city by air-conditioned coach, with all the sounds and smells blocked out so that perception is reduced purely to sight.

Inverting the old idea of Joseph Alois Schumpeter, who held that capitalism is best understood as a process of 'creative destruction', we could say that tourism practices 'destructive creation' as the economic growth and development it produces destroy the bases on which that growth was premised. For example, the North Coast of Crete was once characterised by agricultural and livestock production and fishing, as well as by poverty. But today Northern Crete has become a vast periphery of faceless apartment blocks extending along the whole of its coast. The same has happened to large chunks of Tuscany, where the old farmsteads have been steadily replaced by upmarket estates with their own olive groves and top-quality vineyards (and have perhaps even been declared UNESCO World Heritage sites, like the Val d'Orcia), which sell their produce directly to tourists or as high-end exportation abroad. More often, however, the old farmhouses, or even whole villages, have become simply second homes, done up and well kept with their original wooden ceiling beams exposed and their external walls stripped of plaster to reveal the raw stone. The vegetable plot has been supplanted by an ornamental garden, immediately recognisable from miles away because olive and fruit trees have been replaced by soulless silver firs. These houses are empty, dead, for eleven months of the year, and a good part of the Tuscan countryside (and the same is true for Provence) has become a vast residential complex, cleaned up, painted over and restored, with vases of geraniums at the windowsills, morphed into a holiday destination for affluent Germans or Brits. Indeed, Tuscany has acquired the very apt nickname of Chiantishire.

8

UNESCO's Urbicide

It is devastating to witness the death throes of so many cities. Splendid, opulent, hectic, for centuries, sometimes millennia, they survived the vicissitudes of history: war, pestilence, earthquakes. But now, one after another, they are withering, emptying, becoming reduced to theatrical backdrops against which a lifeless pantomime is staged. Where once life throbbed and cantankerous humanity elbowed its way forward, pushing and shoving, now you find only snack bars and stalls – all of them the same – selling 'local specialities': muslins, batiks, cottons, beach wraps, bracelets. What was once a rushing river, full of shouts and fury, is now safely enclosed in a travel brochure.

The death sentence is delivered from an elegant building in Paris – Place Fontenoy in the seventh arrondissement – after a long-drawn-out bureaucratic process. The verdict is a label that cannot be removed – a brand, stamped forever. UNESCO's 'World Heritage' listing is the kiss of death. Once the label is affixed, the city's life is snuffed out; it is ready for taxidermy. This urbicide – horrible word – is not perpetrated deliberately. On the contrary, it is committed in good faith and with the loftiest of intentions: to preserve, unaltered, a 'legacy' of humanity. As the word suggests, to 'preserve' means to embalm, to freeze, to save something from temporal decay; but here it also means halting time, fixing the object as in a photograph, protecting it from growth and change. There are, of course, monuments that need to be looked after. But if the Acropolis had been under a conservation order in 450 BC, we would not now have the Parthenon, the Propilaea or the Erechtheion: when these wonders were erected, the ruins of previous temples, which had been destroyed by Xerxes' troops when they sacked the city in 480 BC, were removed or salvaged for materials. UNESCO would have been horrified by the Rome of the six-teenth and seventeenth centuries, which produced an admirable potpourri of neoclassicism, mannerism and the baroque. Thank heavens the Marais in Paris was not declared a World Heritage site, otherwise we could forget the Beaubourg.

The idea that ancient monuments should be protected and/or restored only came into being in the nineteenth century. In fact, the modern notion of the monument dates to the same century – another heirloom bequeathed to us by Romanticism. And from the very beginning, a conflict arose between two opposing camps, the traces of which are still visible in contemporary discussions on the conservation of the antique. In his *Dictionnaire raisonné de l'architecture française du XIe au XVIe siècle*, Eugène Emmanuel Viollet-le-Duc (1814–1879) opened his entry for 'Restauration' with the following:

> Both the word and the thing are modern. *Restoring a building does not mean maintaining it in good condition, repairing it or doing it up. It means reconstructing a state of completeness that cannot at any time have really existed.* The urge to restore buildings of another epoch has only existed since the second quarter of this century, and as yet we are unaware of any precise definition of architectural restoration ... We have said that the word and the thing are modern, and indeed, no previous civilisation has ever pro-posed to carry out a restoration as we understand the term today.[1]

Viollet-le-Duc's vision of restoration was radical and 'modernist', entailing the re-creation of a monument in its totality, even where that totality 'cannot have ever existed'.

Meanwhile, across the English Channel, John Ruskin (1819–1900), in *The Seven Lamps of Architecture* (1849), was putting forward a vision of restoration antithetical to Viollet-le-Duc's. Ruskin 'hated' the concept of 'restoration in any form':

Neither by the public, nor by those who have the care of public monuments, is the true meaning of the word restoration understood. It means the most total destruction which a building can suffer: a destruction out of which no remnants can be gathered; a destruction accompanied with false description of the thing destroyed. Do not let us deceive ourselves in this important matter; it is impossible, as impossible as to raise the dead, to restore anything that has ever been great or beautiful in architecture.[2]

Observing the garish colours and coarse lines of the late-twentieth-century restorations of fourteenth- and fifteenth-century frescos, we can be forgiven for sympathising with Ruskin's extremism. But his vision goes well beyond the offences he feared well-meaning restorers would inflict on the antique. John Ruskin was the man who believed that train travel transformed passengers into 'living parcels'. Hence we must at least credit him with consistency. Ruskin is the forebear of a long line of 'restoration fundamentalists'.

It is his ideas that provide an authority for die-hard conservationists: with UNESCO's blessing many little Ruskins flourish in the guise of 'superintendents' of fine arts and architecture, regional and national ministers for urban planning, culture and the arts (though, as we will see in the next chapter, there are also many disciples of Viollet-le-Duc fighting from their corner under the UNESCO banner).

But a balance needs to be struck between constructing and preserving. We want to live in cities that include museums and works of art, not in mausoleums with dormitory suburbs attached. It is an inhuman punishment to spend one's life in the guest quarters of an endless museum. And the smaller the city the more complete its demise. There are now countless replications of San Gimignano – and these are not to be found only in Italy.

The city of Luang Prabang, Laos, has suffered the same fate. Its historic centre is now a tourist trap. Its houses have been converted into hotels and restaurants, with the usual street market – identical the world over – selling the same necklaces, woven bags and leather belts. Paradoxically, the unintended consequence of wanting to preserve the uniqueness of a place is to produce a 'non-place', one that is replicated at World Heritage sites across the planet. Just as one has to leave the medieval walls to find the true inhabitants of San Gimignano, so one has to cycle a mile along the Phothisalath Road, beyond Phu Vao, to find where the Laotians live.

Or take Portugal: walking through Porto, the invisible frontier of the World Heritage quarter is immediately perceptible: the heterogeneous humanity of its urban fabric gives way as if by magic to a monoculture of innkeepers, bartenders and waiters, touting for customers who are instantly recognisable by their clothes – shorts and hiking boots – which are radically unsuitable for city wear.

In Britain, few places are as deadly as the historic centres of Bath and Edinburgh.* Nor is it pure coincidence that both host famous festivals, the inevitable function of a World Heritage city. Venice hosts not only the Film Festival, but also the art and architecture Biennale. Avignon, whose centre has been a World Heritage site since 1995, is home to one of the world's oldest festivals of theatre (founded in 1947 by Jean Vilar), while Salzburg, given World Heritage status in 1996, was already home to the world's most prestigious music festival. To this we can add the *Festival dei Due Mondi* (Festival of the Two Worlds), which takes place in Spoleto, Umbria (whose San Salvatore basilica was declared a World Heritage building in 2011); a Wagner Festival is held in Bayreuth, Bavaria (whose Margravial Opera House was declared a World Heritage site in 2012). To fully appreciate the synergy between the UNESCO label and the organisation of festivals, suffice to know that 'the 16 festivals organised in the Scottish capital between 30 July 2004 and 31 May 2005 attracted

---

* There are thirty UNESCO World Heritage sites in the UK but only four of these are urban sites. Curiously, only two of them are in England (Bath, and Liverpool's 'Maritime Mercantile City'), one is in Scotland (Edinburgh) and one is in the overseas territory of Bermuda (St George). All the other sites are castles (Durham Castle, Blenheim Palace), landscapes (Dorset and the East Devon Coast), or ruins like Hadrian's Wall and Stonehenge.

3,192,438 visitors', producing 'an economic impact of €249.37 million in Edinburgh and another €20.52 million in the rest of Scotland'.[3] And likewise, 'the 2006 edition of the Salzburg Festival, the largest and most famous opera festival in the world, in 36 days offered 207 events in 14 different venues attracting 244,269 spectators from 65 different nations.'[4]

Festival towns are given World Heritage status because they are already theatrical backdrops, picturesque still lifes; conversely, the theatrical or musical performances the label attracts can afford them a semblance of vitality. In the UNESCO city the 'staging of authenticity' is literal: 'the heritage city is both put on stage and itself converted into a stage: on the one hand it is lit up, cleaned up, neatly arranged and embellished for optimum media exposure; on the other, they become settings for festivals, special events, celebrations, congresses and real and unreal "happenings" that, deploying to best effect the ingenuity of the performers, multiply the numbers of visitors' (Choay).[5]

Papered over with flimsy decorations, this absence of life nevertheless pervades all musealised sites. The old city of Rhodes in the Dodecanese is a World Heritage site. It is true that its stones and walls have been preserved, but these and only these have been saved, and their function has been entirely perverted. Rhodes as it is today can burn in hell, for all I care. This kind of preservation does not give us anything, it is a curing of the disease by killing the patient. Preserving a few stones is not equivalent to saving a city, an urban culture.

In this the analogy between cultural heritage sites and natural parks is misleading. Nature reserves are created to multiply the existing fauna and flora, whereas the human fauna of World Heritage cities is forced to flee as the practicalities of daily life become impossible. Imagine having to install a hot water or sanitary system in a UNESCO-protected medieval building, a dilemma Viollet-le-Duc himself discussed: 'one can understand that an architect might refuse to insert gas tubes in a church to avoid mutilation or accidents because other means of illumination exist, but refusing to install, for example, a radiator, on the pretext that medieval religious buildings were never fitted with this kind of heating system, forcing churchgoers to catch cold for the sake of architecture, is downright ridiculous.'[6]

The most concrete example of the contrast between material life and cultural conservation is the city of Dresden, otherwise known as 'the Florence of Germany'. Dresden, along with the Elbe Valley, was awarded World Heritage status in 2004 – but there was a snag: the good people of Dresden wanted to avoid traffic jams as they crossed the Elbe, so they needed a new bridge. UNESCO was opposed, claiming a bridge would ruin the landscape. The matter was put to a referendum: a majority of the inhabitants voted in favour, even at the risk of losing World Heritage status, which was duly rescinded in 2009. In August 2013, the citizens celebrated the inauguration of their new bridge, to the author's enthusiastic approval.

One might object, here, that there are other ways to kill a city. Indeed, Perry Anderson did just this when he wrote to me:

> Are you not neglecting an equal danger posed by the chaos and disorder of urban life – by the senseless greed of developers who demolish ancient buildings in order to erect horrible banks, apartment blocks and shopping centres in their place? Italy is the best illustration of your point. But any journey through China provides ample evidence of this second scourge. In Latin America, the only capital that has not yet been beaten to the ground is the decadent Havana (though just wait until all that *gusano* cash starts flowing in from Miami), or perhaps colonial Quito and the *beaux quartiers* of Buenos Aires. The sight of Rio, Ipanema or Leblon is enough to reduce one to tears.

The second objection is obviously that it was not UNESCO that created the tourist city, but, if anything, it was the tourist city that created UNESCO.

Certainly, the choice between living in a museum or living in a bank is a difficult one. But in truth, the choice is not a choice at all; the substance is the same. Any environment built to realise the lifestyle aspirations of the corporate élites will always consist of secluded enclaves for living, financial downtowns for making money and cultural Disneylands, again, for making money.

It is no surprise that the World Heritage label was created in the 1970s. In 1972, after many years of discussion, the General Conference of UNESCO adopted the Convention Concerning the Protection of the World Cultural and Natural Heritage, which has since been ratified by 190 countries. In 1976, the World Heritage Committee was established, and two years later it identified its first site. In other words, the brand was 'launched' at the start of the world tourist revolution, representing both its achievements and the key to its continuing self-promotion.

What's more, this UNESCO initiative had been preceded by fervent legislative activity on the part of individual states aimed at preserving their own historical monuments, 'for example the Dutch Monumentenwet 1961, the French Loi Malraux 1962, British Civic Amenities Act 1967, Italian Urban Planning Act 1967 and even Turkish Monument and Historic Buildings Act of 1973', whose 'degrees of congruence' suggests 'an active interchange of ideas among those framing the legislation'.[7]

Across the world, an idea was beginning to take hold: that the past was a resource to exploit and that legal structures needed to be created for this to be allowed and facilitated. It is telling that during the same period that the World Heritage label was being launched, the metaphor of energy extraction had become fashionable among the sector's professionals and government ministers: in 1978, Jacques Duhamel, then French culture minister, made the claim that 'our cultural heritage is a reserve as manageable and exploitable as oil'.[8]

And it was in this same period that Italian ministers began to speak of 'cultural deposits', another elaboration of the fossil fuel analogy (indeed, from a geological perspective, fossil deposits are also an 'inheritance' of the past). Duhamel's wording is especially significant because it is the first instance that the duplicity of meaning of the word 'heritage' is displayed in all its glory, as cultural legacy and patrimonial inheritance. 'Fifty years back, book titles and indexes suggest that heritage dwelt mainly in heredity, probate law, and taxation; it now features antiquities, roots, identity, belonging' (David Lowenthal).[9] Ashworth and Turnbridge write,

> The concept that provides the link between the preservation of the past for its intrinsic value and as a resource for a modern community or commercial activity is *heritage*. The word, although sometimes rather loosely used as a synonym for historic relics, does encompass a meaning, equally present in its French (*patrimoine*), German (*Erbschaft*) or Dutch (*erfgoed*) forms, that adds a significantly different dimension to both 'preservation' and 'conservation'. Heritage necessarily contains both the idea of some modern value inherited from the past as well as a legatee for whom this inheritance is intended ... Heritage not only automatically poses the question, 'whose heritage?', but, even more fundamentally, can only logically be defined in terms of that market.[10]

It is no coincidence in fact that the term 'heritage' has undergone the same transformation as the concept of 'identity', which, ignored for centuries (or at least used in a very limited sense), quite suddenly took on a new meaning and at the same time became ubiquitous and indispensable in any discourse.

For centuries the word 'identity' was used in a purely logical sense. For Aristotle identity was simply the relation expressed in the proposition 'A is A': the identical is that which is always the same as itself, and identity is the attribute of two identical things. Under the entry 'identity', the *Concise Oxford Dictionary of Sociology* (1994) states that 'The term identity came into common use only at the beginning of the twentieth century' thanks to – in psychoanalysis – the Freudian theory of identification and – in sociology – to the theory formulated by Herbert Mead of the Self as a social construction. Eric Hobsbawm dated the spread of the term to the beginning of the 1970s:

We have become so used to terms like 'collective identity', 'identity groups', 'identity politics', or, for that matter 'ethnicity', that it is hard to remember how recently they have surfaced as part of the current vocabulary, or jargon, of political discourse. For instance, if you look at the *International Encyclopaedia of the Social Sciences*, which was published in 1968 – that is to say written in the middle 1960s – you will find no entry under *identity* except one about psychosocial identity, by Erik Erikson, who was concerned chiefly with such things as the so-called 'identity crisis' of adolescents who are trying to discover what they are, and a general piece on voters' identification. And as for ethnicity, in the *Oxford English Dictionary* of the early 1970s it still occurs only as a rare word indicating 'heathendom and heathen superstition' and documented by quotations from the eighteenth century.[11]

Further proof of Hobsbawm's observations is that no entry for 'identity' can be found in either the 1964 *A Dictionary of Social Sciences* (sponsored by the United Nations), in Luciano Gallino's 1978 *Dizionario di Sociologia*, or in the 1982 *Dictionnaire critique de la sociologie* by Raymond Boudon and François Bourricaud, though the first of the three contains an entry for 'identification' as a psychological process. As far as I can tell, the first dictionary to contain an entry for 'identity' was the 1986 *Dictionary of Anthropology* by Charlotte Seymour-Smith.[12]

Thus we find that the terms 'identity', 'ethnicity' and 'heritage' changed their meaning and proliferated in public discourse at the end of the 1970s. The connection is not merely fortuitous, given the nexus between heritage and identity, and the fact that our heritage is what identifies our identity: 'All at once heritage is everywhere – in the news, in the movies, in the marketplace – in everything from galaxies to genes. It is the chief focus of patriotism and a prime lure of tourism. One can barely move without bumping into a heritage site. Every legacy is cherished ... To neglect heritage is a cardinal sin, to invoke it a national duty' (Lowenthal).[13]

Hence, 'In the United States [the term heritage] has been appropriated by the New Right. The Heritage Foundation set up in

1973 has a 12 million-dollar budget to fund a Washington think tank that serves to promote conservative political philosophy on an international scale' (Hewison).[14]

David Lowenthal also points to the proliferation in the 1980s of books and studies dedicated to the topic, among which Lowenthal's own work features, along with titles by Robert Hewison and Françoise Choay. Studies on musealisation also emerged, such as Donald Horne's *The Great Museum: The Re-Presentation of History* (Pluto Press, 1984), *The Museum Time-Machine* edited by Robert Lumley (Routledge, 1988) and Patrick Wright's *On Living in an Old Country* (Verso, 1985; Oxford University Press, 2009).

UNESCO was therefore acting in perfect accord with the spirit of the age, in two different senses: it was in symphony with the conservative turn in the West, conservative both in the political sense with the rise of Thatcher and Reagan and their monetarist economics, and in the preservationist sense. The organisation was also in line with the reconversion of the post-industrial West to tourism: it was Thatcher's Britain that approved the National Heritage Act in 1981. The preservation of heritage functions in both these senses, artistically and economically. The process is complete once cultural heritage takes on a market value.

Functioning as a 'certificate of authenticity', the UNESCO label allows the tourist industry to cash in on the market value of the authentic, as with *haute couture* designer brands or *Grand Crus* wines. In November 2014, the much coveted label of 'UNESCO Intangible Cultural Heritage' was even given to an agricultural practice for the first time, for the particular method of making the Muscat wine of the island of Pantelleria, while in the summer of 2015, the winemakers of Burgundy were granted World Heritage status for their *climats* (small plots of land on which Burgundy vines are cultivated on the slopes of the Côte de Nuits region and around Beaune, just south of Dijon).[15] Just so that no one would feel left out, on the same occasion the *caves* (wine cellars), cottages, and *coteaux* (hills) of Champagne were also added to the World Heritage list.

This brings us back to Dean MacCannell's proposition whereby, in contrast to Walter Benjamin, an original artwork's aura manifests itself only once copies begin to appear and not before (see Chapter 3). In other words, it is the technical replication that confers on a work of art its aura. In this sense we could say the function of the UNESCO label is quite simply to provide an 'aura certification' service. What concerns us, therefore, is not whether the knock-offs preceded the label, but that the existence of knock-offs means that sooner or later the label will come, and where there is the label there will inevitably follow more junk.

The tourist industry is certainly aware of its debt to UNESCO: 'It is therefore logical and legitimate that "in recognition of its outstanding guidance, support and encouragement to 185 countries around the world by establishing and monitoring 878 World Heritage sites, and of *its outstanding accomplishments in the travel industry*" the UNESCO World Heritage Centre was awarded the 2008 World Tourism Award, sponsored by Corinthia Hotels, American Express, *The International Herald Tribune* and Reed Travel Exhibitions and presented annually at the World Travel Market in London' (Choay).[16]

Naturally, the UNESCO brand is not the cause of tourism but rather its stamp of legitimacy and guarantee, the do-gooding institution providing the industry with ideological cover. Here we enter the world of medieval scholastic philosophy: the problem of universals, the relation between names and things. The label is not the thing; but as Austin argued, words have performative power, and a certificate can be a potent instrument indeed[17] (just think, for example, of the power in the title PhD). Tourism and the World Heritage label together constitute a feedback mechanism, mutually reinforcing each other. The World Heritage site brand confers on tourism its title of nobility; we could call it the tourist *noblesse de robe,* the equivalent of what the eighteenth-century French nobility was to the French bourgeoisie. In Krysztof Pomian's terminology, the good version of the establishment of World Heritage sites could be defined as follows: UNESCO sanctions the sacrifice of a monument, a landscape or a city to invisibility, then welcomes it back from the past and preserves it for generations to come. Or, to put it differently, the World Heritage site is the Hegelian *schöne Seele* of the tourist industry, the 'beautiful soul' that allows us to accept tourist devastation in the name of aesthetic conservation.

For this reason, there has never been an antithesis setting Preservation against Profit or Culture against Tourism. There have been no titanic clashes between the tourist operators who, umbrellas held high, lead the attack of the tourist hordes upon our ancient ruins, and the heroic enlightened guardians who salvage the priceless treasures of our past. On the contrary, what does exist is a cultural legitimation of the tourist industry lent by the promotion of the conservation of the very sites that tourism is destroying. Here is Lowenthal:

> Heritage also succumbs to those who love it to death. Devotees wear down old floors, abrade ancient stones, erode prehistoric trackways. Banning hobnail boots and stiletto heels merely retards inevitable decay. Only withdrawal from use avails; as a town clerk said when asked to replace park benches, 'benches will not wear out so fast if people do not sit on them.' The more we learn of the ill effects of light, the less can old fabrics and watercolours be displayed. Since breath is lethal to the cave paintings, legacies like Lascaux are closed to public view; to see Leonardo's *Last Supper* visitors today must first be decontaminated.[18]

Françoise Choay also places emphasis on the destructive effects of preservation at all costs:

> This drive toward the market consumption of heritage is damaging not only for the tourists themselves, who are deceived as to the nature of the thing they are consuming and thrust into such noisy and crowded conditions as to make any intellectual or aesthetic appreciation impossible, but also very often for the sites themselves, due to the new construction required to host visitors (hotels, etc) and to the eradication of any creative activity connected to the

local culture and its identity, transforming them into nothing more than theme parks.[19]

The UNESCO label opened the industry up to a vast and marvellous new hunting ground: why build a new Disneyland when we have a plenty of real, living cities waiting (or indeed begging) to become theme parks through the simple process of mummification, that is, through their emptying out?

If at times there may appear to be some contradictions around the edges between 'conservationists' and 'tourism-ists', these are merely temporary divergences over profit in the long term and investment in the short term. We should bear in mind Pierre Bourdieu's lesson on the role of cultural capital as a sub-fraction of the dominant class, dominant vis-à-vis the other classes but itself subordinate to economic capital, even as it fights to win a greater degree of autonomy and self-determination. Ultimately cultural capital owes its own power over society's dominated strata to economic capital. It is a struggle among the dominant fractions that never calls into question the limits and power of domination.

For the financial markets, tourism is essentially an inexhaustible ATM. It is tourist money that allows speculators the liquidity to invest nonstop, with their speed-of-light algorithms deployed from the steel-and-glass skyscrapers of the financial districts. Just as a corporate manager's perfect week consists of five days of frenetic securities transactions followed by a weekend of reading articles in the cultural supplement to the *Financial Times* on the metaphysics of light or on Kabbalah mysticism, so the corporate utopian city would consist of a financial centre and then a World Heritage Museum City, both of which are hollowed out after dusk and essentially inanimate.

But if the World Heritage brand acts as the ideological diploma issued to the hospitality industry, as the cultured and humanitarian face of the worldwide tourist machine, it also suffers from two potentially damaging contradictions. The first is what we might call chronological fundamentalism, whereby anything older is deemed more worthy of conservation. Thus the excavation of a Roman wall is justification for tampering with a magnificent medieval cloister, as is the case with the Lisbon Cathedral. The second contradiction is of a more philosophical nature: since UNESCO is multiplying its World Heritage sites, and since humanity is continuing to produce works of art (or so we hope), then it follows that in 3,000 years we will be immobilised by innumerable pieces of heritage. What will happen in another 1,000 or 2,000 years' time? Will we all be living on the Moon and buying tickets to visit planet Earth? What use would that be? And what relationship would we have created between the past and the present? The present produces monsters for sure; but then it always has. The same was said about Baroque Rome: *quod non fecerunt barbari, fecerunt Barberini* (what the barbarians failed to do, the Barberini have made up for). But as the past was at least at one point the present, then the past must be guilty of the same, and, as they say, time is not kind. We have been left with piles of third-rate classical literature while who knows how many masterpieces have been lost, and we have been deprived of the entirety of Greek painting and almost all the ancient bronze equestrian statues, and so on.

I am reminded here of the ending of *Digression sur les Anciens et les Modernes* (1688), where Fontenelle finds the courage to think that 'there was once a time when the *Latins were moderns*, and they complained of the obsession with the Greeks who were the ancients'. We are only modern because we came after. As Jean de La Bruyère wrote in the same year, 'We, who are so modern, will be ancient in a few centuries.'[20] And (perhaps) our modern errors/horrors will look no worse than the errors/horrors the ancients created when they were moderns. When I imagine the Greek temples not as I see them today, pure white marble set against the clear blue Mediterranean sky, but as they were twenty-five centuries ago, with oppressive wooden roofs and façades painted red and blue, they would have looked squat, shoddy and garish – the stuff of slums, far removed from the celestial aesthetics of their ruins. Who can tell whether, in 2,000 years' time, today's shopping malls will not be spoken of as architectural masterpieces?

This has already happened to the first-century harbour warehouses in Ostia Antica. And there are examples closer in time: today the Paris skyline would be unthinkable without the Eiffel Tower, but we ought to remember that when the tower was built for the 1889 Universal Exposition, the poor engineer, Gustave Eiffel, was told that it was an abomination that defaced the landscape – a mortal wound for the city.

From a conservationist perspective, everything becomes worthy of being preserved. Conservationists are like hoarders, afraid of throwing anything away in case 'it is lost forever'. On this basis there is no limit to UNESCO's auditing and certifying activity of the world's heritage. The first World Heritage site dates back to 1978, while today, following forty-three ordinary and thirteen extraordinary committee sessions, UNESCO, in 2019, declared 1,121 World Heritage sites in 167 countries. Of these, 869 are classed as cultural heritage, 213 natural and thirty-nine mixed.

The 869 cultural heritage sites include 163 cities (partially or entirely, one district only or simply the historic city centre). Almost half (eighty) of these 'art cities' are situated in Europe. In turn, almost half of the European art cities are in just four countries: Italy (twenty art cities including Vatican City and the Republic of San Marino), Spain (seven), Portugal (seven) and France (six). Considering its relatively small surface area, Italy is the country with the world's highest density of World Heritage sites.

Such reverence for Italy was noted as early as 31 March 1827, when Giacomo Leopardi wrote as follows:

> Those foreigners who most honour Italy with their respect, that is, those who regard it as a classical land, do not consider the Italy of today, in other words we, modern, living Italians, other than as custodians of a museum, of a cabinet of curiosities, or such like; and they have the sort of respect for us which is generally given to that kind of people; the sort of respect that we in Rome have toward the *usufructuaries*, so to speak, of the various antiquities, places, ruins, museums, etc.[21]

The conclusion of *The Futurist Manifesto* comes to mind. Published in *Le Figaro* in February 1909 and written by Filippo Tommaso Marinetti, the manifesto read: 'We want to deliver Italy from its gangrene of professors, archaeologists, tour guides and antiquaries. For too long Italy has been a market of second-hand dealers. We want to liberate it from its innumerable museums, which smother it like so many cemeteries.'

Though I have some sympathy for Marinetti's intolerance of cemeteries and second-hand markets, I do not share his blind faith in the future. If I had to define my own position I would call it 'presentism' rather than 'futurism', hope for and focus on the present, though unfortunately the term is already loaded with other meanings. And I have nothing against many of those 'gangrenous' categories Marinetti was so keen to rid Italy of: 'professors, archaeologists, tourist guides and antiquaries'. Indeed, I have nothing against museums per se. What I am averse to is the museumification as a universal category that – to use the Kantian expression – subsumes the entire life of a city and a society.[22]

The problem with the World Heritage label does not arise when it is decided that a painting, statue or building must be saved. Aside from the fact that the criteria used to determine what must be saved changes rapidly (as with Hercules's genitals, 'carved for London's Great Exhibition of 1851, sawn off in 1883, [and] reattached in 1977 in conformity with shifting mores'), there are many different ways to conserve. But Viollet-le-Duc's proposition seems indisputable: 'the best way to conserve a building is to find a function for it, as long as this does not require changes.'[23] Conserving means bringing back to life, finding a new use that the old form can adapt to. Choay cites the Italian universities hosted in Baroque or Renaissance buildings as a successful example. It is possible to reach an acceptable compromise for individual buildings that allows them to be preserved without turning them into museums.

The problem arises, rather, when the heritage label insists on fixing in time buildings or urban complexes that provide a home to networks of economic activity and human relations evolving over time, making them possible and allowing them to flourish. The problem comes when the anxiety of preservation traps within its net entire urban areas in order to mould them to its own ends. As Ashworth and Tunbridge observe,

> No longer is it sufficient to preserve monuments; areas must be planned for conservation ... This change of emphasis, together with the broadening of the definitions of what was to be conserved, led to the conservation of larger and larger proportions of more and more towns until it became exceptional, in most Western European countries, for a town not to have most of at least its central area under some form of conservation designation. Such planning thus becomes not so much a special sort of planning reserved for a few unique instances in a special category of cities, but a way of planning for cities in general.[24]

To put it brutally, in the planning of the contemporary city, or at least of their centres, the ancient has become the paradigm of the modern. In the same way that for post-1970s America, the phrase 'inner city' became synonymous with a city left for dead, an abandoned, degraded, province of the 'underclasses', as exemplified in John Carpenter's celebrated 1981 film (set in the dystopian future of 1997), *Escape from New York* – so the UNESCO city is also a dead city, abandoned by its natives as it is filled by an 'otherclass': the 'tourists'.

In this dead city the tourist roams eternally between cemeteries and antique dealers. More than a century has passed since the publication of *The Futurist Manifesto*, and yet our cities continue to be eaten up by the process of musealisation. The fact is that the World Heritage branding just keeps rolling on. One might have thought that what there was to be declared heritage in a country like Italy, so packed with history, ought to have already been branded by now. On the contrary: proceeding by decades, in the 1970s just one Italian site had been declared worthy of World Heritage ranking; in the '80s, five more were added; and the '90s witnessed the biggest explosion, with twenty-five new heritage sites. But even in the first decade of our millennium a further fourteen were identified; joined by ten in the second decade. That makes a total of no less than fifty-five natural and art sites.

It is, moreover, tragic that cities, towns and regions are queuing up and canvassing to get themselves embalmed. Like the countries aspiring to host the Olympics, unaware of the consequent ruination that will drag them into the abyss (see what happened to Greece with the 2004 Games or to Brazil in 2016), so our mayors, councillors and tourist offices strive to obtain the coveted status. We ought to be terrified at the prospect of our country being reduced to one vast museum, where we will have to buy a ticket in order to walk around, while desperately looking for a way out. They'll make a movie called *Escape From the Museum* to provide us with a breath of fresh air, a splash of life, the spectacle of cities changing, before we return to our mothballed environs.

9

Lijiang: Inventing Authenticity

At 7:14 p.m. on 3 February 1996, an earthquake registering 7.0 on the Richter scale struck the Chinese city of Lijiang in the mountainous region of South Yunnan, wedged between Tibet and Burma to the west and Laos to the south. Three hundred and nine people were killed and 17,057 injured across the region. In addition, 186,000 houses were destroyed and 300,000 people were made homeless. In the twenty-six hours that followed the quake, there were 184 aftershocks, eighteen of which registered between 4.0 and 4.8 on the Richter scale. On top of this, the monsoon rains that fell in the ensuing months triggered many landslides.

At the time Lijiang municipality was home to about 10,000 inhabitants.* The quake completely wiped out the modern parts of the town. Of the older buildings (mostly one or two storeys high) the most resistant proved to be the houses made of wood, which had more 'give'; those made of mud or clay did not survive. After the quake, the aftershocks and the landslides each did their bit, and Lijiang was reduced to little more than a pile of rubble.

And yet from a tourist's point of view the earthquake was a godsend, even if it had been coughed up from the bowels of the earth, because a year later UNESCO declared Lijiang's historic centre, the 'Old Town', a World Heritage Site. The designation served as proof that UNESCO's 'crusade' to patrimonialise

---

* If you do not read Mandarin it is very difficult to find coherent statistics for the area, either on the demography of the local population or on the numbers of tourists. It seems that the Chinese authorities are intent on muddying the waters about the numbers. As such, the data used in this chapter has been obtained by piecing together disparate sources and should be taken with caution.

human history 'does not even shrink from falsehoods' (Choay), for in Lijiang there was nothing to 'conserve' or 'preserve' in the normal sense, as almost everything had been destroyed by the earthquake.[1]

Nestled in a fertile valley 2,400 metres above sea level with a sub-monsoon climate, Dayan, the local name for Lijiang's Old Town, is surrounded by mountains. It is dominated in the northeast by a glacier that flows from the majestic snow-capped, 5,600-metre Yulong peak, known as the Jade Dragon Snow Mountain. Dayan was founded eight centuries ago by the Naxi people, who settled in the Tibetan plateau. Until the arrival of tourism, the Naxi had managed to maintain their traditions and customs alongside the dominant influence of Han culture. Water from the glaciers collecting in the Old Town's Black Dragon Pool (Heilongtan) is distributed among a sophisticated network of canals crisscrossing the city and nearby farming villages, making it the umpteenth place to be nicknamed the 'Chinese Venice'.

Until the 1980s, Lijiang was a small rural town. But at that point Beijing decided to turn it into a tourist attraction as part of its development programme for poor and disadvantaged areas, much like the development programmes of the European Union. In 1985, the central government declared Lijiang Yunnan's fourth tourist destination, following the three other sites identified in 1982 (Kunming Stone Forest, the city of Dali and the Xishuang-banna Dai Autonomous Prefecture). In 1995, Lijiang airport was opened, a rare initiative for 'a town with a population less than 10,000' that did not even have a railway.[2] The arduous two-day bus journey to Lijiang from Yunnan's capital, Kunming, was thus reduced to a flight of fifty-five minutes.

And then came the 1996 earthquake. Here, seismic destruction and the UNESCO World Heritage label came together in perfect harmony to erect an imaginary Lijiang, essentially from scratch. In the name of Ruskinite ideology (preservation of the antique without compromise) the town was renovated à la Viollet-le-Duc, restoring Lijiang 'to a complete state that had never existed at any previous moment'. Thanks to World Bank funding and supervision secured by the UNESCO imprimatur, high-rise buildings damaged in the earthquake were razed and replaced with traditional family houses. The clay and terra cotta of the old houses that had more or less survived were replaced with concrete, and their interiors were completely restructured. As Geoffrey Read and Katrinka Ebbe candidly acknowledged in an essay published by the World Bank, 'in the case of historic cities it is often difficult to strike a sensible balance between replacement and improvement, particularly when existing facilities are outdated or inadequate.' The reconstruction of Lijiang Old Town therefore included the 'safe and aesthetic installation of basic services such as electricity and sanitation', the application of 'design solutions for the installation of street lighting, telephone lines, and water and drainage services compatible with historic streetscapes', as well as 'construction and material improvements to provide thermal insulation and increase wind- and waterproofing'. Most tellingly of all, 'adjustments' were made 'to the traditional layout of rooms to incorporate modern lifestyles'. In short, the reconstruction was used as an excuse to build modern homes in (supposedly) antique shells.[3] This was clearly done with tourists in mind. Authentic antique houses were demolished to be replaced by fake traditional houses[4] and 356 bridges were restored or built from scratch (the number of bridges that existed before the earthquake varies according to the source.)

Monuments were also built that had not existed previously. A prime example of this is the Mu house. The Mu Fu Complex, taken from the name of the family that ruled the area from the fourteenth to seventeenth centuries, was described by Read and Ebbe as 'one of the major tourism sites in Lijiang's Old City'. They also state that 'in 1996 the Mu complex was a large and important, but heavily damaged, site'.

Curiously, however, the 1994 edition of the China *Lonely Planet*, in its three pages dedicated to Lijiang, not only fails to mention the Mu Fu Complex, but also does not list even a single monument, describing only the city's intricate network of alleyways, little houses and canals.

Indeed, once you begin to dig a little deeper you discover that earthquakes are frequent in Lijiang and that each occurrence adds another layer of ruins. Prior to 1996, there had been nine even stronger quakes: in 1481, 1515 (which entirely destroyed the city), 1624, 1751, 1895, 1933, 1951 (when 4,345 buildings were destroyed), 1966 and 1977. Repeatedly damaged by these earthquakes, the Mu residence was then entirely destroyed in the nineteenth century and private housing was built on the site. Furthermore, since 1949, following the advent of the Communist regime, more new buildings were constructed alongside the nineteenth-century houses which were then turned into administrative offices. Essentially then, nothing at all remained of the old Mu residence. And so, when the World Bank–funded 'restoration' was begun, the 'restorers' were able to truly indulge themselves, as they were even able to determine 'the appropriate "restoration date" for different parts of the complex'. The task was also 'complicated by the site's age, its degree of deterioration, and the fact that much historic material had been scattered around the complex and built into later structures'.[5] For all intents and purposes, however, what these 'restorers' did was build a half-scale reproduction of an imaginary construction (24,000 square metres instead of 48,000), a reproduction of what probably *cannot at any time have ever really existed* (Viollet-le-Duc). So much so that the 2007 edition of *Lonely Planet China* described the Mu residence as 'heavily renovated (or indeed built from scratch)'. In fact, Lijiang is full of other 'historical' monuments, such as the Wangu Pavilion, that did not exist prior to the earthquake and which the tourist guides declined to mention before 1996.

Indeed, in their book *The Politics of Heritage Tourism in China*, Xiaobo Su and Peggy Teo cite an *Asian Wall Street Journal* report from 23 November 2001 in their discussion of Lijiang's World Heritage branding. 'Few cities', the newspaper noted, 'have tried to capitalize on that brand with as much zeal as Lijiang.'[6]

Lijiang's tourism stats are indeed eye-opening: 98,000 visitors in 1990, 217,000 in 1994, 1,773,000 in 1998, 3,380,000 in 2002, 4.91 million in 2007, 7.6 million in 2009, and (if the sources are to be believed) 16 million in 2012 and 20.8 million in 2013.[7] In the space of fifteen years, a small mountain town has come to attract more tourists annually than all of Greece put together and around half the number of yearly visitors to Las Vegas.

Neither the UNESCO label nor the World Bank funds could have single-handedly provoked this human tidal wave. The Chinese state has also played its part. In 1999, three years after the earthquake, Kunming and Lijiang were chosen to host the World Horticultural Exposition. Aside from the airport, Lijiang was provided with a railway connection in 2009, the Dali–Lijiang line, used almost exclusively by tourists, as well as a motorway opened in 2013.* Both are majestic constructions; the 165 kilometres of railway includes 98 kilometres of bridges and tunnels, while the 259 kilometres of motorway includes 136 kilometres of bridges and tunnels.

Naturally, an old city that at the turn of this century counted less than 50,000 inhabitants (between 25,000 and 40,000, depending on the source), would never have been able to accommodate millions of tourists. Accordingly, the city has expanded. 'So popular is Lijiang that the "old town" grows bigger every year in order to accommodate the extra visitors', as the 2013 edition of the *Rough Guide to Southwest China* recounts; a new city of skyscrapers has begun to spread like a fungus around the Old Town, making Lijiang into a 'shopping mall decorated with heritage symbols'.[8]

The Lijiang phenomenon is another case of the all-too-familiar litany of commodification that tourism produces, with its corollaries of standardisation, homogenisation and falsification. But more than that, Lijiang begs the question of what UNESCO is really seeking to preserve when it slaps its World Heritage brand onto a city. Here it was justified on the grounds that Lijiang 'is an exceptional ancient town set in a dramatic landscape which represents the harmonious fusion of different cultural traditions

---

* The Dali–Lijiang section of railway forms the southern leg of the Shangri-La–Lijiang line. Shangri-La (the name given by James Hilton to the imaginary land in his 1933 novel *Lost Horizon*) was the new name officially given to the province of Zhongdian in 2001 to encourage tourism.

to produce an urban landscape of outstanding quality'. Yet none of these qualities have been preserved. The stupendous panorama is at risk, as the Jade Dragon Snow Mountain glacier is melting and the streams are drying up. The harmonious fusion of different cultures is also in jeopardy, as the tourist boom has provoked a huge influx of visitors and merchants, driving out the local Naxi population and reducing their culture to pure folklore for tourist consumption. The 500-performer open-air *son et lumière* 'culture show' *Impression Lijiang*, directed by the famous film director Zhang Yimou, is a case in point.

Indeed, the so-called 'traditional culture' of the Naxi people has been swept away with such speed that even UNESCO itself has begun to worry. In 2008, the year UNESCO received the World Tourism Award, a monitoring mission from the World Heritage Centre to Lijiang affirmed that 'while authenticity of the site seems to be at risk, this is partly because of the change of the lifestyle of the local community and partly because of the commodification and commercialization of the Naxi and Dongba culture'. The mission report goes on to note without irony that

> commercial interests have driven measures to facilitate large numbers of tourists, compromising the authentic heritage values which attracted visitors to the property in the first place. In physical terms, architectural and urban authenticity has been affected by widespread rebuilding and redevelopment projects, use of modern building materials and replication of traditional-style architecture, which have been carried out instead of maintaining the historic fabric. In social terms, the property has seen displacement of local populations and the replacement of traditional occupations by tourism-related businesses run by non-local residents.

The report concludes by noting its fears for 'the eventual loss of the cultural identity of the Old Town of Lijiang'.[9]

The UNESCO mission uses (eleven times) the term 'authenticity'. But what is left of Lijiang that is authentic? Quite simply, nothing. On the contrary, Lijiang invites us to question the very

116

meaning of the word 'authentic'. It is in fact the apotheosis of the inauthentic; it could even be considered the Chinese version of the Los Angeles paradox formulated by MacCannell, where the proliferation of markers turns even the inauthentic into something authentic. Once its 'inauthenticities' have been reproduced an infinite number of times through various iterations in the tourist guides, on TripAdvisor and on social media, Lijiang, like Los Angeles, acquires its aura of authentic inauthenticity. In other words, it is only in a very specific sense that the tourist goes in search of the authentic. The authenticity that the tourist visiting Lijiang seeks is not that of the original in contrast to the copy. And indeed, our problem is that we forget that the aura of the original in contrast to the copy is a product of Western Romanticism.

Hence Lijiang poses a third problem, relating to its Chineseness and made evident both by the Mu Fu Complex affair (which has never existed but is nonetheless today offered to tourists as an attraction) and by the *Rough Guide*'s disconcerting observation that 'the Old Town grows each year'. It is a problem borne out of the history of Western culture, and in particular out of Romanticism: Why have broken stones become the object of such intense admiration? It was the Romantic movement that bestowed upon historical ruins the aesthetic value that we Westerners understand to be one of their intrinsic attributes.

Historical ruins made their first appearance on the European scene as a pictorial subject or genre, much like still life or landscape, or rather, as a factor of the *picturesque*. They had slowly become popular around the beginning of the seventeenth century through the paintings of the Dutchmen Gillis van Valckenbroch (c. 1570–1622), Willem van Nieulandt II (c. 1584–1635), Esaias van de Velde (1587–1630), Cornelis van Poelenburgh (c. 1594–1667) and Jacobus Sibrandi Mancadan (c. 1602–80), the Austrian Johann Anton Eismann (1604–98) and the Frenchman Pierre Patel (1605–76). However, it was in the first half of the 1700s that the craze for ruins really took off across Europe, thanks in part to the paintings of the Venetian Gaetano De Rosa

(1690–1770) and above all to the Piacenza-born Giovanni Paolo Pannini (1691–1765), along with his French disciples Hubert Robert (1733–1808) and Jean-Honoré Fragonard (1732–1806). The European penchant for ruins therefore dates back to the period we associate with the triumph of the Enlightenment, but it was also this period that gave birth to the Gothic novel. The progenitor of the Gothic novel, Horace Walpole's *The Castle of Otranto*, was published in 1764, the same year as Diderot and d'Alembert's great *Encyclopédie*, which included an entry on 'ruins' that defined them as follows: 'Only palaces, sumptuous tombs or public monuments can be said to have become ruins. One would never say ruins when speaking of a peasants' or bourgeois home; one would then call them dilapidated buildings.'[10]

Incidentally, it was around the same time that Denis Diderot, the archetypal Enlightenment thinker, introduced the term 'a poetics of ruins' in a review of Robert's paintings for his *Salon de 1767*, a concept indissolubly linked to Romanticism. Which just goes to show that histories of ideas oversimplify when they take for granted the Hegelian dichotomy between 'abstract Enlightenment intellect' and 'Romantic reason'. When standing before canvases depicting the ruins of ancient monuments, Diderot wrote,

> One is struck only by the idea of the eclipsed power of peoples who had erected buildings such as these. It is not the magic of the brush but the ravages of time that grips our attention. The effect of these compositions, good or bad, is to leave you in a gentle melancholy. We fix our gaze on the remains of a triumphal arch, of a portico, of a pyramid, of a temple, of a palace; and we turn back to ourselves; we anticipate the devastations of time; and our imagination razes to the ground the very buildings we inhabit. At that moment, solitude and silence reign. We remain the only survivors of a nation that is no more. And there is the first line of a poetics of ruins.[11]

Diderot's description already contains the Romantic ruin's crucial element: its associated melancholy. The ruin incorporates time into its stones or its bricks, like the face of an old man incorporates it in its wrinkles. The ruin has the capacity to 'transform the contemplation of space in a meditation on time'.[12] It speaks to us of the beauty that once was and how it was swept away by the winds of time, indeed the key word here is *ravages*. The ruins speak to us of ancient empires and *eclipsed powers*. Their very nature places us within a horizon of *grandeur*: 'The ideas that ruins awaken in me are great ones. Everything is annihilated, everything perishes, everything passes. Only the world remains. Only time endures. How old this world is! I am walking between two eternities' (Diderot).[13]

In the second part of the eighteenth century a genuine thirst for ruins began to spread. It was as though only the decayed and deformed could attract interest, precisely because the ravages of time confer temporal depth to an object we are looking at in our present. The viewer is immediately and intuitively presented with what Reinhart Koselleck would in the twentieth century term 'the contemporaneity of the non-contemporary'. Indeed, Diderot's incredible spirit of observation led him to the insight that 'there is more poetry, there are more variations, I do not say in a hovel, in a single tree that has endured the years and seasons, than in every palace façade. A palace has to be dilapidated in order to make it an object of interest.'[14]

The wealthy patricians of the late 1770s put their heart and souls into this task, and into surrounding themselves with fake ruins. Once again then, we see forgery bringing the theme of authenticity to the fore, though here with a level of sophistication unknown to Lijiang. What we are seeing with these eighteenth-century fake ruins is comparable to the operation carried out at Angkor Wat by archaeologists of the French school, where, with the jungle used as a scenic backdrop to celebrate the agency of time and nature, a vision of ancient ruins à la Giovanni Battista Piranesi was constructed. In the same way, eighteenth-century English lords and architects 'collected in their parks fake ruined shrines … Gothic chapels and Greco-Roman shrines, either naturally or even artificially dilapidated, because this made them melancholy and worthy of pity'. Yet, the parks themselves were 'in the English style', that is, artificially wild and untamed.[15] Here it is not simply the ancient that is being mimicked, but the power of time to decompose and disintegrate, a kind of *inauthenticity squared*.

At the beginning of the nineteenth century the fad for ruins had become so widespread that François-René de Chateaubriand was able to make the peremptory claim that 'all men have a secret attraction to ruins'. He even had a moralistic explanation for the phenomenon: 'This sentiment depends on the fragility of our nature, on a secret conformity between these destroyed monuments and the rapidity of our existence. Added to this, moreover, is an idea that consoles our own smallness, seeing that entire peoples, sometimes very famous men, did not however manage to live beyond the few days assigned to our own obscurity. Thus the ruins project a great morality amidst the scenes of nature.'[16]

Ruins had by now become a term for comparing intellectual categories. In 1827, Wolfgang Goethe used it to discriminate between Europe and America:

> Amerika, du hast es besser,
> Als unsere Kontinent, das alte,
> *Hast kein verfallene Schlösser*
> *Und Keine Basalte.*

> America, you've got it better,
> Than our continent, the old one,
> *You have no decaying castles*
> *And no marble.*[17]

The continent of the future has no ruins, says Goethe. Yet, as was shortly to be discovered, the ruins of the future would be imagined, prefigured, 'foretasted'. In 1869, the St Louis publisher Logan Uriah Reavis wrote, 'Before many cycles shall have completed their rounds sentimental pilgrims from the humming cities of the Pacific coast will be seen where Boston, Philadelphia, and New York now stand, viewing in moonlight contemplation, with the melancholy owl, traces of the Athens, the Carthage, and the Babel of the Western hemisphere.'[18]

It is possible to discern here one of the distinctive categories that has circumscribed our thought since the ascent of Romanticism: the future perfect. Reavis imagined a future where pilgrims from an ascendant civilisation across the Pacific would reflect nostalgically on a time that for them was the distant past but for us is still the future, this period of 'will have come to pass' is situated between the future perfect of the pilgrims arriving from over the Pacific to view the ruins and our present, when New York and Boston are prosperous cities. A *nostalgia for the future* thus takes form, a future seen as having already vanished. '*Nous anticipons sur les ravages du temps*', Diderot had written long before. Indeed, it was Mary Shelley who invented one of the prototypes of post-Romanticism: the figure of the last man. In her novel *The Last Man* (1826) Shelley imagined a distant future where humanity – the same humanity the author belongs to – has become extinct and the last man looks nostalgically on its past.

The theme of melancholy, of the coexistence of the living and the dead, and of a nostalgia for the future provoked by reflections on our own yet-to-be-realised demise, are all essential to Romantic music. These themes weave their way through mournful melodies like a leitmotif wrought from a deep Baudelairean melancholy.

Nostalgia – as we have seen – is one of the driving factors in sightseeing. But the tourist's nostalgia is not the same as the melancholy that Diderot spoke of, though it is one of the components. For the spectator in front of a ruined monument to be able to feel melancholy, at least two conditions must be satisfied that do not present themselves to the tourist. Looking back at the entry in the *Encyclopédie* on *Ruine*, the reader will have noticed that it introduced an element of class into the concept. A ruin is not any old ruined building, but rather must be the ruin of a palace, a mansion, a grandiose construction. Ruins speak to us of power because the pleasure of a ruin is accessible only to those with cultural capital. It presupposes that the viewer knows what the ruin is the remainder of, that they know the marvels of its gone-but-not-forgotten past hidden behind the fractured stone.

As Marco Bascetta has noted, the figure that stalks the countless eighteenth-century depictions of ancient ruins is a silent figure. It is the *shepherd* who (with unprecedented frequency in painting, we should take note) grazes his herd among the shadows of tumbling majestic vaults, ignorant of the culture and history surrounding him, whose memory for us the ruins invoke. Though marginal, the shepherd is nonetheless indispensable for restoring to the spectator their class status – their *distinction*, as Bourdieu would say – the thing that distinguishes those with a consciousness of the flow of time from those in blissful ignorance of this melancholic yearning who wander through the landscape without really noticing it.[19]

The ruin is therefore the mirror in which the spectator admires their own classical culture. Not only that but the experience is necessarily solitary ('at that moment solitude and silence reign around us'). The only possible interference between the gaze and the stone is the ignorant shepherd and his herd (washerwomen or oxen would serve the purpose just as well). In the spectacle of ancient ruins, 'a torrent drags nations one over another into the depths of a common abyss; myself, I resolve to stop myself at the edge and divide the waters rushing past either side of me' (Diderot).[20]

It is not just class superiority that is unavailable to the modern tourist. Solitude is also precluded. Viewers of the ruins of Ephesus are not immersed in a silence interrupted only by the hum of cicadas or bleating of goats, nor can they abandon themselves to a solitude punctured only by a flock of sheep or its shepherd. And it is precisely this absence of solitude that is at the root of tourism's inexorable depreciation; the modern tourist is reduced to the status of a shepherd among other shepherds. The nostalgia of tourism is nostalgia for that past and for a social order in which the ruling classes are still able to experience the nostalgia of an ancient ruin. This nostalgic programme (or perhaps programmed nostalgia) is unrealisable when 20 million tourists visit Lijiang each year and 10 million visit Venice (which in comparison to Lijiang now seems meagre!). From here we get the reiterated advice to visit Venice in autumn, Angkor Wat during the hottest part of the day, Machu Picchu at dawn and Lijiang out of season, in order to regain at least a semblance of solitude.

But up to this point we have been concerned purely with the fondness for ruins and with Romantic civilisation. The ruin becomes as unreachable as Novalis's *Die Blaue Blume* (the blue flower), like searching for that faraway blue, or the bluish-grey of mountains on the horizon that ceases to be blue when we get closer.

This is not the case in Lijiang, where solitude certainly does not abound, and where the ruins have all been swept clean away and substituted by new-build (that is, fake) ancient buildings (and not by fake ruins as was the case with the eighteenth-century English gardens). And where melancholy, if a factor at all, has a very different meaning. Pannini and Goethe are afflicted by a presence, the presence of the past, of the wrinkles manifest in the ruins. The only sense of melancholy that could be experienced in Lijiang (and more and more often in other cities) is a melancholy of absence, brought on by the realisation of what is missing. There are no old houses, there is no gurgling of the ancient canals where housewives rinsed their laundry surrounded by flapping chickens. Rural life exists no longer, and there is no 'harmonious fusion of different traditional cultures' (UNESCO dixit).

Without wanting to pose as a Sinologist, I think we can say that the evidence points to China having a relationship with its past that is very different to the one we have in the West. In China, the past is everywhere, in its traditions, in its etiquette, in daily conversation, in people's behaviour, in its proverbs and in the public imagination, and yet at the same time it is nowhere, as its physical traces are nowhere visible. The Lijiang experience is repeated in cities across the country, where you often read that a pagoda was built in the third century BC by the emperor Qin, but then destroyed and rebuilt under the Han in the second century AD, then demolished by an earthquake during the Ming period in the fifteenth century, and so on, until finally they tell you that what you see in front of you dates back to 1974. Even the Great

Wall has never existed as a single monument and is essentially a modern myth instigated by the Jesuits who drew the first map of it.[21] So much so that the stretches of the wall that the Chinese are most insistent you should visit are the parts near Beijing that have been completely rebuilt and where the 1987 Citroën commercial was filmed. One stretch of wall has an inbuilt lift (Badaling), and the other a cable car (Mutianyu).

It seems that in China, the past is not a physical presence made of stone, bricks and marble (though perhaps the fact that the Chinese built mainly in wood plays a part in this), but rather an immaterial presence that saturates the air they breathe. Perhaps it is for this reason – I am hazarding a hypothesis here – why a need is felt to picture this past that hangs over the present, to represent it as it was, or as we imagine it was, to rebuild à la Viollet-le-Duc, even to the point of reinventing it.

Maybe for this reason, the Chinese view ruins as simply a pile of rubble and cannot understand or explain why they might be an attraction. How many times have I been asked by Chinese acquaintances visiting the Roman Forum 'why don't they just rebuild it all?' (Incidentally, this problem presents us with a further enigma: how is it possible that Chinese pianists are able to play Romantic music so well when its cultural roots are completely extraneous to them?)

The Chinese indifference to ruins explains their divergent conception of the authentic. To the eyes of Chinese visitors, the fact that the Mu residence was built entirely anew does not detract from its authenticity, or, rather, from its veracity. It is not only Lijiang's old city that grows every year. Even the famous terra cotta warriors have suffered the same fate, as new warriors are routinely 'discovered' or 'unearthed'. If many of these warriors have also been 'restored' or built from scratch, to Chinese eyes this again would not take away from their veracity. The only difference is the very conception of veracity.

10

Relearning from Las Vègas

Toward the end of his book *The Tourist*, Dean MacCannell writes:

> It is evident from the behaviour of global corporations during the
> last thirty years that they are being driven half mad as they circle
> the human relation at the heart of the world's largest 'industry';
> that is, as they attempt to come to terms with the fact that the eco-
> nomics of sight-seeing is ultimately dependent on a non-economic
> relation.[1]

That is, corporations struggle to come to terms with the idea that
the largest source of income and cash flow in the world depends
on noneconomic factors, because the Grand Canyon, the Parthenon, the banks of the Seine are not the product of rational,
planned investment; they are not controlled or controllable by
investors used to mastering situations from head to toe.

This is why tourist attractions are defined as cultural deposits,
because in this way the attraction (a complex sign, as we have
seen) is reduced to its accounting dimension. It becomes a raw
material to be extracted and exploited, and as such, it becomes
understandable and manageable by accountants (and by government ministers), because it is brought within the industrial logic
of the market.

Of course, tourism is not the only field of economics in which
noneconomic factors play an important role, as shown by, among
others, the economists Kenneth Arrow, Michael P. Todero and
Amartya Sen. Tourism, however, is the only economic field in
which commercialisation is taken to such an extreme that it has

bled the original source dry. It has essentially killed the goose that laid the golden eggs. The various Disneyland cities are based on the principle of pretence, freely accepted by creators and visitors alike: a kind of role play where both sides understand that what they are seeing *is not authentic*, but they play along nevertheless.

The tourist that plays along with this inauthenticity has been described by Maxine Feifer as the 'post-tourist'. She summarises this idea in the last paragraph of *Going Places*: 'Above all, though, the post-tourist knows that he is a tourist: not a time traveller when he goes somewhere historic; not an instant noble savage when he stays on a tropical beach; not an invisible observer when he visits a native compound. Resolutely "realistic", he cannot evade his condition of outsider. But, having embraced that condition, he can stop struggling against it and … then he can turn it around.'[2]

The problem with Feifer's term, however, is that from the nineteenth century onward, tourists have always had such a playful or easy-going attitude, a holiday attitude, if you like. We should never forget that tourists dedicate the precious little spare time they have during the working year to the exhausting activity of sightseeing. What is surprising is not that they want to have fun, but that they do so by trying to learn at the same time. This has always been the real ambiguity of the tourist. As early as Twain's time, the tourist was making fun of the tourist-pilgrim, prompting many an essay on the topic of Mark Twain as history's first post-tourist.[3]

To borrow from Roland Barthes's celebrated title, nobody stops at *tourism's degree zero*. Rather, everyone's sightseeing is stratified by different levels of experience: first-grade or second-grade tourism. Only a few academics wearing blinkers could believe that real tourists in any way correspond to their oversimplified and caricatured conception of such a fragmented, differentiated and articulated human condition. For tourists know very well that what is offered to them as authentic is not actually authentic at all – or perhaps is, but only very slightly. They know that what they are seeing is staged and that they are considered useful idiots, but they play along nevertheless and do not worry about it. Not only post-tourists, but indeed all tourists are aware 'of the iniquities of tourism, yet prefer to make light of them, transforming the sustained moral indignation of the anti-tourist tourist into moments of melodramatic anguish'.[4]

This is not to deny that, parallel to this ludic dimension, there also remains the persistent search for *some level of authenticity*. Even the Chinese tourists who visit The World to see miniature copies of Venice's St Mark's Square or Paris's Eiffel Tower will then save for years to be able to go and see the real thing, to climb the 'real' Eiffel Tower or walk through the 'real' St Mark's Square. Without this search for *authenticity* and its *aura*, there would be no tourist cities. The Roman forums must be at least 2,000 years old and the *Mona Lisa* must be the original, even if you can only just about make it out through the crowd. Even Lijiang must convey its own (peculiar) authenticity. It is the aura of the authentic that ensures that throngs of visitors exert themselves to go and *not* see the Sistine Chapel among a mass of people whose presence make it impossible to concentrate. They could just as easily have stayed home, put on a DVD and admired the details on a screen.

There is, however, at least one place on earth where the big corporations have managed to resolve this ambiguity. That place is Las Vegas, Nevada, where second-grade tourism does not run parallel to its zero-grade but *is* zero-grade tourism. Here, it is the inauthentic par excellence that is authentic. And vice versa: the authenticity sought after in Las Vegas is the authenticity of the completely, perfectly and radically inauthentic.

If it is the case elsewhere that the tourist industry has 'touristified' urban centres that already existed, subjecting them to a process of Disneylandification, Las Vegas is a tourist city created from scratch in the middle of the Mojave Desert, designed purely for the function of drawing in and accommodating tourists.

Founded in 1905, when a forty-five-acre lot of land close to the Union Pacific railway was put up for auction, the town became an autonomous municipality in 1911. Its precipitous ascent began in 1931, when the state of Nevada legalised gambling and construction began on the Hoover Dam which spans the Colorado River on the border between Nevada and Arizona, thirty-eight kilometres southeast of Las Vegas as the crow flies. By 1936 the city, whose name means 'the meadows' in Spanish (that is, an oasis in the desert), had a constant supply of water and electricity, where previously the only source of water had been a few wells able to sustain perhaps a few hundred ranches but certainly not a metropolis. In the 1930s, casinos began springing up in the city centre, and in the 1940s they began to proliferate along what is now called the Strip, a wide avenue around seven kilometres long. By 1940, the city already had 8,422 inhabitants; ten years later it had 24,624.

In the 1940s, '50s and '60s, the development of the gambling industry was under the control of organised crime, for the most part the Cosa Nostra. The Flamingo opened in 1946 and the Desert Inn in 1950, both casino hotels run by the New York gangster Bugsy Siegel. It was during this period that Sammy Davis Jr, Dean Martin and Frank Sinatra – the latter linked to the Cosa Nostra – established a kind of monopoly over Las Vegas's nightlife. Their legacy was such that when each singer died, the lights on the Strip were dimmed; in the case of Martin and Sinatra, roads were renamed in their honour in 2005.

The era of machine-gun mobsters came to a close toward the end of the 1960s, giving way to the era of rapacious financiers, as exemplified by figures like the investor Kirk Kerkorian and the eccentric millionaire Howard Hughes. Hughes, known for his extreme secrecy, bought the Desert Inn in 1967, and by 1968 had become the city's biggest casino operator. Yet he abruptly abandoned it in 1969 when the newest magnate, Kerkorian, came onto the scene. Kerkorian was an Armenian-American ex-pilot who began his career in the 1940s with a small airline specialising in transporting pro sports players from Los Angeles to Las Vegas.[5] In the 1960s he bought the land on which he would later build Caesar's Palace and, in 1968, the Flamingo. Finally, after having bought the Metro-Goldwin-Mayer film studio, he built the MGM

Grand Hotel and Casino in 1973, at the time the biggest hotel in the world with 2,084 rooms.

A third phase began in 1989 with the opening of the Mirage by a company called Wynn Resorts Ltd. By 1990, the population of Las Vegas had grown to 258,295, and its target market began to shift toward progressively wealthier clients. Rooms in the Wynn Las Vegas, which opened in 2005, are no smaller than fifty-eight metres square, the hotel itself covering an area of eighty-seven acres and including an eighteen-hole golf course, eighteen restaurants and an art gallery housing works by Picasso, Vermeer, Cézanne, Gauguin and Rembrandt.

The success of Vegas (to use the familiar abbreviation) has been resounding, but most of all it has been lasting. In 1970, when it had 125,000 inhabitants, the city brought in 6.8 million tourists. Ten years later the number had risen to 11.9 million, in 1990 20.9 million, in 2000 35.8 million and in 2018 42.1 million, according to the Las Vegas Conventions and Visitors Authority. To give an idea of how this compares, Italy's biggest tourist hot spot, Venice, had 9.5 million visitors in 2017, which means that for every visitor to Venice there are four to Las Vegas! What is more, Las Vegas has fought off all competitors to come forward so far: first, Atlantic City in New Jersey, where the Cosa Nostra decided to transfer its business interests; then the casinos that opened on Native American lands; and finally the invention of riverboat casinos on rivers marking the borders between various states, where local gambling restrictions cease to apply. The key to Vegas's success is its ability to diversify and to excel at convention tourism (see Chapter 5). While in 1950 only one in every twenty-five tourists to Vegas travelled for a convention, in 2006 this had risen to almost one in six, and the number of convention participants hosted by the city was 6.3 million.

Vegas has also proven to be relatively resilient in overcoming economic crises. Compared to the 2007 threshold of 39.2 million visitors, 2009 (Vegas's worst pre-pandemic year) saw only an 8 per cent drop. In 2012, numbers surpassed the 2007 record and in 2015 surged beyond the 42 million mark. The impact on convention tourism was starker: after a peak of 6.3 million convention attendees in 2006, Vegas dropped to a low of 4.5 million in 2010. It took until 2017, with 6.5 million convention-goers, for Vegas to surpass its 2006 record – a long recovery, but an impressive one.

In short, if we were to compare the city to a device for producing tourism, then Vegas would be an extraordinarily efficient product, easily achieving all its objectives. The strategies thought up by Las Vegas's planners deserve to be studied with the same respect due any successful enterprise.

Las Vegas is one of the most striking cities I have ever visited. The impact is truly violent. Arriving in Las Vegas, you are hit by an unimaginable force, whose exact nature you spend the entire duration of your trip trying to determine. One thing, however, you understand immediately: this city has something to teach us. It is this that lends the famous 1972 book by Robert Venturi, Denise Scott Brown and Steven Izenour its title, *Learning From Las Vegas,* the manifesto that laid the foundations for a doctrine of postmodernist architecture. Indeed, when the book was reviewed for republication it was given the fuller title of *Learning From Las Vegas: The Forgotten Symbolism of Architectural Form.*[6] The authors' argument was that we have as much to learn from Las Vegas as we do from classical architecture, or ancient, Renaissance or Baroque Rome, and that these lessons consist in a re-evaluation of 'vulgar' architecture, for instance commercial or functional architecture, and, most importantly, in restoring iconography (graphics, paintings and statues) to its rightful standing within the field of architecture. In this sense, for the husband-and-wife team of Venturi and Scott Brown, Las Vegas represented a counterweight capable of neutralising the legacy of modernism, identified in particular with Ludwig Mies van der Rohe. The authors counterpose, on the one hand, the precepts laid down by the great Latin architectural theorist Marcus Vitruvius (85–10 BC), who believed that architecture was:

Firmitas + Utilitas + Venustas
(Stability + Comfort + Pleasure)

against the specific industrial lineage of Walter Gropius and the Congrès Internationaux d'Architecture Moderne (CIAM) – a lineage that came to be known as the International Style, according to which

Stability + Comfort = Grace (which can also be expressed as 'structure plus programme results rather simply in form'.)[7]

To this Venturi and Scott Brown added: 'The architecture of the Modern movement ... developed a vocabulary of forms based on a variety of industrial models' to which its buildings were explicitly adapted 'because industrial structures represented, for European architects, the brave new world of science and technology'.[8]

For Venturi and Scott Brown the problem was that the International Style adopted the forms of industrial language without its function, despite claiming to be functionalist. Or rather, that the industrial model had become a symbolic affirmation, something that the likes of Mies and Gropius nevertheless remained unconscious of. *Learning From Las Vegas* therefore counterposed 'commercial jargon' with 'industrial jargon'. And Las Vegas was proposed as both the prototype and the most advanced realisation of commercial jargon. While the CIAM favoured space as the 'essential ingredient that separates architecture from painting, sculpture, and literature' and considered 'sculptural or pictorial architecture ... unacceptable', for commercial jargon to be effective, symbols must take precedence over form, and painting and decoration are then given renewed importance. What purpose did the bas-relief designs on Roman triumphal arches serve if not as prototypes of the *billboard*, 'mutatis mutandis for scale, speed, and content'? After all, they also served to mark out a space, in their case for processions.[9] Even 'Amiens Cathedral is a billboard with a building behind it'.[10]

The problem, however, is that Venturi and Scott Brown them-selves build logical chains. According to their logic, by abolishing the iconographic and ornamental element of architecture, the industrialism of the International Style confines itself to a reduc-tionist and instrumentalist rationalism, while the prototype of commercial postmodern architecture represented by Las Vegas apparently revalorises the superfluous and decorative. If the former corresponds to the logic of production and efficiency, then the latter corresponds to the logic of consumption. If the former is concerned with function, the latter is concerned with seduction (an architecture 'of propaganda'). To Mies's famous motto 'less is more' Venturi retorted 'less is a bore'.

When I arrived in Las Vegas it certainly made an extraordinary impression, but one totally different from what Venturi and Scott Brown had led me to expect. Of course, later on, they recognised that

> In 1965 we witnessed the expansion of Route 91, the Strip. That street was the peak of neon, the archetype of suburban commerce, whose polychrome signs stood out against the blue sky and heaped scorn on architects' dreams. 'Do you love it or hate it?' we asked one another. We returned in 1997. Much of the neon had disap-peared, replaced by more suffuse LED lighting, and the parking lots had been replaced by Disneyland scenography. The communicative installations had been cut back and the city had little to teach us. The Strip had become a conventional urban element. Big hotels had replaced the parking lots. The new Las Vegas, massified at dizzying speeds, was completely different from the non-city of the 1960s. And it had a nineteenth-century aspect.[11]

But the gulf between expectation and material experience con-cerns more than just the changes a city has undergone. It also concerns language. It is true that Las Vegas is an apotheosis of signs. And it is true that these signs (those that in the 1970s were billboards) are overwhelmingly predominant, something you understand seeing the city at night, when the buildings behind the signs disappear so that the signs no longer indicate the buildings but simply themselves: they are self-sufficient.

It is the nature of these signs that gives rise to difficulties. In contrast to Venturi and Scott Brown's belief, Las Vegas's signs have no symbolic, metaphoric, allegorical or decorative function – rather, they are decisively functional. Indeed, they are not even signs but rather metonyms, abbreviations or acronyms. Vegas is a kingdom whose parts stand in for the whole. Thus, Paris Las Vegas has in front of it (though it would be better to simply say *is*) a small Eiffel Tower, the Luxor is a pyramid (complete with a Sphinx and an obelisk in front), New York is a Statue of Liberty, Caesar's Palace is the classical pediment imprinted with Caesar's emblem and the Venetian is the bell tower of San Marco. All of these are markers plain and simple (according to MacCannell's definition) that reproduce with full force the logic that means the markers themselves become the attraction. As for real tourists the Eiffel Tower is Paris's marker, so the Tower's reproduction, once it has been lit up, is the marker of the casino, yet the Tower itself then becomes an even greater pull than the casino. It is this collection of markers that is Las Vegas's real tourist attraction. In this sense, Las Vegas's iconography is functionality in its purest state. It is the expression of a doctrine of economic efficiency. And the lasting success of its 'tourist mission' is proof of this.

The question is relevant because Las Vegas is the 'intentionally tourist city' par excellence. And because at first sight tourism can seem like the quintessential postmodern economic sector, as not only is it determined by extra-economic factors but also, the commodity being consumed (acquired?) is immaterial. What the 'tourist package' sells is the chance to see the Acropolis, or a tree among the ruins of Machu Picchu, or a sunset over the steps of Rome's Trinità dei Monti church. If that were the case, then the equation would be oriented toward a postmodern economic sector, with the city structuring itself according to postmodern architecture and urban design for which 'disorder [is] an order we cannot see'.[12] But what we see with Las Vegas is that its system of signs has an efficiency and a rationality that is in all respects industrial. Behind the appearance of glitz and excess lies a real economy of means.

This contradiction is resolvable only if we understand the modern and the postmodern not as contrasting but as tendencies that overlap or perhaps intertwine. The postmodern considers the modern as the great narrative of progress, of industrialisation and scientific rationality, the symbol of which is the great factory with its Taylorist workers. But in Las Vegas, tourism means precisely this. The point at which Venturi and Scott Brown's reasoning begins to crack is when tourism (postmodern) becomes an industry (modern). We have already seen how tourism is a heavy industry because it requires a great amount of infrastructure and it exploits and squanders great amounts of raw materials and creates great amounts of pollution. But in Las Vegas we see an additional dimension to the tourist industry.

There are 104 registered casinos in Vegas. In 2017, these casinos, including ones that are also hotels, directly employed 166,000 workers in addition to another 80,000 hired by companies linked to these hotel-casinos (restaurants, franchised bars, and so on), for a total of 246,000 workers. If we limit ourselves to the Strip alone, its forty-five casinos directly employ more than 98,000 workers, with an astonishing average of 2,189 employees per business.[13]

Six casinos – open 24 hours a day, 365 days a year – have more than 5,000 employees: the Mirage, a Polynesian-themed resort and casino, employs 5,700 workers for its 3,044 rooms, 17 restaurants, 109 gaming tables and 1,300 slot machines; the Venetian has 6,000 employees; the Aria Resort & Casino employs 7,750 people; the Mandalay Bay Resort 8,100; the Bellagio (inspired by Italy's Lake Como) 8,200; and the MGM Grand Hotel & Casino (4,962 rooms, 22 restaurants, 4 bars, 14,000 square metres of gaming space, 1,770 slot machines and 170 gaming tables) has 9,300 employees.[14]

Each casino therefore has more workers than a reasonably sized factory, and those toward the top of the scale could even compete with a medium-sized industry. Just as the hangars containing the metalworks in Flint, Michigan (at the heart of North American car manufacturing), look colossal to us, so these plants created for tourism are so big that it seems reductive to call them hotels.

The proof that tourism is anything but postmodern in nature, that it is indeed heavily industrial, is in the fact that Las Vegas is the US city that over the last thirty years has seen the highest rates of labour conflict; it is practically unique in America for experiencing a modern class struggle led by trade unions. The reason for this is simple: the megahotels of Las Vegas are the only truly great industrial sites remaining that cannot be delocalised. In other sectors, strikes have been neutralised through the threat of offshoring, by moving the theatre but leaving the puppets behind, at first to the Mexican *maquiladoras*, then to China. This was what happened with the electronics industry, the computer industry and the car manufacturing industry. But it is not possible to move a casino elsewhere, as the Las Vegas label would be lost. The only way around it would be to build another Vegas in another desert, but then the problem would simply arise again.

The dimensions of the leisure industry, its spatial concentration, its economies of scale, have created a condensed rather than dispersed workforce which, for the first time in modern history, has allowed for the organisation of unskilled service-sector workers: kitchen porters, chefs, cleaners, porters, and so on. The sheer number of employees in a single casino means that the situation found inside the factories is recreated, and it is for this reason that it has been possible to unionise workers – a rare occurrence in the US. It is a particularly difficult task because a good part of the workers are immigrants and many undocumented. In other parts of the world these conditions have prevented unions from organising workers. In Italy, for example, the union confederations have struggled to organise migrant workers. In Las Vegas, however, it is the industrial dimension of its service sectors that has compacted this new working class.

The trade union that has carried out this miracle is the Culinary Workers Union, or Local 226 to be precise. The union offices are on the ground floor of a squat building that lies in the shadow of a towering casino. As I walked into the building during my visit in 2008, a long queue of men and women were waiting to enter, most of them Hispanic, to ask for information on refunds for health care, on pensions or on annual leave. Twenty-five years ago, the Culinary Workers Union (or 'the Culinary', as it is commonly known) had 10,000 members. Today, it has 60,000. What brought it to prominence was the New Frontier strike, 'the longest strike in US history', as Chris Bohner, the union's spokesperson, described it to me, 'six years, four months and eleven days'. The New Frontier was the second big casino built in Las Vegas in the 1940s; the strike involving its 550 employees began on 21 September 1991 and ended on 2 February 1998. It was the first time that pregnant strikers walked picket lines to stop strikebreakers from going to work, and during those six years 106 children were born to strikers. Today the majority of workers in the hotels and casinos on the Strip are unionised.

Las Vegas is to tourism, therefore, what Detroit was to car manufacturing. They both involve mass production and megafacilities (in Detroit's case factories; in Vegas's case hotels and casinos), and they share the same labour conflicts (in Detroit it involved blue-collar workers; in Vegas it is service staff). It begs the question of whether Las Vegas will meet the same horrible destiny as Detroit. After all, every city based on only one economic activity risks becoming the devastated ghost town that Detroit became.

A preview of this fate took place in the spring of 2020, when the coronavirus pandemic emptied Las Vegas from one day to the next and left practically all the city's population out of work, so much so that it was dubbed the ground zero for the US job crisis.[15] The situation was so desperate that at the end of May ten hotels were ready to welcome tourists with coronavirus.[16] And while the virus was still reaping lives, as early as 4 June 2020 the casinos of Las Vegas reopened. It took Las Vegas four years to recover from the 2008 financial crisis – which affected only one particular sector, business tourism and conventions; it is likely that the city will take much longer to recover from the pandemic, if ever. Although, as we have seen, on more than one occasion this artificial metropolis in the middle of the desert has shown an extraordinary resilience.

From a structural point of view, however, in Las Vegas there is an additional risk, created by the overexploitation of the Colorado River, which, in addition to cities in Nevada also feeds Phoenix and Los Angeles and provides irrigation for farms through a vast area of southeastern California. Water levels have been dropping for decades; Lake Mead (created by the Hoover Dam) has not been full since 1983. Since that year, its level has dropped by almost fifty metres (from a maximum depth of 162 metres) and its volume has fallen by 40.4 per cent.[17] In just the last ten years the lake has lost sixty-three cubic kilometres of water. For the moment Vegas is not under threat, for one because it stores recycled water in underground tanks capable of meeting the city's needs for sixteen months.[18] But in the long term, the prospects are bleak. And at the point when those prospects become a reality, Las Vegas will truly become a mirage in the desert.

11

The Zoning of the Soul

No matter how often we tell ourselves that tourism is an industry, we never quite manage to picture it as such. In our minds, industry remains inextricably linked to hangars full of machinery, smoke-stacks and sulphuric fumes – and not to sandal-wearing shirtless hordes in their short trousers. Even if thousands of workers were on strike in Las Vegas for years, the tourist city still seems post-modern. Yet tourism's similarities with industry are not down solely to their reiterated seriality; the automation of the tourism process, for instance, gives it a passing resemblance to industrial assembly lines. Rather, these similarities are also the result of the very principle that shapes the cities where tourism and industry thrive.

Here, I am speaking of the principle of zoning, which governed the urban planning of the twentieth century. As the word suggests, zoning divides the city into zones, each of which is devoted to a different function. It seems that the first municipal zoning ordinance was issued in New York in 1916, and 'established a series of boundaries in the city, creating and separating districts in which different uses of land were permitted'. As an urban policy measure, zoning's novelty was that it was 'applied to all property in a municipality, whether publicly or privately owned' and that it provided a legal codification for the separation of space into monofunctional districts, with each area devoted to a single func-tion, be it housing, commerce, industry or recreation. The practice caught on quickly, and 'by 1929, over 750 American communities had adopted similar zoning ordinances'.[1]

At first glance, zoning seems like a reasonable activity. For millennia, cities had practised what we could call a 'wild', spontaneous zoning: in medieval and Baroque Rome all the chairmakers and repairers made their home in the Via dei Sediari (*sedia* means chair) and the hat makers in Via dei Cappellari (*capello* means hat). Other trades were also reflected in street names: via degli Acciaioli (knife-grinders), Cartari (paper makers), Catinari (jug makers), Chiavari (locksmiths), Cimatori (cloth clippers), Coronari (rosary makers), Falegnami (carpenters), Fornari (bakers), Funari (rope makers), Giubbonari (corset cutters), Leutari (lutists), Pettinari (comb makers), Staderari (steelyard workers), Vascellari (potters).

But the resemblance is deceptive, for this premodern spontaneous zoning was not exclusive or monofunctional: the potter not only worked in the via dei Vascellari; he also lived there, and the locksmith not only made keys on via dei Chiavari but also stayed there to buy his dinner. Conversely, in the zoning peculiar to the modern city, each area fulfils one function alone: a financial district, a commercial district, a residential district, an industrial district – districts that never intersect or overlap. The principle that you do not sleep where you work, you are not entertained where you sleep, you do not shop where you are entertained, is the reason why you will never find a bar in an American suburban subdivision.

Zoning is much more than a planning technique. It is a specific and singular form of *spatial rationality*. And just as always happens in too familiar a setting, we struggle to recognise how odd its peculiarities are. It is a reductionist rationality, in harmony with industrial rationality. Just as it is more 'economic' for a worker to be devoted to one job alone (always the same) and for a machine tool to fulfil a single function, similarly an area is destined for a single use. The two-way correspondence between space and function appealed to the *esprit géométrique* of the urbanists of the Modern Movement. Grouped around the Congrès Internationaux d'Architecture Moderne (CIAM) between 1928 and 1959, this movement's leading lights included Walter Gropius, Le Corbusier and Mies van der Rohe (as touched on in the previous chapter).

Le Corbusier explicitly associated *zonage* with the use of time and with the four phases of the day he linked to each of the four functions he imputed to the city. For Le Corbusier, zoning 'is based on necessary differentiations between the various human activities, each of which requires its own specific space: residential quarters, industrial or commercial centres, halls or grounds intended for leisure hours'.[2]

This spatial scansion of time is the reason why US downtowns are completely deserted at night, or better, are occupied by a humanity completely different from that which crowds it during the daytime. Saskia Sassen observed how at night office buildings are often attended only by cleaning staff – usually poor and immigrant women – while in daytime their population is predominantly male, native-born and of medium to high incomes.

The Situationists maintained that 'architecture is the simplest means of *articulating* time and space, of *modulating* reality'.[3] But precisely because, in its separation of space, it articulates and segments time, staggers humans' actions over this time and segregates their spaces of existence, zoning is first and foremost a political operation. It is, perhaps, the primary form of biopolitics. 'Appropriated space is one of the sites where power is asserted and wielded, and no doubt under the most invisible form, that of symbolic violence as unperceived violence: Architectural spaces – whose silent injunctions are directly addressed to the body … are no doubt the most important components of the symbolism of power because of their very invisibility' (Bourdieu).[4] When someone lives in a block of flats, in a neighbourhood served by a certain street layout, they do not thereby think that they are living in a specific power structure, in a social order – and yet they are doing exactly that. This violence exercised over the individual is totalitarian in tendency, as it pre-orders, pre-constitutes, predetermines and moulds the whole context in which the human being lives. It is curious to note that zoning, this 'Soviet' form of city planning that applies to all areas of either private or public property, was launched – almost simultaneously with the October Revolution of 1917 – in the world capital of capitalism, New

York City. Through the act of separating, zoning exercises an absolute power which reminds us of the blunt sentence passed by Horkheimer and Adorno: 'technical rationality today is the rationality of domination itself'.

The arbitrary dominion to which the planner arrogates himself over individual human beings was clearly formulated by Le Corbusier, as we have seen in the 1933 CIAM manifesto, the *Athens Charter*, cited above. For him, 'zoning is an operation carried out on the city map with the object of assigning every function *and every individual to its rightful place*' (my italics). The absolute arrogance of such dominion could not have been stated with any more disarming candour. He speaks of 'assigning' every individual to their 'rightful place' because up above there is someone who knows what *juste place* pertains to each person. Someone up there knows, as the expression goes, 'to put them in their place', which is to say, to remind them of their subalternity within a precise hierarchical arrangement.

Indeed, entomological metaphors recur throughout Le Corbusier's works: citizens are arranged in 'tribes of worker bees: order, regularity, justice and benevolence'; 'the human animal is like a bee, a builder of geometric cells'; 'man is an ant with precise life-customs, a unanimously-shared behaviour'. He frequently exalts the virility of leaders and chiefs, referring to the 'elite individuals who make up the world of industry and business and who thus live in this virile atmosphere'. And he speaks of how 'we are virile men in an epoch of the heroic reawakening of the powers of the spirit'.[5] The authoritarian paternalism implicit in this conception helps explain Le Corbusier's persistent fascist sympathies and his concern for directing urbanism toward eugenicist purposes.

It is, therefore, hardly coincidental, as Kenneth Jackson points out, that while 'in theory zoning was designed to protect the interests of all citizens by limiting land speculation and congestion', 'Southern cities even used zoning to enforce racial segregation'.[6] Zoning is one of the most potent instruments in the hands of the urban planner to carry out a *political construction of space*, whose effect is a 'construction of spatially based homogeneous groupings' (Bourdieu).[7] Zoning passes seamlessly from the separation of functions to the segregation of humans.

Also interesting is the contrast with the segregation practices of previous eras. Obviously, any society will seek to reflect its social hierarchy in a spatial configuration and order, therefore spatialising its forms of inclusion and exclusion. Although it is difficult to prove, Hippodamus of Miletus (498–408 BC) is considered history's first 'urbanist', or rather the first formulator of zoning. He divided out his ideal city state (*polis*) – and we should emphasise the word *ideal* – in this way, described by Aristotle: 'His system was for a city with a population of ten thousand, divided into three classes; for he made one class of artisans, one of farmers, and the third the class that fought for the state in war and was the armed class. He divided the land into three parts, one sacred, one public and one private: sacred land to supply the customary offerings to the gods, common land to provide the warrior class with food, and private land to be owned by the farmers.'* But as we can see, this zoning (if we wish to call it that) corresponded not to different functions but to the different kinds of expenditure to which revenues from the various territories were to be assigned: this had nothing to do with the modern separation between housing, working and manufacturing functions.

Subsequently, in the Middle Ages, from the ghettos that spanned half of Europe to Paris's Court of Miracles, what was directly segregated was a social group. This could mean a social caste or ethnic or religious group, even if it was a non-existent group. In eighteenth-century Rome, for instance, a specific cemetery was built for 'non-Catholics' (that is, Protestants). Conversely, in the modern metropolis, it is the separation of functions that generates, as its by-product, ethnic, caste or class separation. The difference is very clear when we look at Suburra, the most hunger-stricken,

---

* Aristotle, *Politics*, ii.8 (1267b). This is almost the only source we have on Hippodamus's theories, as his own writings have not been handed down to us. It is worth noting, in any case, that here he speaks not of different neighbourhoods, but of the entire territory of the city-state.

plebeian neighbourhood of ancient Rome, which, nonetheless, extended right up to the Forum: two simple doorways next to the Temple of Mars connected the slum to the centre of imperial power, the patriciate and the plebs. Unlike in the modern world, the rationality of classical Hellenic and Latin dominion was not a technological rationality or the fruit of a productivist reductionism.

Like all forms of domination exercised by 'symbolic violence', the rationalist reductionism proper to zoning has been internalised by all of us who practise – to greater and lesser degrees, and in the United States more than elsewhere – a 'zoning of the soul'. Through this latter practice, a certain attitude is permitted only in certain times and in certain situations, a little like the nudity allowed only at the seaside or the swimming pool, or the clothing worn by tourists that we would never put on in our everyday lives.

The problem is that zoning, in its apparently bureaucratic character, in fact harbours a cold violence. It is a bit like how the meticulous taxonomies of race provided a framework for pogroms. Zoning separates and isolates with the stroke of a pen, and it is no exaggeration to say that zoning imposes a symbolic violence. By 'symbolic' I do not at all mean to imply something immaterial or unreal, but rather a form of domination that acts by convincing the very people it is exercised upon of its own legitimacy. Not monarchy as such, but the rule 'by divine right' – the fact of the unchangeability and irreversibility of this rule – is what constitutes the core of the symbolic violence.

The soldier subject to military discipline obeys orders not only because he risks being shot if he deserts, but also because he is deeply convinced that he is a coward if he does not prove himself to be heroic enough. It's like how a worker laid off by a firm raises no objection to the rationality of 'redundancy' – in the interests of 'cutting labour costs' – or how in a patriarchal society a woman subject to male tyranny tears herself up for not being feminine enough. Subjected to symbolic violence, 'the dominated apply categories constructed from the point of view of the dominant to the relations of domination, thus making them appear as natural' (Bourdieu).[8]

This is also how the symbolic violence inherent to zoning operates, making urban solitude seem to citizens like something ineluctable, even though it is the effect of a deliberate act. But when has the city ever been a realm of solitude (or alienation)? Has anyone ever seen a Parisian of the eighteenth century – a Diderot – or a Londoner of the seventeenth century – Samuel Pepys – or a Roman of the first century BC – a Horace – complain about urban solitude?

We take for an intrinsic property of the city something which is, in fact, the result of a policy, of a repressive spatial violence that separates bodies and subdivides lives and times. Just as the modern metropolis needed a Baron Haussmann to gut and dismantle the alleyways where it would have been easy to set up barricades, and to free up spacious, straight boulevards in order to allow the artillery to fire cannons at those in revolt, so, too, did the great industrial city need zoning to separate what continuity would have brought together, to isolate what would otherwise have become mixed. Indeed, we should not forget that zoning was introduced when (and because) the panic instigated by the crowd – by its 'irrationality', violence and brutality – was at its height. And perhaps it is not such an accident that it appeared at the same time as the Russian Revolution, which magnified enormously the fear of socialism and of working-class revolt. The imperative was to induce separation, so that the mass did not become a crowd, so that isolated actors did not join together. Guy Debord writes,

Urbanism is the modern fulfillment of the uninterrupted task which safeguards class power: the preservation of the atomization of workers who had been dangerously brought together by urban conditions of production. The constant struggle that had to be waged against every possible form of their coming together discovers its favoured field in urbanism. After the experiences of the French Revolution, the efforts of all established powers to increase the means of maintaining order in the streets finally culminates in the suppression of the street.[9]

In the first two decades of the twentieth century, the tireless researchers of the Chicago School described what was, in truth, the effect of a determined and coordinated course of action as a phenomenon of 'natural differentiation' (with the accent on the 'natural'). They could see that the 'urban-segregation process' generated what the founder of urban sociology Robert Park called 'a mosaic of little worlds which touch but don't interpenetrate' in the big city – like worlds which are 'contiguous but otherwise widely separated'.[10]

Zoning appeared at the peak of the growing fear aroused by the city. This was the fear of an agglomeration that concentrated the 'dangerous classes', the classes of workers dirty with coal or grease, of the crowds made up of what Arthur Rimbaud called the 'darkened men in overalls' (*d'hommes noirs en blouse*) 'rumbling through the musky evening' (*au soir fauve ... les foules grondent*).[11]

For the worried bourgeois, the ('tentacular') city loosened moral ties and generated laxity. The girls who went to work in the city lived alone and gave themselves over to a dissolute way of life. The city was *tempting*: with its anonymity and the co-presence of 'worlds which touch but which do not interpenetrate', the city 'encourages the fascinating but *dangerous* experiment of living at the same time in several different contiguous, perhaps, but widely separated worlds ... It introduces, at the same time, an element of *chance* and *adventure*, which adds to the stimulus of city life and gives it for *young and fresh nerves* a peculiar attractiveness' (Park).[12]

In this vocabulary we find indestructible puritan moralism that fears the *diabolical*, tempting and thus *dangerous* element of the city in particular for 'young and fresh nerves'. For the German spiritualist sociologist Georg Simmel, the big city entices, seduces; in short, it 'leads us astray' (*verführt*).

Most importantly, the city is *free*. And it was precisely this freedom that worried Simmel. In his 1903 description of the effects of the metropolis on the life of the mind he wrote how the big city 'grants to the individual a kind and an amount of personal freedom which has no analogy whatsoever under other conditions ... The small-town life in Antiquity and in the Middle Ages set barriers against movement and relations of the individual toward the outside, and it set up barriers against individual independence and differentiation within the individual self. These barriers were such that under them modern man could not have breathed.'[13]

What the clerks of the establishment insist on presenting to us as the terrible fate, the unhappiness, the 'inhumanity' of the big city – *indifference, anonymity* – is, conversely, a key factor in its *freedom*. Anonymity, after all, is the other face of the absence of *social control*, of continuously being under surveillance, of the oppression of not being able to escape the village panopticon (something quite different than the kind of disciplining apparatus analysed by Foucault). This 24-hour multi-eyed inspection, even according to Simmel, makes us 'miss the fresh air'.

Freedom should not be interpreted in a purely metaphorical sense. Regarding the air, the medieval German proverb *Die Luft der Stadt macht frei* ('The city air gives freedom') ought to be understood literally. Max Weber explains:

> The urban citizenry therefore usurped the right to dissolve the bonds of seigneurial domination; this was the great – in fact, the *revolutionary* – innovation which differentiated the medieval Occidental cities from all others. In the central and northern European cities appeared the well-known principle that *Stadtluft macht frei*, which meant that after a varying but always relatively short time the master of a slave or serf lost the right to reclaim him.[14]

However, the city air makes us free in a much wider and deeper sense – one that involves the whole individual personality and cuts through to the very core of politics. Without again digging up the well-worn Greek etymology which connects politics to the city (the *polis*), it is worth noting that before the modern era the great theorists of politics were always 'citizens' and, moreover, citizens of 'republican' cities: Aristotle (a 'metic', Athenian by adoption) and Machiavelli (a Florentine). Conversely, to my knowledge, other civilisations instead saw great treatises in military strategy, ethics and morality and, indeed, of metaphysics, mathematics, geography, astronomy and astrology. These latter themes do brush up against the question of 'good government', but not 'politics', as an autonomous discipline that studies the differing typologies of power and of regimes, having as its object not only the exercise of power but also how one can succeed in conquering it and managing not to lose it.

The city air makes us free because it is the city from which every revolt against oppression rises – or rather, because it is here that freedom 'finds refuge in revolt', as the Florentine *segretario* himself acknowledged:

> he who becomes master of a city accustomed to freedom and does not destroy it, may expect to be destroyed by it, for in rebellion it has always the watchword of liberty and its ancient privileges as a rallying point, which neither time nor benefits will ever cause it to forget. And whatever you may do or provide against, they never forget that name or their privileges unless they are disunited or dispersed, but at every chance they immediately rally to them.[15]

But to what does the city's extraordinary liberatory power owe its existence? To the loosening of social control of the village, obviously. However, this alone does not suffice to explain the fear that the city inspires in its rulers, or their untiring attempt to discipline it. Guy Debord provides us with one cue to answering this question when he says that the repressive effort is concentrated above all in a work of *isolation*, in blocking the 'possibilities of encounter' provided by the city.

Of course, if we look at cities from the outside, with the gaze of stunned Earthologists, then they are probably the most accomplished, most versatile human artefact that our species has ever conceived and produced, an artefact that continues to change while managing to remain very much itself. The city can be thought of as a technological product, a rather complicated mechanism, but its main function has always been that of being an enormous communication factory – a huge 'dialogue mill'. Communication, dialogue, the interaction of bodies and of words – this was and is the essence of the concept of urbanity. And herein lies its intensely political character.

For this reason, Le Corbusier sends a shiver down the spine when in the 1933 *Athens Charter* he enumerates four – and only four – functions of the city: 'habitation/leisure/work/traffic'.*

Once again, as on so many other questions, the much-venerated Charles-Édouard Jeanneret (Le Corbusier's real name) dropped a clanger. He forgets what is perhaps the most important function of cities and has been since their birth, when the first *site of encounter* was organised in the first open space. Indeed, a city that fulfils only the four functions listed above provides no place, use or function for squares or plazas – only flyovers and roundabouts.

With zoning, CIAM's urbanism brought to completion what Guy Debord saw as the characteristic trait of the present moment: 'the self-destruction of the urban centre'.[16] Indeed, zoning works against the very objective for which cities were invented and constructed, which was precisely the opposite: that is, humans invented cities in order to have meeting points, points of articulation between heterogeneous human activities. The city was born as a multifunctional, multitasking operation, to join together *the different functions*, to make contiguous the office, the home, the market, the workshop, the café, the store, the cinema. The city was invented precisely in order to be 'multi-zoned' in a single zone. It is thanks to this characteristic that the city has survived and is surviving the repeated declarations of its death and resists all the outsourcing, the remote working, the Edge Cities and the IT revolutions.

---

* Le Corbusier, *La Charte d'Athènes*. The second part ('État actuel des villes, critiques et remèdes') is divided into the following sections: 'Habitations, Loisirs, Travail, Circulation, Patrimoine historique des villes' – as we see, right from the first formulation of modern zoning, beyond the functional districts of the city there is also a 'heritage' district. *La Charte d'Athènes* was published only in 1942 at the height of Marshal Pétain's Vichy regime. It is worth noting that Le Corbusier himself became 'heritage': in 2016, UNESCO declared his architecture 'World Heritage'.

Le Corbusier has none of all this. Against any urbanity, he draws up the plan for the 'self-destruction of the city' through a threefold reductionism: 1) first, he formulates a reductive sense of the term 'function'; 2) he then reduces the number of functions; 3) lastly, he establishes a reductive (that is, strictly two-way) relationship between function and space. But the demiurge-urbanist is sure he knows how to put each moment of time and every life in its proper place – in its *zone*. Because to each urban function there corresponds a moment of the human being's day, because, therefore, to each function there corresponds a time, because an exclusive zone is dedicated to each function, to each zone there corresponds a moment (and vice versa). And, therefore, the subdivision of space transforms into a government of human time: the articulation of space and time, proper to each architecture, here transforms into a *dominion over time by means of space*. It is this juncture that allows a technique of urbanism to become a zoning of the human soul.

The rigid separation between working time and free time is the first zoning of the soul imposed by the social order – as was already clear in the century of the Enlightenment: 'The temporal schema that determines man's ordinary day, entirely dominating him – that *repartition* of life posed and imposed from the outside – always appeared to Rousseau as an unbearable *compression* of life.'[17]

The repartition (zoning) of time, the compression of life, is characteristic of the city: when we work we don't amuse ourselves; and when we amuse ourselves we are useless. This watertight compartmentalisation produces the infernal cycle identified by Henri Lefebvre:

> leisure appears as the non-everyday in the everyday. We cannot step beyond the everyday. The marvellous can only continue to exist in fiction and the illusions that people share. There is no escape. And yet we wish to have the illusion of escape as near to hand as possible. An illusion not entirely illusory, but ... both apparent and real ... we work to earn our leisure, and leisure has only one meaning: to get away from work. A vicious circle.[18]

It brings to mind the stupendous French expression *gagner sa vie en la perdant*, where *gagner* has the double meaning of 'earning' and 'winning'. Hence, one is 'winning one's life by wasting it' or 'wasting one's life to earn a living'.

As for the other practices of free time, this logic is extended to its furthest consequences by tourism: the same intensified exploitation of time that governs the working day also patterns the tourist's 'vacation'. Even without reaching the heights of the organised tours for Japanese tourists, executed like military manoeuvres, tourists must in any case maximise their sightseeing. They always have to see more galleries and museums, more monuments, more panoramic views, accumulating as many memorable experiences as possible, in a frenetic accounting exercise that turns their so-called 'break' period into an unending toil. To recover from the work we do at work, we do the work of tourism. This logic of productivity was well expressed by a young Frenchman who told me: 'Last year I *did* Brazil, now I'm *doing* Southeast Asia, next year I'll *do* Central Asia.'

It's extraordinary: this tourist work, organised as a tourist industry, creates tourist neighbourhoods with the same modalities with which manufacturing industries create working-class *banlieues*. For Guy Debord, 'Integration into the system requires that isolated individuals be recaptured and *isolated together* – 'tourist resorts and housing developments are expressly organized to serve this pseudo-community that follows the isolated individual right into the family cell.'[19]

This puts things masterfully: the planning of tourism, like that of zoning, produces 'individuals *isolated together*'. The tourist resorts are as self-segregated as the American suburbs. And the popular apartment blocks that follow one after another without interruption along the coasts of seaside resorts (in Andalusia, in Turkey, on the Adriatic) look identical to the high-rise projects of the United States or the rent-controlled housing (*habitations à loyer modéré* or HLM) of France's *cités-dortoirs*, the commuter towns (literally, 'dormitory towns') of the metropolitan hinterlands. This, then, functions as a demonstration that class structure

replicates itself in any given space and in any given moment –
even in the afterlife, as a visit to any cemetery will prove. They,
too, are always divided into neighbourhoods, one made up of big
luxurious villas (monumental mausoleums), another of small, dig-
nified single-family lodgings (family graves, with a stone and at
most a statue), a third of multi-floor condominiums crowded with
a series of recesses, with photos and little flames playing a cameo
role – a posthumous tripartition between capitalist remains,
middle-class corpses and proletarian bones.

But even within the everyday city, tourism – as a peculiar form
of the zoning of the soul – in turn produces a zoning of its own,
continuously slicing out tourist districts which no longer have
anything to do with the 'real city' in which the residents live,
work and interact. We have seen how already in his time, in his
zonage, Le Corbusier inserted a 'heritage' district into the city
alongside the others. Just as zoning defines industrial districts
in the industrial city, so UNESCO and the relevant authorities
delimit the tourist district – the 'preserved' area – in the tourist
city. And what is the 'old city' when it is declared a World Heritage Site, if not a supra-national form of zoning? Now, there
is not a city in the world that is not rethought and replanned
around – and a function of – its protected area, which constitutes
its *patrimony* in both senses of the word, as a heritage of memory
but, most importantly, as capital from which to draw profit. Districts in the agglomerations of the United States are as isolated
from the rest of the city as our historic centres, which are defined
by Lefebvre as 'cultural cemeteries under the guise of the human'.
He continues:

> As social text, this historic city ... takes the form of a document,
> or an exhibition, or a museum. The city historically constructed
> is no longer lived and is no longer understood practically. It has
> become nothing else than a consumption item for tourists, for aes-
> theticism avid of spectacle and picturesque. Even for those who
> seek to understand it with warmth, it is dead.[20]

From the human point of view, tourism also becomes an instrument of separation between residents and visitors. This is by no means a relationship between 'hosts and guests', as anthropology pretends, but rather and precisely the coexisting without touching described by Park. Indeed, even if they occupy the same physical space, it seems that residents and tourists evolve in two parallel universes, unable to communicate with one another. Putting aside sex tourism (see Chapter 5), it is very rare that a tourist will make the acquaintance of a native who is not employed in tourist services. Besides, even with sex tourism the only 'host' people the tourist gets to know are those hired for sexual services for tourists – and besides, this is usually not much in the way of making someone's acquaintance, other than the impersonal contact made.

This is the last sense in which tourism kills the city, for it erases its *urbanity*, de-activates its function as a contact-multiplier or, rather, functions as an invisible wall between the group of temporary residents ('visitors') and those settled there (the 'autochthonous'). When the former are present in greater numbers than the latter, it creates paradoxical situations – as anyone who has spent a little time in Venice will know. There, the few inhabitants go about their lives as if the crowds of tourists around them did not exist, like scuba divers swimming indifferently between indifferent swarms of fish. Once again, we see that tourism is far from peculiar – rather, it has its own place in our society's overall dynamic, namely the dynamic of the modern, of industrialised capitalist civilisation, even in an apparently post-industrial and postmodern sector.

It is an amazing dynamic, since this irreducible hostility to what is urban is driven precisely by a system that was born in the city, with the city, and that would be unthinkable without the city: the bourgeoisie is the urban class par excellence, inconceivable in a rural environment. The hostility to everything that is urban is therefore linked to a problem of power, rather than to a specificity of the dominant social class. To isolate subjects requires a technique of domination more than a vocation. Every technological innovation can be exploited so that subjects are 'isolated together' (to use Debord's extraordinary expression). For example, the telephone, TV, hi-fi and video recorder were all used to lock up the middle-class family in its little suburban house (we will come back to this point). But even tragic events can be bent to the same purpose. The most recent demonstration took place in 2020, when the Covid-19 pandemic became the occasion for a gigantic social experiment on an unprecedented scale (billions of human guinea pigs in one fell swoop) to test mass teleworking, the abolition of physical contact, the cancellation of all social events, the end of socialising – all of which made isolation (this time literally) a universal condition. In short, it was an urban-phobic exploitation of the virus. The result mirrored that of tourism: two opposite, and converging, forms of urbicide.

To the modern industrialised capitalist civilisation, tourism is therefore only the magnificent mirror, better allowing us to distinguish its salient traits. And as such, it also brings into relief the process of the 'self-destruction of the urban centre'.

In its final stage, in zoning brought to its furthest consequences, every other activity is expelled from the city and the city becomes fully, totally, a tourist city. Las Vegas is tourist zoning exaggerated to the extreme, extrapolated into an entire city. From this point of view, the killing of the city, perpetrated by tourism, is rather similar to that carried out by financial districts: urbicide by monoculture, monofunctionality, rationalist reductivism. Detroit died while Chicago survived because it was the mono-occupational, monofunctional Motor City that depended on one industry alone: General Motors made Detroit rich, but then it packed up and left, and Motown became for a time an abomination of desolation, a human desert. Chicago, conversely, based itself on differentiated activities, agriculture, varied industries (chemicals, food processing, steel), finance and culture (various universities and research centres). Any city that depends on one industry alone (be it tourism, finance, cars or fashion) is destined for an early death. Already today, Venice is a dead city: as one sees walking from canal to canal on a November night without finding a single window lit up. Florence is already far down this slippery slope – and Rome is heading along the same path.

Naturally, the larger and more diversified a city is, the slower will be its deterioration and suffocation at the hands of tourism. But this makes the big metropoles feel a false sense of security, because for them the road downhill is still a long one – even if for London it is a less distant prospect than it is for New York, and for Paris it is closer still. For all three of these cities, it is less remote a future than it appears: after all, at the end of the fifteenth century Venice was still the capital of global capitalism, the 'universe's market', and less than 150 years later, there was already agitation to put its own Carnival to profitable use, as I have discussed above (see Chapter 7).

Just as the departing car industry left behind in Detroit a mass of gutted buildings, shattered windows, streets with massive holes and burnt-out single-family homes, the same can happen to tourist cities. When the wind changes and the hordes choose other destinations, the only traces left will be broken bottles, rusted cans and chunks of plastic, like debris washed ashore by the incoming tide.

12

Long Live Alienation!
Or, Peeling the Hegelian Onion

Taking pot shots at tourists seems like the world's most popular sport. Fire and brimstone abound (even in this book). To say something is 'for tourists' means it's a scam – a 'tourist trap'. We're not far off the tourist playing the same role as an Irishman in an outdated English joke. But behind its apparent pan-class connotations, the fun to be had from hating tourists is hardly innocent. As one article wittily noted in 1983, 'The leisure of the masses, a most recent phenomenon, has received more criticism from the intellectuals in ten years than the aristocrats' has in two thousand.'*

Nearly forty years on, this quip remains just as cutting – and as true. And it offers a clue for deciphering the impatient dissatisfaction we are left with by all the studies and analyses, even ingenious ones, of tourism and the tourist city. Each time – it's obligatory at the start of the discourse, almost a banality – we are warned that tourism depends on class structure and the class dynamic. But then a priggish silence envelops the real, material meaning of modern tourism's mass nature. There is just an allusion to the complex variety of those on the purchasing end, a little like a stuffy New England matriarch embarrassedly saying that a district is 'so diverse!' – meaning there are too many black people.

But once this warning-upon-entry has been offered, then everyone hurries ahead using the term 'tourism' as an undifferentiated

---

* Jean-Maurice Thurot and Gaétane Thurot, 'The Ideology of Class and Tourism: Confronting the Discourse of Advertising', in *Annals of Tourism Research*, 1983, no. 10, p. 184. It is worth noting that the French term *loisir* (hence the English *leisure*) derives from the Latin *licere*, 'to be permitted'.

mass. It is this unmooring from the dynamic of class and its associated interests that grants the discourse on tourism all its sheer immateriality and, at the same time, condemns it to social scorn.

For example, let's take Culler's sensible and subtle argument, according to which pot shots taken at tourism make up part of tourism itself:

> Ferocious denigration of tourists is in part an attempt to convince oneself that one is not a tourist. The attempt to distinguish between tourists and real travellers is a part of tourism – integral to it rather than outside or beyond it ... Once one notes that disliking tourists, wanting to be less touristy than other tourists, is part of being a tourist, one can recognize the superficiality of most discussions of tourism, especially those that stress the superficiality of tourists ... part of what is involved in being a tourist is disliking tourists (both other tourists and the fact that one is oneself a tourist). Tourists can always find someone more touristy than themselves to sneer at. The hitch-hiker arriving in Paris with a knapsack for an undetermined stay feels superior to his compatriot who flies in on a jumbo jet to spend a week. The tourist who comes on a package tour that includes only air travel and a hotel feels superior, as he sits in a café, to the tour groups that pass by in buses. Americans on bus tours feel superior to the groups of Japanese on bus tours, who seem to be wearing uniforms and obviously do not understand the culture they are photographing.[1]

All true enough – but Culler's problem is that he speaks of 'tourists' as if they belonged to an undifferentiated social group, with similar incomes, equal types of insertion into the labour market and comparable cultural capital. But even if the hitchhiker who reaches Paris is destined for the same future as the professional who arrives in a jumbo jet, the hitchhiker is probably – at least for now – outside the labour market, perhaps for the British gap year or the New Zealander Overseas Experience, and thus has a relationship with time wholly different from that of his compatriot who arrives (perhaps with the family in tow) for a week's holiday torn from under the fingernails of a tyrannical boss. What differs here is not only their relationship with time but also their relationship with money: even in the unlikely case that the hitchhiker and the traveller in the jumbo jet had the same budget, their spending criteria would be wholly different. For the former, this money needs to last as long as possible, to stay longer at each stop and visit as many places as possible, while the latter wants to use it to make the vacation as comfortable and trouble-free as possible, in order to avoid returning to work exhausted and stressed.

How different their aesthetic criteria, the clothes they wear, the books they do or do not read, the music they listen to, the souvenirs they buy, the photos and the selfies they take: a whole galaxy of practices sets them apart. The same destinations, or 'attractions' or sights, are different for each of them: in Paris the hitchhiker will seek out the basement dive bar in a bohemian district (which once meant the Latin Quarter, today Ménilmontant in the twentieth arrondissement) that the traveller in the jumbo jet would turn his nose up at; while the hitchhiker would sarcastically deride the candlelit dinner on a *Bateau Mouche* on the Seine that the jumbo jet man would choose as the quintessential Paris experience. Behind the word 'tourist' we can separate out different positions in each of the different fields which define a person's social being. In this dynamic, the emulation of one class by another, as materialised in tourism, is concretised in a variety of different cases, in function of the different conscious or unconscious strategies adopted toward this same emulation. For instance, the choice of the terrain of social competition: the hitchhiker cannot compete at the level of luxury but can make the best of the one resource she has in abundance: time. She can stand out not in terms of the star rating of the hotel where she stays, but in terms of making it to the most difficult-to-reach places.

Yet the disdain which every tourist feels toward tourists, and her anxious concern to differentiate herself from them and conceive herself as a 'traveller', is just one of the countless ways in which individuals perceive themselves as taking up a different position to the one they really occupy in social space. It's just like how a low-level state employee disdainfully remarks on the 'public', which he is absolutely certain he is not part of. Tourism thus takes the form, at the same time, of an activity practised by all classes – thus something that unites them – but which is practised in a differentiated way, and thus also as a field of confrontation for the differentiation between, and of, classes. It is, therefore, both a shared terrain and a site of conflict: the different tourisms *distinguish* the various tourists, in the sense that they make them more or less *distinct* (in Bourdieu's sense) and thus more or less 'common'.

Thus, in tourism, too, a 'hierarchy of contempt' is built that gradually unfolds, according to various coordinates, from the least to the most organised trip, from the most hard-to-reach destination to the easiest to find, and from greater to lesser time available. The hierarchy of tourist contempt appears in various configurations, just as happens in societies in general: for instance, in the hierarchy of contempt concerning immigrants or ethnicities, the targets of greatest contempt may be black and Native Americans (in the United States) but elsewhere people of mixed black/indio blood (as in Brazil) or Moroccans (in the Netherlands, where Maghrebians tend not to speak Dutch but the black Surinamese do) or Albanians (as in Italy, where there prevails a diffuse criterion that whoever arrived last is the object of most contempt). The specific subjects change, but their *relational* position remains the same.

This demonstrates, once more, that tourism operates like any other generalised social practice – that is, it functions as a *mirror* or *magnifying glass* for society. For it is the field in which the processes also constantly reappearing elsewhere are most visible – processes which, however, generate no similar astonishment or reproach in other fields.

Take the much-despised staging put on for tourists. It is true that in a Naples restaurant someone *has* to play the mandolin (because the mandolin and "O sole mio" are unavoidable markers of *napoletanità*). But it is also true that as Erwin Goffman – the theorist of the role-playing of everyday life – puts it, the representation of the self is not an optional extra, it isn't something that can be suspended or interrupted, as if at a given moment I can choose to stop playing a role. As a social being, the individual cannot enter into relation with others other than by putting on an act: we do so just as we breathe and find it impossible to put our self-presentation to sleep. As Jean-Paul Sartre conveyed in his famous passage on the *garçon de café*, this act is itself always true:

> Let us consider this waiter in the cafe. His movement is quick and forward, a little too precise, a little too rapid. He comes toward the customers with a step a little too quick. He bends forward a little too eagerly; his voice, his eyes express an interest a little too solicitous for the order of the client ... All his behavior seems to us a game ... But what *is* he playing? ... he is playing *at being* a waiter in a cafe ... plays with his condition in order to *realize* it. This obligation is not different from that which is imposed on all tradesmen. Their condition is wholly one of ceremony. The public demands of them that they realize it as a ceremony; there is the dance of the grocer, of the tailor, of the auctioneer, by which they endeavour to persuade their clientele that they are nothing but a grocer, an auctioneer, a tailor. A grocer who dreams is offensive to the buyer, because such a grocer is not wholly a grocer.[2]

In the case of tourism, there is a double act – an 'act squared' so to speak. For not only is the waiter playing the role of the waiter; he is moreover playing the role of the Parisian or Spanish or Thai waiter. When the Greek grocer serves a tourist she doesn't just have to dance the dance of the grocer, she has to dance it to the rhythm of *sirtaki* (and there's a reason why she can't sell anything other than Greek specialities). Meanwhile the Brazilian tailor will dance the dance of the tailor, yes, but to the beat of the samba drum. But conceptually speaking there is nothing different in the tourist show than what is produced in any other branch of society: it seems to us like more of a caricature, more exaggerated, because it is a literally 'exotic' act put on for outsiders. It is this, above all, that draws attention (and criticism), not its theatrical nature – which in itself is innocent, being intrinsic to sociality itself.

But what makes it glaringly clear that tourism partakes of the general characteristics of our society is the incessant accusation that it commodifies beauty. We get this even from the insightful Françoise Choay, when she rails against the 'market consumption of heritage'. There is no doubt of the existence of commodification, and that ineffable masterpieces and monuments of human society are, indeed, becoming a mere source of earnings and sustenance for countless beauty merchants. Firstly, in our society, to say that something is 'commodified' is like discovering that the sea is wet: 'Recreational travel is, then, along with professional sport, outdoor recreations, music, food catering, films, videos, books, magazines, television, art, and numerous other leisure activities, an avenue for the pursuit and accumulation of profit ... In an unambiguous way, capitalist relations of production are an integral part of our "free time", just as they are an integral part of tourism' (Britton).[3]

Nor should we be surprised that free time is a commodity like all the others, given that the 'commodity-form' subsumes everything and that the commodity is the form in which social relations become things – are reified – as Marx wonderfully showed us in one of his most famous passages:

A commodity is therefore a mysterious thing, simply because in it the social character of men's labour appears to them as an objective character stamped upon the product of that labour; because the relation of the producers to the sum total of their own labour is presented to them as a social relation, existing not between themselves, but between the products of their labour. This is the reason why the products of labour become commodities, social things whose qualities are at the same time perceptible and imperceptible by the senses ... it is a definite social relation between men, that assumes, in their eyes, the fantastic form of a relation between things. In order, therefore, to find an analogy, we must have recourse to the mist-enveloped regions of the religious world. In that world the productions of the human brain appear as independent beings endowed with life, and entering into relation both with one another and the human race. So it is in the world of commodities with the products of men's hands. This I call the Fetishism which attaches itself to the products of labour, so soon as they are produced as commodities, and which is therefore inseparable from the production of commodities.[4]

But caught up in the logic of his discourse, Marx did not note the symmetrical consequence of his statement – he did not see the return leg of his outward journey. Namely, if the commodity becomes a fetish, then the fetish, too, becomes a commodity. To put it using his own words, 'the nebulous region of the religious world' becomes a commodity: and what else is paying to enter a church, if not the commodification of the 'holy'? In Walter Benjamin's terms, this directly leads us to the inevitable 'commodification of the aura' – which is precisely what the beautiful souls are complaining about.

And there's more. Was there really any time in human history where art works were not bought and sold and when beauty (including the beauty of the human being) was not the object of barter and exchange? David Lowenthal writes that 'Jamaicans bluntly say that tourism is whorism ... All these laments have hoary pedigrees. To be sure, heritage today peddles a wider range of goods to more buyers than ever before. But it has long been vulgarized, faked and sold: the medieval relic trade outdid any modern scam. What *is* novel is the mistaken notion that such abuses are new and intolerable.'[5]

But there is a contemporary counterexample of the 'commodification of beauty', on which the silence is deafening, as a tabloid writer might put it. And this counterexample is the art market – a wholly particular market 'where producers don't make work primarily for sale, where buyers often have no idea of the value of what they buy, and where middlemen routinely claim reimbursement for sales of things they've never seen to buyers they've never dealt with'.[6] A market which not only 'commodifies' beautiful objects (and what else could a market do?) but literally confiscates them – for the greater part of the works bought by modern collectors end up in underground *caveaux* in which they will lie until the end of time, if not until the next auction at Sotheby's or Christie's. Indeed, an impressive number of Renaissance masterpieces can today be seen only in the black-and-white photos taken by the nineteenth-century Alinari brothers, because the objects themselves have disappeared from circulation, into private hands. This is a privatisation process which UNESCO protection has nothing to find fault with, even though it has a much more ruinous effect on the 'heritage of humanity' than does tourism, for it literally takes this World Heritage *away from* all human beings.

This is a market, lastly, which has the advantage of labelling each 'beautiful object' with an exact monetary value, down to the last cent. And this is also a disproportionate value, which sets up comparisons between things that can hardly be compared. Such was the *Guardian*'s 2015 list of the ten most expensive paintings in history. Here we discover that the top-ranked work, Paul Gauguin's *When Will You Marry?*, could pay the net annual incomes of around 10,000 Italian workers and thus support around 40,000 people for a year, if each worker maintains a spouse and two children. Meanwhile, the total for the top ten paintings amounts to some 1,820 million dollars – equivalent to the net annual income of more than 60,000 Italian workers, and thus sustenance for some 240,000 people.

The world's largest financial audit agency, Deloitte (more than 300,000 employees worldwide), valued the global art market at 63 billion dollars in 2014.[7] There are some ninety-two countries across the globe, such as Slovenia, Zambia, Afghanistan, Lithuania and El Salvador, with a GDP below this sum. But to my knowledge, no thoughtful censor has ever unpacked the relations established by auction houses between (aesthetic) values and financial interests, analysing the philosophical and sociological implications of the art market. Yet this analysis is constantly going on with regard to tourism.

The Ten Most Expensive Paintings Ever Sold (as of 2015)

Painting	Artist	Price (adjusted for inflation)	Year of Sale
Gauguin – Nafea Faa Ipoipo (When Will You Marry Me?)	Paul Gauguin	$300m	2015
The Card Players	Paul Cézanne	$263m	2011
Women of Algiers (Version O)	Pablo Picasso	$179m	2015
No. 5, 1948	Jackson Pollock	$164m	2006
Woman III	Willem de Kooning	$162m	2006
Portrait of Adele Bloch-Bauer I	Gustav Klimt	$159m	2006
The Dream	Pablo Picasso	$158m	2013
Portrait of Dr Gachet	Vincent van Gogh	$149m	1990
Three Studies of Lucian Freud	Francis Bacon	$145m	2013
Bal au moulin de la Galette	Pierre Auguste Renoir	$142m	1990
Total		$1,820m	

Source: Ami Sedghi, 'The 10 Most Expensive Paintings Ever Sold', *Guardian*, 11 May 2015. Naturally this ranking could not take account of the $450m sale in 2017 of the *Salvator Mundi*, attributed to Leonardo da Vinci but probably painted by a pupil of his.

This silence is all the more ironic given that both the master-piece buyer and the tourist who merely visits those masterpieces that are still accessible set themselves essentially the same social objective, namely a growth in the symbolic capital in their own possession. Just as the European tourist increases his or her social capital by joining the group of Europeans who have visited Borobudur *and* Machu Picchu, so, too, does the art collector find value in community. As Deloitte confirms:

the social value of buying art is a key aspect for art collectors. 61 per cent said this was a key motivation, up from 60 per cent in 2012, while an even higher 72 per cent of art professionals believed this was a key motivation for their clients ... Invitations to art fair VIP openings around the world and gallery and museum dinners for collectors and patrons provide members with an exclusive network, giving access to the artists themselves, but also to other business people and celebrities. Deutsche Bank's sponsorship of the Frieze art fair, the UBS sponsorship of Art Basel and Royal Bank of Canada's sponsorship of Masterpiece highlights the value that such events can bring to their clients, not for the financial benefits, but in terms of the emotional and social value these events provide. The wealth management industry should strategically think about how to create and provide services that offer access to exclusive events and networks for their clients.[8]

But while countless semiologists, anthropologists, sociologists and ideologists have exerted themselves in the critique of tourism, its interpretation and conceptual unpacking, none of them have reserved comparable energies for the art market. More than just silent, they discreetly tiptoe around it, with the delicate non-chalance appropriate when dealing with big sums of cash – the tact that is due real money. Perhaps this contrast arises from the fact – and here we get back to the forms of class discrimination – that the protagonists of the two phenomena are very different from one another socially. Tourists cannot be defined with arcane acronyms. But this is precisely what happens with collectors labelled 'HNWIs' or even 'U-HNWIs', where HNWIs stands for High-Net-Worth Individuals. Indeed, the Deloitte report categorises these latter 'into three discrete wealth bands: those with US$1 million to US$5 million in investable wealth (millionaires next door), those with US$5 million to US$30 million (mid-tier millionaires) and those with US$30 million or more (Ultra-HNWIs)'. For Deloitte – we can read between the lines – whoever has only 1 million to 5 million dollars to invest is little more than a pauper.

It is, moreover, curious how acronyms are fobbed off on the two ends of the social ladder (with a preference for N, to mean both 'Net' and 'Not'). Thus next to (and opposite) the NHWIs are the NEETs, in the sense that the former are at the top of the pyramid while the latter are not even part of it – being Not in

Employment, Education or Training. The only thing that unites the NHWIs and the NEETs is that during part of the year any number of them may become tourists. Once again, tourism is a shared, socially omnipresent terrain, where a conflict is fought which, while symbolic, does not lack in real effects.

Commodification, alienation, inauthenticity – three terms that have always been attached to tourism, and mutually refer to one another. But once we take them all together, they allow us to understand the degree to which all those who have spoken of tourism (this author included) have moved within a Hegelian conceptual horizon. We have all fallen into the venerable Georg Wilhelm Friedrich's trap, and have not yet freed ourselves from it. The beauty of this trap is that even those who perhaps do not even known who Hegel was, or at least have never studied him – including, I suppose, many of the authors cited thus far – nonetheless fall into it. For ideas can be absorbed even just by breathing the air of the times, by imbibing commonplaces and conditioned conceptual reflexes.

The first suspicion about this trap arose when the theme of nostalgia kept recurring in discourses on tourism, and with it, reiterated claims as to the unreachability of the tourist's goals and destination: 'Tourism, human circulation considered as consumption, a by-product of the circulation of commodities, is fundamentally nothing more than the leisure of going to see what has become banal' (Debord).[9] This is only a different, blunt way of saying that modern tourism is one of those activities that, obeying the mechanism of 'social limits' (Hirsch), self-destruct: we can again read Coleman and Crang, for whom tourism 'bears with it the ironic seeds of its own destruction, as the very presence of the tourist corrupts the idea of reaching an authentic and totally different culture. Paradoxically, a *nostalgic* semiotic economy is produced, one that is always mourning the loss of that which it itself has ruined. The really authentic unspoiled place is always displaced in space or time – it is spatially located over the next hill, or temporally existed just a generation ago.'[10] Authenticity is always round the corner, and it is always the authenticity of yesterday or the day before that. Here, how could we not refer to the sharp judgement in the *Dialectic of Enlightenment*, for which the 'promissory note of pleasure' which the culture industry draws on 'is indefinitely prolonged'. If its promise will never be reached, how could we not apply the same judgement to tourism? And how can we not recall the Blaue Blume that appears to the young Heinrich von Ofterdingen in the (unfinished) eponymous novel by Novalis, the romantic symbol of any desire that cannot be fulfilled? But precisely here lies the trap – namely, to represent as intrinsically unreachable, as a general characteristic of the mindset of the generic tourist, what is instead the outcome of class emulation and owes to the fact that 'the élite must always find new locations, uncontaminated by the mass – places which will thus still carry a high level of symbolic capital and which are guaranteed as different by the difficulty in getting there, hardships or cost' (Coleman and Craig).[11]

To put that in other words, the trap lies in representing as a mentality what is, instead, the outcome of a relationship of domination and subordination; in attributing to the tourist – and here Hegel comes in – an *unhappy consciousness*. The unhappy consciousness is defined by Hegel as a split consciousness, which attributes to itself all that which is temporary and contingent and situates outside of itself everything that is lasting and necessary. In placing this latter outside of itself (estranging it), it cannot but constantly and uselessly chase after it. It does nothing other than seek the 'the unattainable other-worldly beyond which, in the act of being seized, escapes, or rather has already escaped'.[12] This consciousness thus has an unhappy, lacerated relationship with the unchangeable. Its attitude toward the transcendent takes the shape of a painful 'nostalgia' for an impossible reconciliation, as 'devotion' for an imagined original unity.

It is with good reason, then, that nostalgia, devotion and the pursuit of the unreachable play a crucial role in all the accredited interpretations of tourism. For the unhappy consciousness, as for the tourist who is never satisfied with the destination accessible to him, 'the actual doing of consciousness becomes a doing of nothing, and its consumption becomes a feeling of unhappiness ... What we see here is only a personality limited to itself and its own petty acts; we see a brooding personality, as unhappy as it is impoverished' (Hegel).[13] The atonement to which the devotee subjects himself becomes the discomforts the tourist has to bear.

We have everywhere encountered nostalgia as the horizon of tourism, as the foundational sentiment of romanticism and of the cult of ruins. Nostalgia is 'the repetition that mourns the inauthenticity of all repetition', writes John Frow, who summarises the history of this sentiment as follows:

> Originally defined in the seventeenth century in terms of a set of physical symptoms associated with acute homesickness, it subsequently came to be closely connected with the 'specific depression of intellectuals,' melancholia. By the nineteenth century it had been extended to describe a general condition of estrangement, a state of ontological homelessness that became one of the period's key metaphors for the condition of modernity (and which is also one of the central conditions of tourism, where the Heimat functions simultaneously as the place of safety to which we return and as that lost origin which is sought in the alien world).[14]

Nostalgia, it has been said, has become a 'social illness'. And I would add that this disease has had a contagious effect on modernity, *contemporary to* the propagation of tourism. Nostalgia for the authentic in an inauthentic world, nostalgia for the unalienated in an alienated era. As the title of the French actress Simone Signoret's autobiography put it, 'nostalgia is no longer what it used to be' – hence we have nostalgia for nostalgia.

The antithesis between traveller and tourist is akin to that between '[a]uthentic and inauthentic experience; community and society; organic and mechanical solidarity; status and contract; use value and exchange value – the structural oppositions through which the relation between tradition and modernity is constructed (or rather, through which modernity defines itself against its mythical Other) are potentially endless but formally homologous' (Frow).[15]

This formal homology between all the oppositions we have encountered obliges us to peel off another layer of the Hegelian onion, to identify the trap that exists one level deeper. It seems obvious that these antitheses are homologous to the one between the Ego and the non-Ego. Less self-evident is the implicit meaning of this homology, which is to say that the moment of the antithesis is negatively connoted: if 'Ego' is homologous to 'authentic', to 'use-value' and to 'unalienated' while 'non-Ego' is homologous to 'inauthentic', to (commodified) 'exchange value' and to 'alienated', then in the unfolding of the dialectic the non-Ego (antithesis) takes on a minus sign, as opposed to the plus sign of the Ego (and of the thesis).

The dialectic ought to be credited with having represented the first serious attempt to answer the question: how can the old be made to give birth to the new? A *real* new, one which is not already contained in the old. In mechanism there is no space for this 'unprecedented' new, because the new is limited to being the successor to some precedent, which always accumulates previously given addenda. Conversely, in the dialectical process of thesis–antithesis–synthesis, the synthesis is a higher, *new* stage, in which something is present which was absent both from the thesis and from the antithesis and which comes into existence only by way of 'dialectical sublation (*Aufhebung*)'. But it is precisely this innovative side of the dialectic that makes it appear to us also as an easy formula. At worst it can be seen as a conjuror's trick that brings back through the window the same vitalist irrationalism that it pretended to have chased out the door, and at best as an example of circular thinking. It is for this reason that no serious materialist has ever managed to truly convince themselves of the dialectic. So much for Marx.

In truth, systems-theory concepts have been formulated which bear a certain analogy with the dialectical process, the concepts of 'non-linear interaction' and 'feedback' – processes in which the action of one agent produces an effect which, through a feedback action – changes the agent itself (which, in turn, acts anew, doing so from the basis of a different and changed state, thus generating yet another different effect, and so on). In feedback as in the dialectic, the process changes the point – or state – of departure from which one first started out, but with a substantial difference: there is no privileging of the ego over the non-Ego, of the thesis over the antithesis – rather, their roles are interchangeable.

In the dialectic, conversely, the Ego is effectively accorded an enormous privilege (if not theoretically so): that, is, the privilege conferred on the initial state that enjoys the pre-eminence of the original; whereas the non-Ego is a becoming-Other, with all its negative connotations, such that to be posed as a non-Ego is defined as 'estrangement' *(Entfremdung)*, as 'alienation' *(Entaüsserung)*, 'expropriation' (where the verb *sich entaüssern* means 'to undo', 'to strip', 'to deprive') and lastly 'cessation' or 'alienation' in the sense of sale or transfer of ownership (*Veraüsserung*). In short, however indispensable the antithesis is considered to the synthesis, as compared to the thesis, the dialectic drags in its wake the curse of the *non*: the *non*-being, the *non*-Ego, the Other apart from the Self, the Foreigner.

Of course, Hegel was not the first to confer primacy upon the Ego and the Subject: he was himself caught in pre-existing traps. For the negativity always implicit in coming out of the self, in becoming another, we need only think of the expression, 'he's beside himself with rage'.

But what Hegel might have thought is important for our purposes only up to a certain point. The problem is that Marx extended the concept of alienation to the economy, yet not in the strictly economic sense that it previously had, when 'alienate' only meant the sale of a good, and alienation was, precisely, a sales contract. Marx carried out an operation that was, so to speak, opposed to the one Rousseau had accomplished in his *Social Contract* when he applied the commercial meaning of alienation to political philosophy, or rather made it the very foundation of any society. Rousseau wrote that the clauses of the social contract 'can all be reduced, of course, to one alone: namely, the total alienation of each associate with all his rights to the community as a whole ... Moreover, since the alienation is made without reservation, the union is as perfect as may be, and no associate has anything further to claim.'[16] We might note that through this move, alienation is attributed a highly positive value. The young Marx, conversely, carried out the inverse process: he imported into the economic field the Hegelian philosophical meaning of the term, alienation as dispossession (the worker dispossessed of his labour), which became alienation as estrangement, as something that separates from the self and thus as an unhappy consciousness. This notion, then, expanded beyond all proportion and became double faced. On the one hand is objective, economic alienation, and on the other a subjective, existential, psychological alienation. The first coincides with the commodity fetishism that 'thingifies' the social relations between human beings (see Chapter 4). It coincides with the worker who finds his own labour expropriated and is enslaved in the 'assembly line' production of a commodity, which he not only produces but is convinced to buy (and to idolise as a fetish).

The other, originating in the first sense of alienation, expresses itself in an estrangement from the self, impotence, isolation, anomie, states of mind which are explored in literature from Franz Kafka's *Castle* to Albert Camus's *The Stranger*. We should remember that before it received the melancholic and existential meaning that it later acquired, the term 'alienation' (which was introduced by Philippe Pinel) was synonymous with madness. Its association with madness can be seen in some Romance languages: *aliénation mentale* in French or *alienación mental* in Spanish. This linguistic connection, however, does not appear in German (*Geisteskrankheit*) or in English (*insanity*). An academic publication founded by Cesare Lombroso in Turin in 1880 was entitled *Archive of Psychiatry, Criminal Anthropology and Penal Sciences to Serve the Study of Alienated and Delinquent Man*. And as late as 1929, the entry in the *Treccani Enciclopedia* for 'Alienazione' read: 'As of 31 December 1926 59,992 *alienati* had been taken into the madhouse ... This figure does not include, it should be understood, the tranquil imbeciles assisted by their relatives at home.'

But even once the concept of mental alienation was freed from the stigmas of the madhouse, it has long continued to serve as a bridge between individual psychology and sociology, because – in a classic feedback process – existential alienation is the condition that allows economic alienation to act with greater potency. This is the mystification discussed by Horkheimer and Adorno, for whom the masses 'insist unwaveringly on the ideology by which they are enslaved'.[17]

But at this point the concept of alienation becomes so all-encompassing that it assumes the rank of a phenomenon intrinsically connected to the capitalist mode of production. Alienation becomes *synonymous with modernity*. To use Paul Ricoeur's words, it becomes 'a "hospital-word" in which all the "diseased" come to recuperate', it becomes 'the slogan for any "civilizational malaise"'. This was what Michelangelo Antonioni's films like *The Night* or *The Eclipse* also showed. The term's field of application expanded beyond all measure and covered ever-new shards of reality: this was the era in which for Franz Fanon and Third Worldism the effect of colonialism was a gigantic alienation of the colonised. As Ricoeur, writing in the 1960s, further put it: 'alienation is today an ill word. It suffers what some lexicologists call a "semantic overcharge"; by dint of meaning too much, it risks not meaning anything anymore. The question posed, facing such a patient, is whether to treat it or kill it off.'[18]

As we ponder whether to kill alienation or to treat it, we can begin to interrogate both its heuristic effectiveness and its intrinsic validity.

What we can first say is that having reached the peak of its glory in the 1930s to the 1960s, alienation has since experienced a rapid decline. Since the beginning of the twenty-first century, only very rarely has alienation been invoked to explain the revolts in the *banlieues* or the other phenomena of social discontent. Similarly, in the arts, literature and cinema, this condition is no longer to be sought out as the psychological key to various characters. It may seem strange that in a globalised world, where the expropriation of the self is thus more manifest, so little recourse is made to this concept. On the one hand there is an inurement effect. Just as no one gets angry anymore about the 'hidden persuasion' exercised by ad men* or protests against the mystification effected by mass culture, it is likewise probable that, precisely because it is synonymous with modernity, alienation is also considered simply a condition of existence, on a par with mortality or limits of space.

But in my view, there's rather more to the question. I have some reservations about saying it, but let's put it like this:

Alienation is good.

It may seem that I want to *épater les bourgeois*. But let's be clear first that for Hegel, the Ego could not but alienate itself, could not but place itself outside of itself – otherwise, there would simply be no world or any history; there is a 'necessary alienation' in which 'the subject realizes himself by losing himself, where he becomes other in order to become truly himself' (Debord).[19] The Ego has no alternative: it can, perhaps, choose *how* to alienate and estrange itself, but not *whether* to do so. In this perspective, it is true that alienation is an ineluctable condition of existence; we are alienated in the same way that we are bipeds.

There's more. All production 'thingifies' its own social relation, reifies human relations: here, too, the problem is how it does so, rather than the fact itself. And it is true that Marx's description of what makes for a non-alienated individual in a communist society is rather ridiculous: 'in communist society, where nobody has one exclusive sphere of activity but each can become accomplished in any branch he wishes, society regulates the general production and thus makes it possible for me to do one thing today and another tomorrow, to hunt in the morning, fish in the afternoon, rear cattle in the evening, criticise after dinner, just as I have a mind, without ever becoming hunter, fisherman, herdsman or critic.'[20]

For the young Marx, who was not yet twenty-seven years of age when he wrote these lines in *The German Ideology*, it is the

---

* *The Hidden Persuaders* is the title of a book by Vance Packard published in the United States in 1957, which had huge resonance at the time.

social division of labour which inexorably produces estrange-ment.* Yet specialisation not only has to do with the capitalist mode of production, but rather with technological progress and the mountain of training, practice or study necessary to master a given field: even an Egyptian embalmer and a Mycenaean vase maker had to be 'specialised'. However, in an even deeper sense, specialisation is a legitimate human desire – as Galileo Galilei said, we humans are far behind God when it comes to the *extent* of our understanding, but we can emulate Him with our *intensive* understanding.† Fully getting to grips with a skill, totally mas-tering a certain technique – *divine* piano playing, fashioning a beautiful piece of furniture, knowing the topological theory of normed rings in mathematics – all activities that require abso-lute dedication and thus unbelievable 'specialisation', can lead to finding the satisfaction that give one's life meaning.

This is a good estrangement. Ricoeur heads back to the gnostic roots of alienation, as an act with which God created the world: God made himself something other than himself, the world. More-over – not to be blasphemous – but what does a person do when they make love, if not estrange themselves ('realising oneself by losing oneself')? What, indeed, would making love be if one was always self-aware, if one did not forget oneself, 'come outside of

---

* In his old age, Marx's opinion became more nuanced, as evidenced in the third volume of *Capital* that deals with the 'realm of necessity' and 'realm of freedom' (chapter 48).

† 'The human understanding can be taken in two modes, the intensive or the extensive. Extensively, that is, with regard to the multitude of intelligible, which are infinite, the human understanding is as nothing even if it understands a thou-sand propositions; for a thousand in relation to infinity is zero. But taking man's understanding intensively, in so far as this term denotes understanding some prop-osition perfectly, I say that the human intellect does understand some of them perfectly, and thus in these it has as much absolute certainty as Nature itself has. Of such are the mathematical sciences alone; that is, geometry and arithmetic, in which the Divine intellect indeed knows infinitely more propositions, since it knows all. But with regard to those few which the human intellect does under-stand, I believe that its knowledge equals the Divine in objective certainty, for here it succeeds in understanding necessity': Galileo Galilei, *Dialogo dei massimi sistemi* (1632); English translation by Sillman Deake, foreword by Albert Einstein, *Dialogue Concerning the Two Chief World Systems*, Berkeley: University of California Press, (1953) 1967, p. 103.

oneself'? The Italian word '*divertimento*' (entertainment, amusement, fun) has Latin origins to do with getting away from oneself – in English, 'divert' shares the same root. Would we really argue that amusement/estrangement is unhappiness?

Obviously, there is a chasm between the alienation of the pianist who obsessively repeats scales over days, months and years, and that of the assembly-line worker constantly tightening the same screws, even if the repetitiveness – the extreme specialisation – is the same. But this is the abyss that separates a *chosen* alienation from an alienation to which one is *subjected*. The bad thing, here, is not the fact of getting outside of oneself, of becoming an other, but the *obligation* to do so in a certain way in a certain moment – being *compelled to do this*. The bad thing is not the division of labour and time, but the coerced division of labour and of time. We might add, in parentheses, that this does not mean that the solution ought to be found in a neither desirable nor possible return to an imagined originary unity when labour was not divided and the Ego did not become another (the little Rousseau of the state of nature nesting within each of us). It means that perhaps we need to further develop the idea of communism, imagining it as a society that allows each of us to choose our own division of labour, our own alienation, rather than as a society that tries to abolish it. In short, if one can choose one's own alienation, then it is welcome!

This is better, in any case, than the unbearable dilettantism of doing a little hunting, a little fishing, a little literary criticism and – why not? – crosswords. Such an idleness reminds us of the unliveable emptiness at the heart of the landowner Eugene Onegin's existence, cruelly described by Pushkin. Looking after the cattle, as Marx put it, seems to have emerged from the same Arcadia that Marie Antoinette imagined when she played at being a little farm girl milking the cows a few hundred metres away from the Versailles palace: it seems that the young Marx was beholden, despite himself, to the trap of class emulation and anticipated the proletarian's life in a future communist society as identical to the aristocrat's life in the now passed feudal society: similarly easy and similarly pointless.

13

Yearning for the Other

A further surprising indicator of the implicit positive value of the term 'alienation' comes from the adjectives that are connected to it. Usually the verb 'to alienate' is used via its past participle – 'alienated' – which then becomes a noun, 'the alienated'. But beyond the alienated there is the 'alien', a word that has undergone a curiously meandering journey. Its Latin dictionary definition reads '*alienus*: of others, strange, averse, hostile, incompatible, unfavourable; *alieni*: strangers, foreigners; *alieno tempore*: at an inopportune moment, out of time'. Hence Terence's well-worn maxim: '*Homo sum, humani nihil a me alienum puto*' ('I am human, and I believe nothing human is alien to me'). In American English legal terminology, 'alien' takes on a more literal meaning: a 'resident alien' is any person who lives in a country of which he or she is not a citizen. Yet from there the term has slipped, coming to designate extraterrestrials (especially in the plural): aliens. Here, alien life is otherworldly. Thus having started life with the meaning of foreigner, restive, hostile, 'alien' has returned to Romance languages as *extraterrestre* in French and Italian, whereas Portuguese has *alienígena*. In the other Indo-European languages, the English word 'alien' has established itself in everyday use (especially after the 1979 Ridley Scott film of the same name) together with terms that have traditionally designated extraterrestrials (like the German *Außerirdische*).

Indeed, what is more foreign than an extraterrestrial? The only possible comparison is that of an interaction between one person who is autistic and another who is not, where the former is unable to decode the body language and the facial expressions of the latter, and vice versa: as one autistic patient once told Oliver Sacks, 'Much of the time ... I feel like an anthropologist on Mars'; that is, she felt that interactions with other people were often as difficult as interviewing Martians.[1]

Aliens are foreigners to us not only because they are totally unknown to us, but, more implicitly, in that they are enemies. As the Canadian philosopher Ian Hacking has written: 'Anthropology and sociology teach that human groups hang together partly because of who they include and partly because of who they exclude. Our instinct has always been to exclude aliens, first the terrestrial ones and then the extraterrestrial'.[2]

It is not surprising, therefore, that in the images of extraterrestrials handed down to us by Western science fiction and everyday mythology, 'alien' civilisation mirrored the representation of communist society broadcast by Radio Free Europe during the Cold War:[*] collectivist insects lacking individuality and, thus, lacking 'humanity'. In the most classic act of denigrating whatever is Other to the Self, all which is alien in nature becomes inhuman in character. Not by accident, the narration of aliens was contemporary with the narration of robots ('intellects without a soul'), insofar as the only recognised form of alienness was that of the unhuman, the unemotional.

But the alien was inhuman in a very terrestrial and anthropomorphic way, inhuman because they lacked sympathy and love, at least until one had a crush on a handsome or beautiful terrestrial, a passion that led them to renounce their own entomological inhumanity and in most cases to perish because of their humanisation. As Roland Barthes observed in a chapter of his *Mythologies* dedicated to Martians and flying saucers, the insurmountable difficulty of conceiving the Other constantly returns:

---

* Radio Free Europe was founded in 1949 as an instrument of anti-Soviet propaganda, and until 1972 it was exclusively financed by the CIA. Long based in Munich, in 1995 it moved to Prague. After the end of the Cold War its direct transmissions to Eastern Europe fell off significantly, while it ramped up its efforts in the area between the Mediterranean and Pakistan.

one of the constant features of all petit-bourgeois mythology is this impotence to imagine the Other. Otherness is the concept most anti-pathetic to 'common sense'. Every myth tends fatally to a narrow and, worse still, to what we might call a class anthropomorphism. Mars is not only Earth, it is petit-bourgeois Earth, it is the little district of mentality cultivated by the popular illustrated press. No sooner has it taken form in the sky than Mars is thus aligned by the most powerful of appropriations, that of identity.[3]

The unbearable banality of so much bad science-fiction, which tends to apply the terrestrial dimension onto the cosmos, also stems from this distaste for conceiving the Different-from-me (from-us): starships really are ships, vessels and freighters, just as interstellar spaces are oceans, solar systems are archipelagos, and extraterrestrials are strange exotic islanders from those archipela-gos or, alternatively, alien invaders and hordes of (communist?) barbarians who threaten the survival of the human race and its planet. Naturally, the space fleets sail through the ether, much like fleets of ships in the sea, and space pirates home in on them just like the buccaneers of Tortuga. A witty parody of this anthro-pomorphism and geomorphism came in Douglas Adams's 1979 book *The Hitchhiker's Guide to the Galaxy*, in which the insig-nificant third planet of a small yellow star on the edge of the Milky Way (that is, Earth) is swept aside in order to make way for a galactic motorway.

Fortunately, not all sci-fi is anthropomorphic. In its best expres-sions, alien characters have the specific function of observing what is alien to them, namely us terrestrials, thus casting an alien gaze on the familiar: that is, the aliens produce a mirror effect. In a lightning-paced story by Fredric Brown, a soldier in the trenches is described as 'wet and muddy and hungry and cold and he was fifty thousand light-years from home'.

He stayed alert, gun ready. Fifty thousand light-years from home, fighting on a strange world and wondering if he'd ever live to see home again. And then he saw one of them crawling toward him. He drew a bead and fired. The alien made that strange horrible sound they all make, then lay still. He shuddered at the sound and sight of the alien lying there. One ought to be able to get used to them after a while, but he'd never been able to. Such repulsive creatures they were, with only two arms and two legs, ghastly white skins and no scales.[4]

But sci-fi as written by its best authors has also proven capable of imagining yet more alien creatures. For example, there is a planet almost entirely covered by an ocean, destination of the starships from the constellation Alpha Acquarii, which revolves around a binary star in a very strange orbit which corrects itself with respect to the normal course dictated by gravity. The planet is called Solaris and it has stirred such interest and so much discussion that there is even a *Journal of Solaristics*. The Solarists have discovered that this ocean is a single, vast, colloidal gelatinous structure, highly organised, and that it is the only living being that resides on Solaris, able to correct its orbit and directly act on space-time. Readers will have recognised this as Stanislaw Lem's 1961 novel, *Solaris*, of which there have been two film adaptations, one directed by Andrei Tarkovsky (in 1972) and another by Steven Soderbergh (2002).[5]

Alien creatures can thus arouse admiration, sympathy, even love. The most fascinating alien creature in sci-fi (as far as I know at least) is without doubt a cloud, or rather a *Black Cloud*,[6] which is the title of a novel by the astrophysicist Fred Hoyle. In this story, a vast cloud of particles enters the solar system and surrounds the Sun, darkening it and threatening the extinction of all life on Earth. But an astrophysicist from the committee called on to confront the planetary emergency understands that the cloud is a giant living being, whose particles are connected in synapses with a complexity that rivals that of the human imagination. The cloud has surrounded the Sun in order to provide itself with the energy that allows its continued wandering through space. The astrophysicist manages to establish communication with the cloud, which is astonished by the idea that intelligent life has evolved on a solid planet. The cloud learns with astonishing speed of all that the human species has ever produced, which the astrophysicist transmits to it by computer. It is particularly fascinated by some of Beethoven's compositions. The astrophysicist, ever more enamoured with the immense cloud, asks it to communicate its knowledge to him. However, his mind cannot withstand the impact of such deep ideas, which have the power to overwhelm the human intellect, and he collapses. The cloud heads away from our Solar System to come to the aid of another cloud that has stopped giving out signals. The astrophysicist's ill-fated love for the cloud is more romantic than any sentiment felt by Tristan, Heloise, Werther.

Fred Hoyle expressed an attitude widespread among humans of the twentieth century, namely a desire to contact aliens. The predisposition toward such an encounter manifested itself in myriad ways. The most obvious – and embarrassing – expression of this anguish over the alien (a fearful desire, a hopeful fear) is, without doubt, the psychosis over Unidentified Flying Objects. Seventy years later, we would struggle to take onboard how widespread belief in 'flying saucers' really was, and how persistent it remained, even after the end of its peak between 1950 and 1970. We ought not forget that these were also the years in which humanity was convinced it had entered the 'space age'.

The first nine flying saucers were seen on 24 June 1947. The wealthy American businessman Kenneth Arnold spotted them hovering in tight formation close to Mount Rainier in Washington state. The Cold War, the space race between the US and the USSR, and the popularity of sci-fi encouraged these sightings to be taken seriously even, at least ostensibly, by state authorities.

The term UFO was coined by the US Air Force (USAF) in 1953, the year after it formed a study group, the Blue Book Project, which continued to conduct investigations into UFOs until 1969. In 1968, the USAF's Condon Committee, named after the influential physicist Edward Condon, had released its 'judiciously skeptical' report on the phenomenon. France had its own study group (Geipan) as did Britain, which curiously enough took until 2009 to declare that it had closed down its unit investigating UFO activity. Although the height of UFO-mania was in the 1950s and '60s, sightings continued and were even officially recorded in 2019.[7]

Like so many other 'inexplicable' phenomena, from Padre Pio's stigmata to precise predictions regarding the end of the world, the interesting thing is not so much whether or not these phenomena are indeed real, but rather why so many people believe in them. And why they are taken seriously, even as a matter of 'scholarly' investigation. From this point of view, UFOs seem like the twentieth-century version of what Spiritism was in the nineteenth century. Positivists who only believed in 'facts' gave credit to Spiritism after photographic plates seemed to be printed with the hypothetical ectoplasms of the dead: the Positivists were always thirsting for 'rigorous', 'scientific' explanations for mysterious phenomena. Such was the case of Cesare Lombroso, who wrote, 'Moreover, just as Hertz's laws of waves largely explain telepathy, likewise the new discoveries on the radioactive properties of certain metals ... showing us that there may be not only brief manifestations but a continuous, enormous growth of energies, of heat and light, without any apparent loss of matter, erase the greatest objection that the scientist had raised against mysterious manifestations of Spiritism.'[8]

Ufology similarly skirted around official science, with both the accredited scientists who concerned themselves with it and others who appeared to support it mounting a campaign to find traces of extraterrestrial life. They did so with more or less ignoble objectives – be it financing the aerospace industry or procuring new funds for the Pentagon. But today it is hard to understand the degree to which the imaginary of the time was really steeped in science fiction and how far science fiction influenced global-scale decisions. We need only think of the Citizens' Advisory Council on National Space Policy, set up in the US at the end of the 1970s by the sci-fi writers Jerry Pournelle, Robert A. Heinlein and Poul Anderson, the astronaut Buzz Aldrin and the retired general

Daniel Graham, along with aerospace industry bosses and scientists.* The Council's contact with the Reagan administration was the national security adviser Richard Allen. Its lobbying efforts achieved the launch of a space-weapons programme, the 'Star Wars' system announced by Reagan in the early 1980s (its official name was the Strategic Defense Initiative, SDI). Here, politics followed the initial *Star Wars* film by serving up space weaponry to the collective imaginary.

Among the scientists who most dedicated themselves to propagandising for human space exploration, the most famous was the astrophysicist Carl Sagan. He was a tireless populariser, NASA adviser, member of the committee to review the Blue Book Project, organiser of the UFO symposium held by the American Association for the Advancement of Science (AAAS) in 1969 (a symposium overflowing with interest), and one of the founders of the Search for Extraterrestrial Intelligence (SETI) project. SETI's website has some 6.8 million followers, and after Sagan's death it dedicated its research centre to him.

Over the years, Sagan became ever more hostile to what he called anthropocentrism, the human-centred vision of life and the universe. Already in the 1960s he joined a semi-secret society which proposed to decipher dolphin language, on the grounds that this would be the key to deciphering any alien language. Along with its key figure, the neurobiologist John Lilly, this society also included the astrophysicist Frank Drake, the evolutionary biologist J.B.S. Haldane, and the Nobel chemistry laureate Melvin Calvin. In subsequent years, Sagan argued that whale hunting was a form of homicide and became an adviser to Cornell Students for the Ethical Treatment of Animals.

Ian Hacking is the only philosopher to have noted the consonance between the search for alien life and the drives of animal liberation movements, and to have formulated a hypothesis to explain both:

---

* This story is told by Norman Spirad (himself a science-fiction writer and for a time president of the American Association of SF Writers) in 'Quand la guerre des étoiles devient réalité', *Le Monde diplomatique*, July 1989.

Once upon a time, people and animals lived in close proximity, sharing in a life. People who were not actually hunters or farmers lived close by hunters or farmers. Now in the increasingly wide-spread industrial world our species is almost all alone. Alone in the sense that there are hardly any species with whom we are or can readily be in daily contact and getting on with our collective lives … For the first time in human history a significant, and in geopolitical terms the currently dominant, part of our species is alone … It has even been suggested to me that one aspect of animal liberation movements is a sort of nostalgia for the time when we, as a species, had company. I could take this one step farther; the recent enthusiasm for aliens and cyborgs may represent a fantasy-longing for new types of beings with whom we can associate. Renewals of a demand for 'cosmopolitics' can be seen as a desire to have a larger cosmos, populated with other beings for which we should make kindred cause, scallops on the verge of annihilation. Or less animate entities: mountains, the atmosphere assaulted by an ozone hole.[9]

If we are tormented by loneliness even on this planet, imagine the solitude we might feel in the infinite expanse of space! This sentiment must be incredibly persistent, if even in January 2000 the US edition of National Geographic was titled 'Are We Alone?', referring to the idea of our solitude in space. That same month, by sheer coincidence, Scientific American ran a story called 'Once We Were Not Alone', alluding to our solitude on this planet and the fact that there were at least fifteen primate 'cousins' who could have evolved along with us, but didn't.

Inevitably, we move in a Pascalian horizon, that of the immense vastness of the cosmos, the insignificance of human beings, the mysteries of the origin of worlds and of our civilisation. Here we run into one of modern civilisation's most stupefying beliefs, namely the 'ancient astronauts' theory, which explained the origins of man by invoking the intervention of mysterious astronauts who came from stars and supposedly instilled the spark of intellect in a species of primates or in ancient civilisations on our planet. Traces of their visit, so the story goes, are to be found on Easter Island, at Stonehenge and at other prehistoric sites. One example of the reasoning behind this theory are the pre-Inca Nazca lines in Peru, which, we are told, were in reality markers to help the starships land. These alien astronauts' visit to Earth, in the remote depths of the past, is supposedly proven by rock paintings in Tassili, in the Sahara desert or in Brandenburg Mountains in Namibia, and by papyrus fragments and scrolls, in addition to references in the most disparate texts, from Maya engravings to the poem *Mahabharata*, in which there is talk of celestial wagons and terrible weapons, and so on. This is a sort of 'occultist archaeology', as the ethnologist Wiktor Stoczkowski calls it; he dedicated a stunning book to the ancient astronauts theory, *Des hommes, des dieux et des extra-terrestres. Ethnologie d'une croyance moderne.*[10] The best-known proponent of this theory, back in the 1960s, was Switzerland's Erich von Däniken, whose books sold a total of 63 million copies in twelve languages and who still continues to take part in TV programmes on this theme. But this theory also had other exponents like Louis Pauwels and Jacques Bergier, whose volume *Le matin des magiciens* (published by Gallimard in 1960) was held in high esteem by Edgar Morin and sold more than a million copies.[11] Pauwels and Bergier moreover founded the review *Planète*, which was translated into ten languages during its publication between 1961 and 1972. In Italy, this belief was spread by the books of Peter Kolosimo (a pseudonym of Pier Domenico Colosimo).

This belief would not be worth talking about if it were not for the fact that it has found enduring success. In 1985, 21 per cent of the population of France thought that aliens had visited Earth in the past. Yet, even more intriguing, the percentage of French students who believed in ancient aliens theory remained stable (around 30 per cent among natural science students) and reached heights of up to 50 per cent (psychology students).[12] This belief is so persistent that according to a survey for the *Huffington Post*, even in 2013 a quarter of Americans held that extraterrestrials had visited planet Earth (and over 40 per cent were uncertain).

Stoczkowski digs out the roots of this belief, going back to the theosophy movement formulated by Madame Blavatsky. In a meeting held in New York in 1875 she founded the Theosophical Society, which influenced such diverse figures as Arthur Conan Doyle, Piet Mondrian and Carl Gustav Jung, before later re-emerging in New Age philosophy. Many of the archaeological and textual 'proofs' later adopted by von Däniken and Kolosimo had already appeared in Madame Blavatsky's books – she used them to accredit the idea of divine messengers. This idea of intermediaries between divinity and the world down here goes back to ancient Gnosticism (which we already encountered with our discussion of Paul Ricoeur in the previous chapter, and the origin of the idea of 'becoming an other'). The theosophical substrate, the cultural patrimony of science fiction and the flying saucer craze all conspired to create and spread ancient astronauts theory.

This belief has the characteristics proper to modernity: it presents itself not as a faith but as a 'scientific' theory with its welter of 'proofs', reading lists and charts – apparatuses that pseudo-science has learned to use and which apes legitimate academic knowledge. It picks up on the tradition of Spiritism, which claimed a scientific status on account of the imprints on the photographic plates. But at the same time, it is a sort of religion, with its implicit messianism – which is sometimes explicit, when it expresses hope that extraterrestrials will return, just as Blavatsky and her followers awaited the Maitreya.

But the striking thing about this modern faith – in which aliens have the same function as the intermediaries between god and the world in Gnosticism – is the fact that Otherness is turned on its head: not only is the Other more evolved than we are, but we are ourselves the fruit of this alienness, the product of the light that the ancient astronauts inculcated in still-semi-bestial primates. This is what is portrayed in the first scenes of Stanley Kubrick's 1968 film *2001: A Space Odyssey*, adapted from a story by Arthur C. Clarke. From this point of view, ancient astronauts theory takes to an extreme the 'desire for the Other' that we encountered in more reasonable forms in figures like Carl Sagan, whose only screenplay was adapted for the 1997 film *Contact*, starring Jodie Foster, which was based on an earlier script and his 1985 novel of the same name. Obviously, the 'contact' in question is with extraterrestrials.

The stigmata of modernity are visible even in the original title of von Däniken's biggest-selling book, *Erinnerungen an die Zukunft* (Memories of the Future),[13] which came out the same year as Kubrick's film. Here, in this modern belief, we again find the category of *past future* which the contemplation of ruins imposed on the collective mindset and which occupies such importance in the 'tourist gaze'.

However, the most interesting aspect of this 'yearning for the Other', from sci-fi to UFOs and the ancient astronauts, lies in the dates – which coincide with the boom in global tourism. The contemporaneity of these phenomena does not stem from any visible connection or any common causal relation. The link between them instead lies in the fact that they both make up part of the Zeitgeist, in the fact that each metabolises in its own way a common problem, namely the problem of the Other and of the Alien. What we are seeing is a yearning for the Other, the discovery of the Alien within us, and becoming familiar with the Other.

At the time, we were all convinced that we were at the dawn of the space age: we began to observe the Earth *from outside*. The most striking image to come from the first Moon landing in August 1969 was the enormous Earth hovering in the jet-black lunar night. I remember how on the following New Year's, on 1 January 1970, we physics students at university promised one another that we would spend the New Year of 2000 on the Moon. This seemed to be in the order of things, just as in the first half of the twentieth century commercial flights became widespread only thirty years after the first aeroplane flight. Instead, within a few years, it had become apparent that the 'space age' was the briefest of parentheses. With the Apollo 17 mission in December 1972, the era of human missions to our only natural satellite came to an end, and with it the illusion of 'colonising space'. But at the time, we considered it a reasonable prospect that we would soon be able to buy a Hitchhikers' Guide to the Solar System (if not the galaxy) and become tourists of the infinite.

Time has been a cruel master and in a mere five decades has drastically scaled back our ambitions. Forget galaxies, the outer limits of the solar system and even the closer planets within it: today, tycoons are rushing to book their places in Earth orbit as the final frontier of class emulation. This is ridiculous, from a cosmic point of view: Earth has a radius of around 6,371 kilometres. An orbit at a 400-kilometre altitude would be like orbiting at 2.5 centimetres' distance from a ball measuring one metre in diameter. What does it matter? The thing that counts is to observe Earth from the outside, so that we can be the aliens.

14

The World at Our Disposal

No doubt, tourism (and the tourist) is alienated – doubly or even triply so. Tourism is alienated because it is commodified. Alienated, we have seen, because it is a zoning of the soul. It is alienated because it is regimented in order to escape regimentation. And it is alienated because it is constantly pursuing an authenticity that incessantly becomes inauthentic as soon as we access it.

The tourist is so alienated that at the end of the nineteenth century he became so in a clinical sense – that is, tourism entered into official diagnostics in the guise of a new syndrome, that of the 'mad traveller'. This syndrome was officially introduced by the Bordeaux psychiatrist Philippe Tissié, who published *Les Aliénés Voyageurs* in 1887. Ian Hacking recounts this in his fine book on 'transient mental illnesses'. By this he means the illnesses that appear in a certain time and place, and perhaps in a given class or gender. They then enter into diagnostic dictionaries, and after a certain period, disappear from them again (with hysteria serving as the most famous example).

Hacking tells us how in Bordeaux's Hôpital Saint-André, Tissié attended to a tearful patient, Jean-Albert Dadas, an employee of the local gas-fitting firm, who 'had just come from a long journey on foot and was exhausted, but that was not the cause of his tears. He wept because he could not prevent himself from departing on a trip when the need took him; he deserted family, work and daily life to walk as fast as he could, straight ahead, sometimes doing 70 kilometres a day on foot, until in the end he would be arrested for vagrancy and thrown in prison.'[1] During his many trips, Dadas suddenly found himself in places he had never heard of: Paris,

Marseilles, Algiers, Frankfurt, Vienna, Moscow, Constantinople (and Hacking provides us with a map of his movements). Dadas did not remember much of these journeys, but under hypnosis he revealed the bare details. Tissié diagnosed a form of 'hysteria', observing all the symptoms enumerated by Charcot. The following year, Tissié presented the case of a second 'pathological fugitive'. Many similar cases then proliferated in the clinical literature, and new definitions were coined from *dromomania*, *poriomania* and *ambulatory determinism* (in Italy) to *Wandertrieb* (in Germany). In 1893, Henry Meige published *Le juif errant à la Salpêtrière* (The Wandering Jew in the Asylum),[2] a study of a sample of 'neuropathic Jewish travellers'. After 1910, the syndrome began to disappear, though for a long period it remained in the diagnostic manuals. In truth, dromomania had already served its purpose – namely, to provide a first clinical justification for the medicalisation of homelessness.

Whatever interest there was in the case of the lamplighter Dadas, it is clear that the mad traveller or compulsive fugitive syndrome could never have entered a doctor's head before tourism became widespread. What made Dadas 'alienated' was not his travelling itself: his destinations were, essentially, the same as those of many well-heeled, bourgeois travellers. But what unequivocally proved his madness was that he travelled as a poor man, a proletarian without means.

But the tourists are also alienated in a more literal sense: for what are they doing if not 'going away', if not 'going abroad/to the outside world', if not deliberately 'getting outside of themselves'? In truth, we see the tourist caught in a double alienation – in one way compelled from the outside, but also in another way that is voluntary, or rather actively sought out. Freedom exists also as potential – not only the freedom to go to a place, but the freedom to be *able* to get there. Very intentionally, I started this inquiry into tourism with the collapse of the Berlin Wall, an event hastened by an unstoppable avalanche of tourist visa applications. In common wisdom, in the unwritten constitution of the modern, totalitarianism and dictatorship are summed up in prohibitions against travel. This conception of freedom as the 'possibility to go' has its roots in the origins of the modern and it is connected with geographical discoveries and great journeys. As the ineffable Michel de Montaigne said more than four centuries ago: 'I am so enamoured of liberty, that should I be interdicted the access to some corner of the Indies, I should live a little less at my ease.'*

It is an act of freedom, but a disciplined one: therein lie all the insoluble contradictions of the tourist practice. We need only compare today's free time to the Carnival, which constituted feudal society's principal means of organised recreation. The Carnival was not only an event in which all groups and social ranks participated, but also the moment in which it was permitted to transgress the codes that normally governed social life. Conversely, in modern society, leisure time is segmented into different activities among different groups, and it is *regulated*. There is no anarchic break in the established order, no messing with conventions. Not only that, but it never involves society as a whole. Rather, it obeys the iron rule that the recreation of the groups who are involved must not disturb society as a whole, or cause inconvenience for those who are not involved. Implicit in this is that it must not subvert the established order or its dominant ideology. What is more, each particular leisure activity must obey behavioural conventions and norms of participation. 'Contemporary organised tourism, along with its historic antecedents, is no exception. It involves specific cultural practices governing what is seen, how it is seen, the composition of tour groups, the behaviour of individuals and the group during the touristic experience, and so on' (Britton).[3]

The 'organised trip' is both the apotheosis and the parody of this discipline, which has given rise (as it still does) to the obsessive use of the 'herd' metaphor. This is the most irrefutable example of what Henri Lefebvre calls a 'bureaucratic society of

---

* And he adds: 'All my little prudence in the civil wars wherein we are now engaged is employed that they may not hinder my liberty of going and coming.' Michel de Montaigne, *Les Essais* (1588), Gallimard, Paris, 1965, book III, chapter XIII, vol. III, p. 316; *The Essays of Michel de Montaigne*, translated by Charles Cotton 1877, book III, chapter XIII 'Of Experience', available from the Gutenberg project at gutenberg.org.

guided consumption'.[4] The only transgressions that tourists do allow themselves are those related to dress code – going around in the flip-flops, shorts and baseball caps they would never wear in everyday life. They are not in fact exceptions or infractions, but rather make up the parts of the 'tourist outfit', a sort of uniform whose shabbiness seems obligatory, just as the (frayed) jacket, shirt and tie were for the clerks in the City of London. The only thing that the modern-day tourist holiday has in common with the old Carnival is this new costume. For when it comes to transgression, the present-day carnivals of Venice and Rio do allow a limited transgression, but only to foreign tourists – thus reminding us of the Cold War joke where an American says, 'We Americans are free because we can say we don't like Nixon', and the Soviet replies, 'But we can say we don't like Nixon, too.'

So far, so good. But once it has been ascertained that tourism is not the best of all possible travel, we somehow feel driven to put up a defence of a much-maligned term. The first line of defence is the question: in a society dominated by market logic, how could we have a free time that wasn't commodified? In other words: is a non-capitalist use of time really so realistic in a capitalist society? Obviously not. But then the critique itself must be ill formulated, since it ends up cutting itself with Occam's Razor: after all, it criticises a concept (tourism) by taking recourse to a more general universal (capitalism). If we had to wait for the defeat of global capitalism before we could correct everything wrong that its critics have imputed to tourism, then we'd certainly need a lot of energy.

There is something derisive and cruel about this critique. After the human race has been forced for millennia to live in economically tight circumstances, often relegated to ignorance and brutalised by the hammering of the ad industry, these critics then are amazed that this same brutalised, ignorant, wretched and immiserated humanity lacks the mental agility to enjoy the towering expressions of the human soul with sufficient refinement. This is, again, a fresh incarnation of the age-old contempt for the spat-upon plebs – but translated into an 'unsparing critique' of the wrongdoings of a capitalism they take care not to challenge.

This brings us to the second line of defence of tourism, which makes use of concepts developed by marginalism, which is to say the dominant economic theory. When one invests in a certain asset (bonds, equities, real estate, futures, and so on) what counts is not its absolute yield but rather its relative yield – that is, as compared to what the same sum would yield were it invested in some other asset. What counts, then, is not how much a certain operation yields, but rather *how much more* it yields relative to other equities. This is the principle that despotically governs all of our lives. So we might ask ourselves why it should not also apply to tourism. The right question then becomes: if terrestrial bipeds did not invest their free time in tourism, in what other occupation could they invest it, which would yield them something more, that is, which would yield them more happiness. Puzzles, perhaps, or pedalling away on an exercise bike at home?

The futility and the superficiality of the critique of tourism become unassailably clear as soon as we pose the question of the alternatives. Who on earth is able to offer billions of humans an alternative use of their own free time? Or perhaps they contend that it would be better not to have free time at all?

But the spread of tourism on a global scale does much more: it blurs the distinction between hosts and guests. This blurring is the foundation of the 1977 book *Hosts and Guests: The Anthropology of Tourism* edited by Valene L. Smith. Like the distinction between indigenous and foreigner, that between host and guests, appeals to concepts which describe as *conditions* what have now – thanks to the statistical reversibility of roles – instead become *situations*. For each person is a tourist for some spell in their life and a native at another; each of us experiences the situation of the visitor and that of the indigenous, with the effect that what Urry calls the 'tourist gaze' is now used even when we are at home: there is thus created, in Sartre's terms, a 'theatre of situations' in which the shopkeeper, who for one part of her life 'dances the shopkeeper's dance', then enters another shop where she observes another human being dancing the same dance. The very notion of indigenous or native proves misleading. This was clearly asserted by the Indian writer Amitav Ghosh in 1986, when he recounted the moment of his arrival in Egypt, where he had headed for his research on the fellahin for his PhD dissertation in social anthropology at Oxford University:

> When I first came to that quiet corner of the Nile Delta I had expected to find on that most ancient and most settled of soils a settled and restful people. I couldn't have been more wrong.
>
> The men of the village had all the busy restlessness of airline passengers in a transit lounge. Many of them had worked and travelled in the sheikhdoms of the Persian Gulf, others had been in Libya and Jordan and Syria, some had been to Yemen as soldiers, others to Saudi Arabia as pilgrims, a few had visited Europe: some of them had passports so thick they opened out like ink-blackened concertinas. And none of this was new: their grandparents and ancestors and relatives had travelled and migrated too, in much the same way as mine had, in the Indian subcontinent – because of wars, or for money and jobs, or perhaps simply because they got tired of living always in one place. You could read the history of this restlessness in the villagers' surnames: they had names which derived from cities in the Levant, from Turkey, from faraway towns in Nubia; it was as though people had drifted here from every corner of the Middle East. The wanderlust of its founders had been ploughed into the soil of the village: it seemed to me sometimes that every man in it was a traveller. Everyone, that is, except Khamees the Rat, and even his surname, as I discovered later, meant 'of Sudan'. Well, never mind *ya doktor*, Khamees said to me now, 'since you're not going to make it back to your country by sundown anyway, why don't you come and sit with us for a while?' He smiled and moved to make room for me.[5]

All of us are a little bit fellahin and a little bit Indian anthropologist – and we exchange the roles between us and even with our own selves.

There is good reason for this comparison with the anthropologist. Walker Percy argues that when they see some ritual dance, tourists 'need the ethnologist to certify their experience as genuine'.[6] He sets out the idea of an 'ethnologist friend who accompanies tourists'. Meanwhile, for Simon Coleman and Mike Crang, 'anthropologists themselves are sometimes better seen as a variant of tourists. Both are seeking to create symbolic capital from travel and both work by translating foreign experience into domestic categories.'[7]

Yet this means that the so-called 'tourist gaze' is nothing but the 'modern gaze'. Such an idea already flashed by when Walter Benjamin associated the flâneur first with the detective and then with the journalist: 'Preformed in the figure of the flâneur is that of the detective. The flâneur required a social legitimation of his habitus. It suited him very well to see his indolence presented as a plausible front, behind which, in reality, hides the riveted attention of an observer who will not let the unsuspecting malefactor out of his sight'. Moreover, '[t]he social base of flâneurie is journalism. As flâneur, the literary man ventures into the marketplace to sell himself.'[8]

Who knows what Benjamin would have said about the millions of self-appointed autodidact reporters represented by the tourists who write reviews on TripAdvisor? An anthropologist, ethnologist, investigator and a journalist, the tourist becomes synonymous with each form of modern curiosity for the Other.

And here we get to the decisive question: after all the ill that has been spoken of tourists, all the aspersions heaped on them, is the tourist in fact moved by a positive motive?

One hint in this direction is provided by the poet Giacomo Leopardi (1798–1837), who taught himself classical culture and spent the first part of his short life holed up in Recanati, his 'wild native village' in the Marche region of Italy. A rural economy, far from any artery of communications and distant from the industrial and technological revolution that was then spreading from England to extend its grip over the rest of the world, it was what he defined as the 'European centre of barbarism and ignorance'. Thus Leopardi looked on the modern as one might observe it from the Moon, making both vast blunders and showing unexpected insight. In the age of romanticism and the triumph of sentiments, that of Schumann and De Musset, the young man from Recanati was convinced that in the world of the 1820s, the flames of life were going out and that given 'the need that all have for warmth', each person would go off in search of it and bundle together 'that little life that is to be found'.

> And thus beyond the recourse to all the genres and areas of human knowledge, where what is called the encyclopaedic takes form, and it is today much in use, beyond travel to the furthest climes, commerce of all kinds, more alive than it ever was, between the most disjointed and diverse nations, each nation is now intent and desirous of knowing the customs, the literatures, all that belongs to other nations, and partaking in it as much as possible, which is to say being occupied with it. Ancient and modern foreign works, never hitherto known in this or that nation, and which would never have been [known] in other circumstances, are translated, compiled and spread; [works] perhaps barely worthy of being known by nations, never mind pass the borders of their nations; all the cultured languages are studied; there is a multiplication of newspapers that give account of foreign works and things, and of their exactness, expanse of vision and carefulness in so doing.[9]

The motivation that Leopardi advances for this – that sentiments and passions were disappearing from the modern world – is an odd one. But the phenomenon he captured is real. And the only people who could grasp it were those who stood above this overwhelming deluge of journeys, exchanges, relocations and translations, observing its currents as if watching from the riverbank. Leopardi saw that 'all nations' had been swept along by an unprecedented, insatiable curiosity for the world, what Michel Foucault would have called a 'will to see'. He recognised that never before had there been such an aspiration to know the Other:

In this current century, both for the increase in trade by exchange and the use of travels, and for that of literature, and the encyclopaedism that is now widespread, such that each nation wants to understand as deeply as it can the languages, literatures and customs of other peoples … the civilised nations of Europe … have put aside a large part of the ancient national prejudices unfavourable to foreigners, of the animosity and aversion toward them, and above all of the disdain toward them and toward their literatures, civilisations and customs, however different they may be from their own. The taste for knowing them has grown together with the esteem for them and the fairness of the judgement upon them; there are infinite volumes published in each nation as to inform it on things in the others.[10]

Perhaps Leopardi was too optimistic, and perhaps unfavourable prejudices regarding foreigners had not declined as much as he believed. But without doubt the 'taste' for knowing these foreigners had increased; the desire to 'partake of them' and 'be occupied with them' had as well. Without knowing it, Leopardi was giving an explanation of tourism as a 'good thing'. Without knowing it, he was providing a splendid example of 'positive alienation'.

For among all the most varied and subtle explanations of the growth of tourism, one has been so taken for granted that in practice it is erased. So many negative or selfish or self-interested reasons have been sought out that another motivation – the most potent one – is dismissed. This is not simply the 'wish to see the world' or a mere 'hunger for the world' but the inebriating sensation – given to human beings for the first time by the communications revolution – of having 'the world at our fingertips'.

This was the incredible nineteenth-century revolution in our mindset.[11] We no longer remember what it was like to live on a planet where it took a whole day to travel a hundred kilometres. And we are now incapable of reliving the astonished stupor that greeted the first inkling of this revolution, when, driven at the terrifying speed of forty kilometres per hour, the first trains terrorised and excited travellers. It is worth turning to a passage from Heinrich Heine when in 1843 he was shaken by the 'terrible shuddering emotion, such as we always feel when the most tremendous and unheard-of things take place'. He continued: 'What marvellous changes must now enter into our methods of perception and action. Even the elementary ideas of space and time are tottering; for by the railway, space is annihilated, and only time remains.'[12]

Incredulous admiration was also awakened at sea, by the new steamships: as Henry Tuckerman wrote in 1844, 'Steam is annihilating space, and even the devotee of business begins to find it more expeditious to transact his foreign affairs in person than by letter.'[13]

This theme was picked up a few years later by Karl Marx, according to whom 'Capital by its nature drives beyond every spatial barrier. Thus the creation of the physical conditions of exchange – of the means of communication and transport – the annihilation of space by time – becomes an extraordinary necessity for it.'[14]

We are so caught up in our self-satisfaction over *our* communications revolution that we cannot even imagine what a shock *their* revolution was for its contemporaries. It is well known that we humans don't have much of an imagination: when we are young we can't imagine how we will be when we are old, when we are healthy we cannot put ourselves in the shoes of someone who is ill, and few natives are able to empathise with immigrants. For this reason, we do not really succeed in convincing ourselves of what Benjamin somewhere says, namely that each man was modern in his time.

Caught up in our 'web', we do not realise how much the world was changed by the first web spun by humanity, a very material one, with undersea telegraph cables for the first time enabling instant communications across the globe. Benedict Anderson called this the first true 'early globalisation',[15] because the telegram made it possible to buy stocks on Wall Street in real time from Paris, and vice versa. In 1851 the first undersea cable was laid beneath the English Channel. By 1872 over 20,000 cities and villages around the world were connected by more than a million kilometres of telegraph lines and almost 50,000 kilometres of undersea cables. In 1902, the network was completed by the inauguration of the Trans-Pacific cable, as Armand Mattelart tells us.[16] The whole world was united by the telegraphic web: 'In 1903, Theodore Roosevelt sent off a round-the-globe telegram to himself which reached him in nine minutes.'[17]

Indeed, the first transnational community was made up of telegraphists, whose flirtations and expressions of love travelled from Siberia to Australia via the dots and dashes of Morse code. It was also one of the first modern professions to employ a mostly female workforce (on account of the agility of fingers used to sewing, it was said at the time). This was one of the keystones of maritime navigation, with the radio operators and the legendary SOS signal. But nothing can give us today the sense of incredulous wonder with which humans discovered that they could transmit their own thoughts across thousands of kilometres in an instant, such that contemporaries defined the telegraph as the 'instantaneous highway of thought'.[18]

Just as we see best the things at the edges of our visual field, we can make out most clearly whatever is new, while inurement blunts our senses and our perception. Something which is too familiar goes unnoticed because it is now *taken as a given*. Thus the contemporaries of that revolution were acutely conscious of the fact that a new era was coming into being, a new era that we today take for granted. Tuckerman himself claimed: 'Our times might not inaptly be designated as the age of travelling. Its records form no insignificant branch of the literature of the day.'[19] Twenty-four years later he insisted, in the May 1868 issue of *Putnam's Monthly Magazine*: 'If the social history of the world is ever written, the era in which we live will be called the nomadic period. With the advent of ocean steam navigation and the railway system, began a travelling mania which has gradually increased until half of the earth's inhabitants, or at least half of its civilized portion, are on the move.'[20]

The world is within our reach, therefore – not only from a technological point of view, but also in terms of how far our wallets can stretch, with an economy car or with a low-cost flight. To do something only because one *can* do it, just to demonstrate that the possibility is really possible. This is one of the most potent drives to human action. We need only look at how many people speak on the phone just because it is possible to do so, even if they have nothing to say. How many snatches of conversation do we hear going 'Are you there?' 'Yes, I hear you now', 'I'm still here', 'OK I'll ring you in ten'.

Siegfried Kracauer wrote in 1925: 'We are like children when we travel, playfully excited about the new velocity, the relaxed roaming about, the overviews of geographic regions that previously could not be seen with such scope. We have fallen for the ability to have all these spaces at our disposal; we are like conquistadors who have not yet found a quiet moment to reflect on the meaning of their acquisition.'[21] Better than any other word, this concept is expressed by a fantastic slogan seen in a passageway of the Atocha Madrid railway station in October 2018: 'Hay muchas razones para viajar: por exemplo, viajar.' ('There are many reasons to travel: for instance, to travel.')

What headiness, this world at our disposal – all the more so if you can easily set off for London from Tregnago, Pietraperzia or Capistrello as if it were nothing – that is, departing from little villages from which setting off to Britain would once have been an epic adventure and in which this practical impossibility also produced a mental incapacity even to imagine the trip. It wasn't even dreamt of. Thus the world has not only come within reach, but at the same time it has become thinkable, conceivable, not only as an abstract notion (the Aldebaran star) but as a practicable destination (the bar across the street). Simply because tourism had been invented and was now accessible to the more comfortably off middle classes, Oscar Wilde could coin the aphorism: 'When good Americans die, they go to Paris.'

It has become possible for each person – independent of class and income – to be literally a 'man of the world'. Certainly, each person will visit myths rather than places. Otherwise they wouldn't take the trouble to submit the visions in their own imagination to a reality check, as Dr Johnson put it.

But there is nothing improper in all this. Not even if these visions are a little second-rate, crude and kitsch, as might be expected. The pig-headedness and feeble-mindedness of which 'the masses' are accused does not, certainly, owe to the stupidity of the individuals that make up these multitudes, but rather to a millennia-long history of material and symbolic violence, a policy that seems to follow the dictates of a Voltairean mufti. Contrary to what Voltaire thought, this is not reserved to bigots alone, but is practised without discrimination by atheist rulers as well as fundamentalist ones:

> for the edification of the faithful and for the good of their souls, we forbid them to ever read any book at all, under pain of eternal damnation. And, for fear that the diabolical temptation to educate themselves might take hold of them, we hereby ban fathers and mothers from teaching their children to read. And, to prevent all violations to our edict, we prohibit them expressly from thinking, under the same penalties; we enjoin all true believers to denounce to our officials anyone who strings together any four sentences from which a clear and distinct meaning can be inferred.[22]

If we had to compare tourism to some other mass practice characteristic of modernity, we would better insert it in the category of self-help or (economic, bodily, emotional or intellectual) self-improvement. Self-help is a sector supposedly worth around 11 billion dollars in the United States alone, when everything is included (books, seminars, audiovisual products, personal training, stress-management and weight-loss programmes, mail-order and online catalogues, holistic institutes).[23] In bookshops across the US, the shelves devoted to self-help are the fullest, taking up more space than fiction. A glance at a few of these book titles makes clear the expectations of those buying them (and gives justification to the joke that the quickest way to become rich is to write a book on how to become rich). For instance, there is the *Handbook to Higher Consciousness*; *The Seven Pillars of Success*; *Use Your Body to Heal Your Mind*; *Waking the Tiger*; *Think and Get Rich*; *How to Survive the Loss of a Love*; *Battlefield Mind*; *The Six Pillars of Self-Esteem*; and *Awaken the Giant Within*.

If the large majority of humanity did not consider tourism a form of self-improvement, it would be impossible to explain the scrupulous intransigence with which parents force their children to visit museums and galleries during their holidays, even though these same parents would never dream of looking at a painting in their everyday lives. There is something touching in the confidence that going to visit a city, a monument, a country can open your mind, make you better: here, too, we are emulating the class structure, where the dominated chase after the dominant.

15

Life's Menus

Italians call it a hunger for the world: an expression that can also be taken literally. In running through the various types of tourism (for culture, sports, health or business), I have deliberately left one out, precisely because it is the sort of tourism that is inevitably carried forth by all the others, and which moreover synthesises all of their characteristics and many ambiguities. This is gastronomic (culinary or food) tourism. To evaluate its importance, we should bear in mind that even in the case of business or beach or sex or religious tourism, spending on food amounts to '30 per cent and more' of the total spending on the trip, according to the OECD.[1] With all the ambiguity inherent in this word, one thing is certain: even tourists eat.

For on the one hand we could say even tourists are compelled to put food in their mouths, to tolerate flavours and inhale alien odours, to touch repulsive textures, experience the daily intake of calories, proteins, vitamins and amino acids that they cannot but ingest. Food is the most tactile, most flavourful, most fragrant form in which the Other offers itself up to the tourist – it is thus the object of the most acute idiosyncrasies, the most heinous suspicions, of mistrust rooted even in early childhood. For many, food is the great inconvenience of the journey, something to be tolerated just like the sleepless night on a transatlantic flight, the lumpy bed in the only available hotel or the defective shower that leaks rusty water.[2] This negative bias toward unfamiliar foods comes from the suspicion that an ingredient is not kosher, some meat is not halal, some vegetarian dish will contain animal fat, with the sheer lack of familiarity, like the Italian who attacks

French cuisine because she can't find a decent pasta dish in Paris at a decent price. This extends to the various diarrhoeas referred to as a 'revenge', from 'Montezuma's revenge' in Mexico to the 'pharoah's revenge' in Egypt – and it's a long list.

But on the other hand, food may itself constitute a reason for the trip (and often it is both an inconvenience as well as an attraction). Food has to be part of the trip, or rather is itself 'visited': there is no sightseeing without taste-tasting. We visit a country not only to see its monuments, wander through its cities, admire its countryside and bathe along its beaches, but also to taste its 'specialities', to try its 'typical' cuisine. In this sense, gastronomic tourism is the indispensable complement to any tourism.

Just as artistic tourism can be anything from an add-on to a beach holiday to a key point of the journey, so, too, can the gastronomic visit become the main purpose (even if 'peppered' with excursions to museums, cities and beaches, which here become collateral goals). It is here that tourism becomes culinary, with cuisine considered a decisive element of a certain culture. Rather, precisely because it is practically the only interaction that goes beyond a purely visual dimension and becomes flesh, consistency, elasticity, the act of tasting being the main way to 'sample' *another culture*. Again, we get back to tourism as a global strategy invented by the modern in order to confront and, in a certain sense, negotiate the irruption of the Other into our lives, brought about by the revolution in transport and communications.

Or better, English-speaking anthropologists have coined a neologism along the same lines as the expression 'way of life', namely the 'foodway',[3] which involves not only ingredients and recipes, but the times, the modes, the forms, the taboos, the ritualisations of the preparation, presentation and, indeed, the consumption of food. Culinary tourism thus becomes, in Lucy Long's words, 'the intentional, exploratory participation in the foodways of an other':[4]

Culinary tourism is about food as a subject and medium, destination and vehicle for tourism. It is about individuals exploring foods new to them as well as using food to explore new cultures and ways of being. It is about groups using food to 'sell' their histories and to construct marketable and publicly attractive identities, and it is about individuals satisfying curiosity. Finally, it is about the experiencing of food in a mode that is out of the ordinary, that steps outside the normal routine to notice difference and the power of food to represent and negotiate that difference ... I define culinary tourism as the intentional, exploratory participation in the foodways of an other – participation including the consumption, preparation and presentation of a food item, cuisine, meal system, or eating style considered to belong to a culinary system not one's own.

This is why culinary aspects are inextricably bound to tourism in general and mark all of its different levels. Like almost all the processes we have visited thus far, the critical moment of the new, literal 'hunger for the world' again came at the beginning of the nineteenth century. At precisely the moment that the notion of historical monuments was taking form and becoming specified, in these same years the poet Joseph Berchoux (1760–1839) summarised the Greek term 'gastronomy' (literally, 'government of the stomach') with the new meaning of 'the art of eating well'. 'The 1807 eight-volume edition of the *Almanach des gourmands* evoked the first notion of a "monumentalisation" of food specialities ... Formulating the desire for a map of France featuring "the gastronomic productions that made our cities famous", it proposed "thus instead of the Amiens bell tower, we would see in its place a duck paté; in Nérac a partridge terrine; in Toulouse a duck liver terrine; pig shin and cheese in Troyes; a jar of mustard and another of barberry jam in Dijon".' With the same criteria with which buildings were entered onto the list of historical monuments, in 1809 Charles-Louis Cadet de Gassicourt produced the first 'Gastronomic Map of France'. It was described by Julia Csergo as 'this gastronomic land-registry in which the monumental edifice, local glory, cultural heritage, become the truffle, the pâté, the poularde, all these notable products of culinary art whose notoriety sometimes goes back to the Middle Ages and which the traveller ought not miss any more than he would a site, a fortress, a cathedral.'[5]

Today we are so accustomed to finding a section in a tourist guide dedicated to the cuisine of a single country, region or city, that we no longer even notice. But the mapping of taste, the cartography of the tastebuds, is a process that helped to mould what we might call tourist culture. For example, the *Michelin Red Guide*, created for car users in 1900, with logistical information on petrol pumps, garages and tyre-fitters, rapidly came to integrate gastronomic recommendations. In 1914, reconnecting with the culinary cartography launched by Gassicourt more than a century earlier, it published a map of 'gastronomic France'. In 1926, it introduced its stars for restaurants and in 1931 it fixed a classification system based on stars. Tellingly, two stars indicated that the restaurant was 'worth a detour' whereas three stars made it 'worth the trip'. Since the number of stars was usually more or less proportional to the price, gastronomic excellence was accessible only to the deepest pockets, restoring a clear economic hierarchy between the various gastronomes and the different tourists.

It is almost superfluous, here, to underline the importance of the 'distinction' factor, in Bourdieu's sense, which permeates food practices and, at the level beyond that, culinary tourism. Precisely because every social practice immediately becomes a marker signifying the subject who practices it, gastronomic habits are among the most accurate indicators we have in order to situate a person's place in society. Brillat-Savarin's famous (and overused) formulation 'Tell me what you eat and I'll tell you who you are'[6] here acquires a specific sociological importance which its formulator could not have suspected.

Going to certain restaurants, being a connoisseur of wines and their vintages, knowing certain foods and how to get to grips with them (knowing how to empty out a lobster claw with the pincer and the little fork suited to this task, or shelling shrimp or deboning a quail with a knife and fork), all become instruments of social differentiation (distinction), indicators of an exact position in the evolution of the social hierarchy. Further, when we invite guests over for dinner 'the style of the meal that people like to offer them is no doubt a very good indicator of the image they wish to give or avoid giving to others, and as such it is the systematic expression of a system of factors including, in addition to the indicators of the position occupied in the economic and cultural hierarchies, economic trajectory, social trajectory and cultural trajectory' (Bourdieu).[7]

If food choices and consumption in everyday life constitute a factor of distinction, culinary tourism is a factor of distinction to the power of two, because it demonstrates the mastery and knowledge of exotic codes. For example, in ancient China, 'the importation of Indonesian and other spices during the T'ang period emphasised the differences in the cuisine of the rich and the poor. Rich households were generally addicted to foods from abroad; foreign food (to say nothing of foreign clothes, foreign music, and foreign dances) was rigorously required at tastefully prepared banquets and this necessarily included dishes cooked in the Indian style.'[8]

Knowing that harissa (a medium-spicy chili sauce) ought to be mixed into the broth before it is poured over the couscous shows that you are familiar with Maghrebian foodways; folding a Vietnamese spring roll in a lettuce leaf before biting into it displays an acquaintance with Indochinese customs; avoiding planting one's chopsticks in the rice bowl shows respect for Chinese etiquette: all so many bricks in helping to build your cultural and social capital.[9]

If culinary tourism breaks down into different sections of society, so, too, do its guidebooks: for example, in Italy, the *Gambero Rosso* guidebook has split into a guidebook for (more expensive) *ristoranti* and another for (cheaper) *trattorie* and *osterie*. This will continue so long as the economic and social hierarchy is internalised, as the patrons who themselves become food critics make it their own, in statistical terms, self-selecting based on their own tastes and income. They do this thanks to the mechanism – noted already by Hans Magnus Enzensberger – according to which tourists are themselves agents in the tourist industry and become a living testimonial to it. In 1979, the Zagat family launched guides for restaurants in different cities, the evaluation of which was decided by customer reviews – a method that would later take off online, with TripAdvisor. In 2011, the Zagat group was bought up by Google, though it did not manage to carve itself a niche in the space that TripAdvisor had already conquered.

Here, the process identified by MacCannell replicates itself: food is a marker of a culture which itself mutates into a tourist attraction and in turn creates its own markers, thus becoming a 'heritage' product. Indeed, gastronomy is becoming an object of patrimonialisation just as monuments are, and like them it needs safeguarding, to the point that UNESCO has declared the vineyards of Burgundy and Champagne in France, and of the Langhe in Italy, World Heritage Sites. Meanwhile, here are some of the 'intangible cultural heritages' of humanity, according to UNESCO:

> Traditional Mexican cuisine
> Shrimp fishing on horseback in Oostduinkerke (Belgium)
> Kimjang, making and sharing kimchi in the Republic of Korea
> Gingerbread craft from Northern Croatia
> Gastronomic meal of the French
> Traditional agricultural practice of cultivating the 'vite ad alberello' (head-trained bush vines) of the community of Pantelleria (Italy)
> Mediterranean diet
> Palov culture and tradition (Uzbekistan)
> Turkish coffee culture and tradition
> Art of Neapolitan 'Pizzaiolo' (Italy)
> Nsima culinary tradition of Malawi

Without wishing to go overboard with sarcastic remarks on the eccentricity of what is included and excluded from this list, a

French gastronomic meal is anything but 'intangible' – as is well known to anyone who has had to stomach one. In any case, there's a rosy future in store for the UNESCO bureaucrats: opening up in front of them in an endless list are the boundless pastures of processes for admitting other candidates for the 'intangible culture of humanity', from Spanish *jamón serrano* to Maine lobsters, the oysters of Oléron and the cherries of Traverse City (Michigan).*

With intangible heritage, the accent is laid on tradition: among the 549 candidates admitted onto the UNESCO list via various routes (and they are not only food), the words 'traditional' or 'tradition' appear in some ninety-nine cases. Here we enter that universe where bread must be 'rustic' or 'homemade', a pie is always 'mom's' or 'granny's', the recipe invariably 'ancient', invariably cooked 'like once upon a time' and – there can be no doubt – 'in a wood oven'.

The theme of authenticity thus bursts into the realm of tastes and aromas. Arjun Appadurai writes:

> Few words play as important a role in the vocabulary of the food critic as does the word 'authenticity' … Authenticity measures the degree to which something is more or less what it ought to be. It is thus a norm of some sort. But is it an immanent norm, emerging somehow from the cuisine itself? Or is it an external norm, reflecting some imposed gastronomic standard? If it is an immanent norm, who is its authoritative voice: the professional cook? the average consumer? the gourmand? the housewife? If it is an imposed norm, who is its privileged voice: the connoisseur of exotic food? the tourist? the ordinary participant in a neighbouring cuisine? the cultivated eater from a distant one? These questions lead to the first puzzle of authenticity. Authenticity is typically not the concern of the native participants in a culinary tradition, except when they (and the food) are far from home. It generally arises in the contexts of export, tourism, gourmandise, and exoticism …

---

* The banners greeting visitors to this pleasant beach resort on Lake Michigan read 'Traverse City: Cherry Capital of the World'.

The second puzzle about authenticity is its relationship to quality. Quality is typically the insider's concern, authenticity that of the culinary tourist. We often admit that there is food that, though inauthentic, is good. But can we as easily speak of food that is authentic but bad? It is difficult to come up with examples of the latter sort ... The final puzzle about authenticity reminds us of Hegel's observation about the 'Owl of Minerva'. Authenticity as a criterion seems always to emerge just after its subject matter has been significantly transformed. How is one to generate stable criteria of authenticity for traditions that are always changing? All cuisines have a history: tastes shift, regional distinctions go in and out of focus, new techniques and technologies appear. New foods come in and go out of vogue in all complex culinary traditions. The idea of authenticity seems to imply a timeless perspective on profoundly historical processes.*

As in all the other forms of tourism, in gastronomic tourism, too, the authenticity is staged. Not only that, but it is above all negotiated, to use a verb that is all the rage in cultural studies (and which reveals the shopkeeper ideology standing behind it). Staging is fundamental to decorating an eatery in such a way that its culinary 'identity' is obvious, from the inevitable red lanterns outside Chinese restaurants to the red-and-white checked tablecloths and walls adorned with wicker wine bottles in 'real Italian trattorias', and from the painted blue stripes in Greek places to the terminology on some menus.

More generally – through a process which we have already witnessed in many other sectors – the last two centuries have seen a touristisation of everyday cuisine. As tourists explored ever more diligently the foodways of the lands they visited, these cuisines became ever more tourist-oriented. First of all, the local cuisines changed, blurred so to speak, in order to win the acceptance and approval of tourists. Faced with a previously untasted dish in

---

* Arjun Appadurai, 'On Culinary Authenticity' (letter), *Anthropology Today*, 1986, vol. 2, no. 4, p. 25. It is interesting that Appadurai here makes explicit the Hegelian trap within which the whole discourse on authenticity operates.

which repose the flesh of unknown creatures, the tourist's curios-ity is torn between the call of the exotic and the savouring of the tasty, and a concern for what is edible and what is not. American palates will appreciate a stew until they know there is rabbit (or cat) in the sauce, or that what seemed like a thin eel turns out to be a snake.

'Authentic Chinese food' is purging itself not only of scorpions and cockroaches but also hens' feet and roosters' wattles. Fish will be served without their heads (though they are considered a delicacy in China) and tripe will be mentioned in the menu, but only in Chinese. Peruvian restaurants will avoid serving roast *cuj* (guinea pig or rat). A southern African restaurant would never think of preparing fried caterpillars for European tourists, even though they have a delicate taste similar to almond paste.[10] Staying with the subject of insects as ingredients, we will never find locust ravioli in a Magrebhian restaurant or red ant chutney in an Indian establishment or a plate of aquatic roaches in shrimp sauce in a Laotian.[11]

Even without arriving at these extremes, things are already toned down when it comes to the use of spices: an Indian restau-rateur will never offer Westerners the red-hot sauces that cause tears to stream down their cheeks, inflame their eyes and give them hiccups. The Korean kimchi served to tourists has rarely been marinated in a brine of fermented shrimp.

Rather, we could say that the more theatre there is to the staging of authenticity, the more its 'typical' character is stand-ardised and limited: the stronger the signs of Chineseness (red lanterns out front, dragons on the walls), the more the Chinese-ness of the food itself is diluted and limited to pure markers of Chineseness in a paradox we can call 'glocalisation'. So, dump-lings and 'spring rolls' … 'the twin processes of homogenisation and heterogenisation have "become features of life across much of the late twentieth century world".'[12] Homogeneous in its heterogeneity, 'ethnic cuisine' is the gastronomic equivalent of 'ethnic music', that is, a traditional music rearranged for an inter-national and contemporary audience – Celtic music that can go down well in Okinawa. Thus ethnic cuisine is a new form of global gastronomy.

Gastronomic tourists find themselves in the same situation we have encountered many times before, which is reminiscent of Achilles chasing the tortoise: these tourists are ever in search of a 'true flavour' beyond the toned-down cuisine prepared for them. The tourism industry runs to their aid, multiplying its initiatives and gimmicks, putting into people's heads the idea that the disappointments of gastronomic tourism ought to be redeemed by even more culinary tourism.

Hence the proliferation of itineraries designed to take us to the ultimate authentic flavour, genuine pilgrimages to taste and aroma. We see this also in wine routes, not only those in Old Europe with its Rutas de la Rioja Alavesa, les Routes des vins d'Alsace and la Strada del Vino della Costa degli Etruschi, but also on most continents, from the 2,000-kilometre Argentinian Ruta del Vino through Mendoza, to the routes fanning out from Stellenbosch (not far from Pretoria) in South Africa, the Wine Roads in Sonoma and Napa Valley in California and the Australian wine circuits of the Margaret River near Perth, in Western Australia.

Each of these itineraries involves a guided tour of the cellars amid the great oaken barrels, where not only wine but enological guides and volumes of literature vaguely related to Bacchus are for sale. Courses are also offered in enological acculturation such as training in the use of retro-olfactory perception and distinguishing bouquet. Tools of the wine taster are also displayed, from tastevins and corkscrews of various levels of technological sophistication to decanters and enormous tasting glasses (which might also harbour a Bordeaux).

But there is another way to attract tourists, including culinary ones – and it lies in organising gastronomic events. The most established and, to my knowledge, oldest and biggest beer festival in the world is Munich's Oktoberfest, which attracts around 6.5 million visitors a year. The first Oktoberfest – and again, here, we head back to the decisive period of the early nineteenth century – was laid on by the Bavarian King Max Joseph for his subjects, upon the wedding of his son, the Crown Prince Ludwig (later, Ludwig I) and Princess Therese von Sachsen-Hildburghausen. The festivities culminated in a series of horse races, and it was repeated in subsequent years in order forever to commemorate that unforgettable matrimony.[13] Just as the October Revolution in fact broke out in November (because of the offset with the Orthodox calendar), likewise Oktoberfest, which lasts for sixteen days, plays out through late September and ends on the first Sunday of October, to avoid the uncertainties of the Bavarian autumn.

Oktoberfest immediately found imitators on the other side of the ocean. German immigrants in Wisconsin had barely the time to found the city of Milwaukee on Lake Michigan in 1846 before the first local Oktoberfest was celebrated. Today it is held in July, attracting an average of 100,000 visitors. Each year some 430 Oktoberfests are celebrated in the United States. The model has also been copied in Asia. Qingdao, China, a coastal city of 8 million inhabitants where Tsingtao is brewed, hosts the biggest beer festival, with 3 million participants each year.[14]

Another event that magnetically attracts tourists is the trade fair, with which business and gastronomic tourism cross paths – for instance, Vinitaly, an international wine and spirits exhibition that has been held in Verona, Italy, since 1967. More than 2,600 journalists cover this event, which is visited by 150,000 people and 4,300 wine producers from thirty countries.[15]

Gastronomic events are the terrain on which the untrammelled fantasies of local councillors and regional officials can be let loose, on the basis that holding the most improbable of festivals will turn around devastated local finances. This is a surreal example of the febrile bureaucratic imagination – a sample of which we find in the list of gastronomic events organised in Italy each year. The following list of festivals is by no means exhaustive:

There are 8,662 events dedicated to wine, 3,120 dedicated to beer, and 734 to grappa.

1,515 festivals (fairs, exhibitions, markets, meetings, parties) are dedicated to polenta,

    621 festivals devoted to gnocchi,

    338 to noodles,

    229 to bruschetta.

Among meat, there are:

    1,040 sausage festivals,

    576 pork,

    217 piglet,

    49 kid,

    16 lamb,

    17 ossobuco,

    plus 732 ham festivals,

    629 salami

    and 147 mortadella.

These ones celebrate creatures from the sea:

    271 tuna festivals,

    215 for mussels,

    195 for anchovies,

    126 for cod

    and 101 for clams.

Cheeses are also not forgotten:

    732 ricotta festivals,

    562 for parmesan,

    495 for pecorino,

    334 for mozzarella,

    228 for gorgonzola

    and 174 for fondue.

Among vegetable festivals, there are:

    5,790 truffle festivals (white, black, Alba, summer, scorzone, and so on),

    754 for pumpkin,

    633 for chestnuts,

    527 for onions,

    341 for garlic,

328 for chillies,
318 for porcini mushrooms,
247 for broad beans,
229 nuts,
97 for fennel,
72 for peppers
and 52 for aubergines.

These amount to over 34,000 events, more than four for each of Italy's 8,003 municipalities. But the food festival is also sometimes coupled with a cultural discussion or a concert, such as the Feste de l'Unità, the local festivals connected to the Communist Party and its former newspaper *l'Unità*. Music festivals can also be modelled on these, like the one I had the chance to witness in Pensacola, Florida, where the Christian rock festival was often deserted in favour of the neighbouring crayfish festival.

These events, festivals, fairs and gastronomic destinations face an insidious and inexorable competition. It comes in the form of ethnic restaurants that are now such an indelible part of twenty-first-century urban life. For there is no medium-to-large-size city in the world that does not display a more or less vast panoply of exotic cuisines. Even staying in the same city, we have 'world food at our disposal'. We can have Moroccan tajine, an Indonesian rijsttafel, Argentinian carne asada, Mongolian fondue, Turkish mezze, Hungarian goulash, Tamil daal, Alsatian choucroute, Galician octopus, Portuguese cod, Greek dolmades, Thai tom yum soup, Russian blini, Peruvian tamales, Scandinavian herring or Mexican empanadas. Just as the zoos of the nineteenth century made it possible to experience the thrill of wild animals without leaving town, thus the metropolis of the new millennium offers us a boundless array of exotic flavours, even as we remain *chez nous*.

For once, the phenomenon of ethnic restaurants does not date to the early nineteenth century. Rather, it goes back to what Benedict Anderson has called 'early globalisation', with its first global migration and the new dislocations of power. Indeed, the Yankees visiting Louisiana, after buying out Napoleon Bonaparte a few decades earlier, could by 1840 savour French-Cajun cuisine at Antoine's in New Orleans (and it was, indeed, Antoine's rather than the French *chez Antoine*). Up until a few years ago one could still dine at the Fiore d'Italia, which from 1886 proclaimed itself San Francisco's oldest Italian restaurant. Even in a smaller Midwestern city like Des Moines, Iowa, the first Chinese restaurant opened in 1930.

Across the twentieth century, immigration continued to land at the beachheads of ethnic dining in former colonial powers or hubs of industry (Arab restaurants in Paris, Indian ones in London, Turkish ones in Berlin, Indonesians in the Netherlands, Mexicans in the US). Yet, it is no accident that it exploded in concomitance with the great tourism revolution of the post–World War II period. This is demonstrated by the extraordinary spread of Thai cuisine in the United States, notwithstanding the fact that Thai immigration to that country is relatively small outside of Southern California (and some Thai restaurants in America are run by Chinese people). Rather, it owes to the fact that Thailand is a popular mass tourist destination for Americans, a pattern partly set by the spells of leave spent in Bangkok by US soldiers fighting in Vietnam. Ethnic restaurants are the product of a boomerang effect: once they have returned home, tourists want to experience again the flavours they tasted on holiday just as they want to bring back memories of their trip by looking at the photos and videos they shot. Or this may simply be an effect of their widened culinary horizons. For instance, despite the heightened attention Peruvian chefs have recently received in the *New York Times* and elsewhere, only those who actually have been to Peru really know the extent to which its extraordinary cuisine is one of Latin America's best-kept secrets.

Not by accident, cookbooks for visited locations are among the mementoes most often present in the luggage of those returning from trips, as they seek to reproduce those hitherto unknown aromas. Appadurai is right when he says that ethnic cookbooks 'belong to the literature of nostalgia',[*] for they satisfy the need to re-create a flavour that is now pined after. Often those who visit an ethnic restaurant want to rediscover the flavours and the atmosphere they experienced as tourists on holiday.

Just as tourists bring another little part of the world home, so ethnic restaurants in big cities put the world within reach of your taste buds. In ethnic cooking, we find proof of the metaphor that often recurs in studies relating to this theme: 'eating the Other', as the title of an essay by bell hooks puts it. 'Within current debates about race and difference, mass culture is the contemporary location that both publicly declares and perpetuates the idea that there is pleasure to be found in the acknowledgment and enjoyment of racial difference. The commodification of Otherness has been so successful because it is offered as a new delight, more intense, more satisfying than normal ways of doing and feeling. Within commodity culture, *ethnicity becomes spice, seasoning that can liven up the dull dish that is mainstream white culture.*'[16]

If racial, ethnic or cultural differences are accepted, recognised and 'savoured', they are then able to spice up an otherwise bland social life. One book by Panikos Panayi (Reaktion Books, London, 2008) bears the title *Spicing Up Britain: The Multicultural History of British Food*. The notion of adding spice makes its way even into more bureaucratic circles. A women's project financed with European funds was titled 'Recipes for making a multicultural Finland soup'. Salla Tuori observes:

> This choice of words is interesting. On a general level, the title reflects the way in which 'multiculturalism' is often domesticated into consuming 'others' through food, music and other cultural products, both concretely and metaphorically ... offering 'recipes for a multicultural Finland' suggests that the project can give exact directions for successful 'multiculturalism'; multiculturalism can be as easy as cooking a soup.[17]

---

[*] Appadurai is referring in particular to Indian cookbooks and is even more drastic: 'cookbooks appear to belong to the literature of exile, of nostalgia and loss'. 'How to Make a National Cuisine: Cookbooks in Contemporary India', *Comparative Studies in Society and History*, January 1988, vol. 30, no. 1, p. 18.

Thus ethnic food and cuisine seamlessly precipitate us into the whole discussion around multiculturalism. For ethnic cuisine is both a metaphor for multiculturalism, as in bell hooks, or a metonym as in a part representing a cultural whole. Ethnic cuisine provides us with a celebratory image of a multicultural society, one that would supposedly enrich our lives with the possibility of choosing between tonight's meal being zighini in an Eritrean restaurant, sushi in a Japanese outlet or tandoori in a Punjabi place. Carried along by the metaphor, this vision suggests that a multicultural society is as easy to throw together as a soup. In the description of the Finnish project, the European bureaucrats' language is light-hearted and unbridled, filled with metaphors of metaphors:

Dear Reader,

We here at [the Kitchen] in [the city] have cooked a multicultural soup for everybody to taste. The cooks [keittäjät] are our immigrant mentors. The main ingredients used are: paying attention to gender equality, finding one's own strengths and capacities, and grassroots wisdom. Spices are the colours that different cultures bring to the Finnish society and the salt in the bottom is support and help for each other.[18]

Now, not only do cultures become spices, but spices become colours. The culinary metaphor lends itself to an idyllic, well-meaning idea of a multicultural society: what a marvellous planet we would have if peoples and cultures could mix with the same facility that the aromas and flavours of multi-ethnic cuisines blend together! 'Ethnic food is eaten with such joy, and with such pride, it makes you wonder what could happen if politics, the arts, academia, the media and education were to be transformed in an equally positive way.'[19]

Just as the French Communist Party's leader ordered his militants in 1936, 'You have to know when to end a strike', so too should scholars be told to calm it with the metaphors. But this isn't happening. Instead, the culinary metaphor has intervened to distinguish between the two basic models of multicultural society: the salad society and the hotchpotch society.

The first has been evoked by Angela Davis: 'The metaphor that has replaced the melting pot is the salad. A salad consists of many ingredients, is colorful and beautiful, and it is to be consumed by someone. Who consumes multiculturalism is a question begging to be asked.'[20] In a salad, the tomato remains a tomato, the cucumber remains a cucumber and the lettuce remains lettuce. It is a heterogeneous combination made up of ingredients that remain distinct from one another. This type of society can be compared not only to a salad but also to a mosaic, as in *L.A. 2000*, a report on the future of Los Angeles commissioned by the city administration: readers were told to think of Los Angeles 'like a mosaic, with each tile a different, vibrant colour essential to the whole'.[21] The economist Amartya Sen defines this salad (or mosaic) society a 'plural monoculturalism'.[22] It is a society made up of so many sub-societies, each of them monocultural: this is essentially the model practiced in many English-speaking countries, and can be seen to be an example of 'little worlds which touch but don't interpenetrate' as discussed by Robert Park.

The culinary metaphor also sets out a second model of multicultural society, one that Salman Rushdie defended during the controversy and ensuing fatwa over his *Satanic Verses*. The novel 'celebrates hybridity, impurity, intermingling, the transformation that comes of new and unexpected combinations of human beings, cultures, ideas, politics, movies, songs. It rejoices in mongrelization and fears the absolutism of the Pure. *Mélange*, hotchpotch, a bit of this and a bit of that is *how news enters the world*.'[23]

Long digressions on this hotchpotch society, this 'culinary melting pot', are bursting from the pages of Donna Gabaccia's book. She begins her work with a dedication to her son bordering on the ridiculous:

Mangiando, ricordo:
Dedicated to Tamino,
my German-speaking,
Italo-Polish-American child,
who eats Ethiopian and cooks Cuban
and who grew up with this book.

Amartya Sen instead maintains (with some measure of exaggeration) in the article cited above (not by accident subtitled 'Chili and Liberty') that from a culinary point of view,

> Indian and British food can genuinely claim to be multicultural. India had no chili until the Portuguese brought it to India from America, but it is effectively used in a wide range of Indian food today and seems to be a dominant element in most types of curries. It is plentifully present in a mouth-burning form in vindaloo, which, as its name indicates, carries the immigrant memory of combining wine with potatoes. Tandoori cooking might have been perfected in India, but it originally came to India from West Asia. Curry powder, on the other hand, is a distinctly English invention, unknown in India before Lord Clive, and evolved, I imagine, in the British army mess.[24]

If the notion of 'plural monoculturalism' introduced by Sen is illuminating, his culinary examples of *real* multiculturalism are, however, misleading. I do not think that Germans are multicultural just because they eat potatoes, or Turks because they smoke tobacco, or Neapolitans because their cuisine would be blown apart if it were not for tomatoes (and yet potatoes, tobacco and tomatoes all come from the Americas, just as chili came to India). Nor does the fact that Neapolitans speak with a dialect full of French-cognate words make them multicultural, because then the very word would lose meaning and all peoples and societies on Earth would be multicultural. How multicultural were the Britons in the twelfth century with those Celts, Angles, Romans, Saxons and Normans all together? In Italy there is no region as monoidentitarian and closed (to the limits of impenetrability) as

Sicily, yet according to these criteria it should be a triumph of multiculturalism, with its Greek, Roman, Arab, Norman, Angevin and Spanish hybridisations.

When the tomato gives flavour to a pizza *alla napoletana*, its Amerindian origin is completely forgotten. Like ethnic cuisine, society is multicultural so long as the little clot of otherness remains. Only, that is, before the Other is dissolved into the solution, fused into the melting pot. Sticking with the US metaphor, a melting pot is another word for crucible, and when metals have fused in the melting pot there is just a single substance produced, a new culture, just as there is no longer copper and tin but only bronze. Once again, we run into the problem of the Other. The question of multiculturalism is posed when there is a margin of irreducibility between one social group and another.

Thus, multiculturalism is just one phase in the evolution of a society, which ends when no one in the Po Valley is any longer able to distinguish the descendants of the Longobardi from the Latins or other Italic peoples, or when in Spain no distinction is made anymore among Iberian, Vandal, Latin or Arab communities. But multiculturalism is precisely the political proposal that tends to make a temporary phase into a permanent order of things. Not by chance, the most radical champion of multiculturalism, the Malaysian-origin Australian Chandran Kukathas, conceives society as an archipelago in which the state is reduced to the minimum of the minimum,* making Robert Nozick look like a Jacobin statist by comparison.

An archipelago society must necessarily be made up of separate islands, in the most extreme example of what Sen calls plural monoculturalism. The accent, therefore, is laid on what separates the various groups from one another and holds each of them together, namely their traditions. For this reason, multiculturalism

---

* Chandran Kukathas, *The Liberal Archipelago: A Theory of Diversity and Freedom*, Oxford University Press, Oxford, 2002. Not surprisingly, Kukathas is associated with the most conservative of US think tanks, the Cato Institute founded and financed by the billionaire Koch brothers.

appears as a 'multiconservatism',[25] with each group conserving its own traditions as if they were precious treasures and heritages: 'For example, Chandran Kukathas has argued for a strong version of libertarianism that would allow maximal autonomy for individuals and groups. Thus, parents would be free to force a child into marriage, or deny her life-saving medical treatment, or have female genital mutilation (FGM) performed upon her' (Brent Pickett).[26]

We understand why many women have rebelled against this conception of multiculturalism: when Susan Moller Okin posed the (rhetorical) question 'Is Multiculturalism Bad for Women?', Katha Pollitt replied that it is: 'Fundamentally, the ethical claims of feminism run counter to the cultural relativism of "group rights" multiculturalism.'[27]

This multiculturalism has considerable philosophical implications. In the first place, with multiculturalism – like any position concerning the theme of the other (and thus the authentic/inauthentic pair, with the unhappy consciousness correlated to it), we are back within the Hegelian horizon. Indeed, in his essay cited above, Brent Pickett observes:

> Redistributive thinking is frequently grounded in Kantian moral philosophy, which holds that persons should treat one another as beings of equal moral worth, but which does not want to dictate what sort of life is the best. In the parlance of moral philosophy, Kantianism offers a theory of the right, not the good. In contrast, philosophical theories of recognition typically have their source in Hegel's philosophy of consciousness, which emphasizes how individual identity is socially constructed. Given this social construction of the self, the misrecognition by others is (potentially) profoundly damaging, and can deprive persons of the best sort of life. Hegel's philosophy is oriented toward the good, rather than emphasizing the right.[28]

Secondly, for this extreme multiculturalism, society is no longer made up of individuals, but of groups, of islets, each of them self-managing according to their own rules. The most untrammelled laissez faire attitude takes us back to a caste conception of society such as the Indian castes which tend not to overlap, but rather remain separate, each with its own different religion and foodway. For this reason, in Kukathas's sense of multiculturalism, if a subgroup stipulates the existence of an out-of-caste, a pariah (dalit), the untouchability of this pariah must be guaranteed and made to be respected (even by those rebellious pariahs who would protest against such a fate) in the name of the group's freedom to associate among their own.

It is curious that in the interminable debate on multiculturalism, no one has ever mentioned the peculiar nature of multiculturalism in the Roman Empire, according to which all the subject (or 'allied') people's gods were equally worthy of veneration, to the point that a temple 'to all gods' (*Pan-theon* in Greek) was built in Rome on a circular plan in order to avoid giving pre-eminence to one god over another. This multiculturalism is interesting because it consisted of two great unifying principles, namely obedience to the emperor as if he were a god and learning the Latin language. Not by accident, in the modern world it is an imperial civilisation, the Anglo-Saxon one, which most forcefully supports multiculturalism à la Kukathas (even to the point of allowing Islamic councils to act as family and financial dispute mediation services for Muslims in the UK).

To my knowledge, only Slavoj Žižek has connected imperialism, multinational capitalism and multiculturalism:

[T]he ideal form of ideology of this global capitalism is multiculturalism, the attitude which, from a kind of empty global position, treats *each* local culture the way the colonizer treats colonized people – as 'natives' whose mores are to be carefully studied and 'respected'. That is to say, the relationship between traditional imperialist colonialism and global capitalist self-colonization is exactly the same as the relationship between Western cultural imperialism and multiculturalism: in the same way that global capitalism involves the paradox of colonization without the colonizing

Nation-State metropole, multiculturalism involves patronizing Eurocentrist distance and/or respect for local cultures without roots in one's own particular culture.[29]

The disdain implicit in multinational and multicultural capitalism is described in the bluntest and most sarcastic form by the most radical critique of multiculturalism that I know of, put in summary form by the late Martin Hollis: '"Liberalism for the liberals" and "cannibalism for the cannibals."'[30] Or, indeed: 'liberalism for us, cannibalism for you.'

Thus after a long pilgrimage around the world we have got back to the human zoos that so excited the crowds of stay-at-home tourists at the great international exhibitions of the late nineteenth century. Multiculturalism as a sociological concept reveals its touristic nature, or rather its original roots in culinary tourism – even in its most extreme, cannibalistic form.

16

Maybe One Day

Maybe one day they'll ask what exactly the activity we call tourism consisted of. And the tourist will perhaps be a rather enigmatic figure from the past, like the haruspex, the almoner or the gleaner. Or perhaps it will be considered a temporary human illness, like that of the mad travellers of the nineteenth century. Or rather, it will be an obsolete profession like the lamplighter, the lacemaker, the donkey-keeper or the wailer. At root, we are witnessing the extinction not only of many living species, but so, too, of many trades – even ones that emerged only recently. The telegraph was the first 'instantaneous highway of thought' but in 1999, after less than 150 years, telegraphists officially ceased to exist. They were replaced on ships by GPS, and there was no longer any need for someone to put out an SOS call. Another casualty: the 'ice harvesters', who once supplied the refrigerated underground ice houses of the Chicago slaughterhouses, among other places. And similarly, closer to our own era, typographers have also disappeared. The journalist and the anthropologist, to which tourists have been compared, are also jobs probably on the road to extinction.

Of course, humans will not stop moving around. But perhaps the 'hunger for the world' will be satiated, or at least this kind of hunger. We do not know when, we do not know how, but just as it had a beginning, what I have called the 'age of tourism' will also have an end. In mathematics there are two types of theorems: uniqueness theorems, which establish that there is one entity and one alone (function, operator, set) that responds to the required conditions; and existence theorems, which establish that there is something (and it is no better defined) that satisfies certain properties. The assertion that the age of tourism will come to an end belongs to this second category. We know that a thing will happen, but we cannot say any more than that. A little like how we know that the civilisation built on cars will not last forever and that it will be replaced by some other way of moving around, yet to be defined. We know it by force of arithmetic, because 10 or so billion people cannot allow themselves 5 billion or so cars. In 2018, some 308 million motor vehicles circulated in the EU among a population of almost 500 million.* We cannot afford it from an economic point of view, nor in terms of space, environment or resources. So perhaps one day our descendants will ask what were all these tin carcasses (those metal exoskeletons) that lay motionless along our streets at night.

For a while recently, it looked as if the age of tourism was coming to an end. In a world that lives confined to the present moment, which forgets each minute as it slips by and fails to look even an hour into the future, it took only a few days of lockdown to declare tourism dead. A few weeks of empty European streets during the pandemic were enough to declare in April 2020 that nothing would ever be the same again, much less tourism. To get the measure of this complacency, to show the fickleness of modern certainties, it is enough to consider a headline from the Italian financial newspaper *Il Sole 24 Ore* just two months later: 'Italy reopens: Escape to the mountains, boom for holiday homes' (5 June 2020): as soon as they can, humans escape from prison, even though prison is their home. Even though they know they will be incarcerated again.

Once again we stumble upon the immense underestimation of tourism, as if a virus were enough to undo a multidimensional, multisectoral phenomenon made possible only by two immense

---

* In 2016, there were 1.32 billion cars, vans and trucks on the planet, to which we should add almost 500 million motorcycles. For Europe, the data are from the European Automobile Manufacturers Association (acea.be) and for the world I have referred to information from Oak Ridge National Laboratory, *Transportation Energy Data Book*, Edition 37, cta.ornl.gov.

revolutions: a technological revolution in transport and communications that made travel shorter, safer, more comfortable and cheaper; and the social revolution that allowed increasing numbers of the world's population to enjoy paid leisure time.

These two revolutions have in turn transformed the collective consciousness, revolutionising common sentiments, the perception of the world, of distances, of otherness, the very concept of one's own freedom. Undoing this pillar of the modern constitution is no small thing: one day or another it will happen, but it will certainly not be due to a simple virus. Our very relationship with the world, with space, with dimensions must change. Some of this is already happening, but it will not be a short process.

In order to get some sense of the forms this process might take, we can examine a specific form of tourism, tiny and dismissible, which has the advantage of already having become extinct. We ought to look back to the second half of the nineteenth century, and the introduction of electric trams.

> The tram expanded beyond all measure the process of suburbanisation that had begun with the horse-drawn omnibus. For the first time it became possible to 'explore' the city. Tram companies published guides and timetables, enabling passengers to vary their routes and change lines. At the end of the lines, huge amusement parks were built with bars (such as New York's Coney Island or Chicago's Riverside). As a result, the number of passengers swelled on Sundays and during the summer as entire families set off on tours to visit quarters of the city, monuments and gardens that had previously been unreachable. What it must have felt like – the sense of anticipation as the tram came into view, the hunger for the unknown and the unexplored, the mixture of apprehension and curiosity that assailed those intrepid tram riders – we can never know.[1]

Today we no longer *set off* on a tram (just as we no longer spend our evenings at morgues). Yet the city has not got any smaller. Nor do we know it better – far from it (and we'll get back to this). But something else has happened. Our curiosity has gone, or more accurately, it has changed. For we have become inured to our gap-ridden knowledge of our own urban habitat. Perhaps the same will happen with our knowledge of the world itself. We will move around, but we will no longer 'set off'.

If we want to uncover the main reason why it will disappear, we should spin out our reasoning further, indeed by returning to the concept of zoning. Digging deeper into its social implications, we can understand why zoning civilisation is in its twilight. For just like Modern urbanism (the CIAM), the social structure of the last two centuries took shape by way of mechanisms that would ensure a *disciplining* power relation. With this term, Michel Foucault designated all those institutions that exercise a total and exclusive control over the individual subjected to them, which identify those subject to power and not those who hold it – unlike royal power, which identifies the sovereign ('the body of the king') rather than the subject and which can coexist with other sovereign powers, like that of the father in the family or the Pope among Catholics. Conversely, the worker in the factory, the pupil at school, the prisoner in jail, the patient in hospital, the lunatic in the asylum and the soldier in the army are each completely defined by the disciplining power that takes hold of them and moulds their bodies. In this mechanism, the family, as the only residual institution of royal power, has the precise function of allowing the transfer from one disciplinary power to another: we leave school and return to the family, from which we go to the factory, only then to return to the family and then go into the army...[2]

Zoning translates the disciplinary structure of society into urban geography, rendering spatially the exclusive monopoly that each disciplinary institution exercises over the individual, mapping the temporal scansion of life. And it is no accident that urban zoning is in decline at precisely the moment when the West's great disciplinary institutions are in crisis.

The number of American cities implementing new urbanism regulations that go against zoning is increasing. Miami did just this in 2009, approving a new strategic city plan, which the

Congress for the New Urbanism (CMU) described in enthusiastic terms:

> The difference between Miami's old and new code is fundamental. Like most cities in the mid-twentieth century, Miami had previously adopted conventional zoning regulations that disregarded traditional mixed-use patterns and divided the city into zones of preferred uses such as residential, commercial and industrial. By contrast, the new code encourages residences, schools, shops, parks and other amenities to be within walking distance ... Instead of separate use zones, Miami is now mapped with 'transect zones' which describe the form and intensity of urbanism from close-knit neighborhoods of two- and three-story buildings to the high-rises of the urban core and of other waterfront areas.

In part, zoning is in crisis precisely because of the objective it has set itself: isolating individual citizens, making encounters and contact difficult and deactivating the 'dialogue mill'. In the long run people rebel, though not violently so: this is not protest (Voice) but defection (Exit), to use Albert Hirschman's typology.[3] They do not put up barricades – they simply move out of the suburbs in which they had hitherto been confined (especially women). For almost three decades after the great flight from the cities that peaked between the mid-1970s and the late 1980s, the inner cities have been repopulating and the urban geography of the United States has begun to look more like Europe's. In Europe, the wealthy class live in the centre and the worse-off in the periphery, whereas across the Atlantic the better-heeled classes had for many decades exiled themselves to the suburbs, leaving behind the urban centre to be inhabited by what they called the 'underclass'. Kenneth Jackson, the most authoritative scholar of suburbanisation, told me: 'Demographic factors will continue to bring people back to the city. People are getting married later and later and, if you're single, you don't want to be holed up in the suburbs ... At first people found malls a novelty – the idea of walking in an air-conditioned indoor street and taking the family to the cinema and ice-cream parlour. It was exciting. But that was decades ago. And then they went to another mall, and it was always the same thing. And then people got bored. The city is much more exciting.'[4] (Once again there is Simmel and Park's notion of the city as temptress.)

But this is just the point – that zoning is being abandoned at just the point when all the great disciplinary institutions are in deep crisis in Western society. It no longer has conscript armies; it is losing its big factories; it is witnessing the (deliberate and encouraged) collapse of the project of universal education; and it is privatising health care systems. Nor is the asylum still central to defining society's relationship with mental illness. It is a society which is witnessing the dissolution of the overlapping disciplinary layers that had hitherto constituted the individual. Where he was once shaped by the layering, one atop the other, of his school book, his work book, his military service status, his police records and his clinical file (which, together constituted his real 'identity'), all synthesised in the vaccinated, educated, employed wage-labourer fulfilling his duties as a conscript – this (male) figure, called the 'citizen' of the nation-state, is vanishing.

But it is not only individual disciplinary systems that are failing. The truth is that the temporal structure of existence which underpinned zoning's distribution of space is double-bound to full-time work, with what Robert Castel calls 'wage-earning society'.

In his 1995 book, Castel notes how for centuries the condition of the wage earner was, perhaps, the most ignoble: 'One was waged when one was nothing and had nothing to trade except the strength of one's own arms. A person fell into wage-labour when his status was degraded: the ruined artisan, the smallholder whose land no longer provided enough food.' Even in 1922, France's Parti Radical proposed 'the abolition of wage-labour, a residue of slavery'.[5] Yet after that, wage labour – defined as full-time work for an indeterminate period – seemed destined to become the very condition of modernity, along with all the protections associated with it (pensions, medical assistance, paid holidays, maternity leave, family benefits):

Wage-earning society seemed destined to follow an ascendant trajectory that, at the same time, would guarantee collective wealth and promote a better redistribution of opportunities and security. To avoid belabouring this discussion and to keep to the main line of the argument, I will confine myself to protections directly linked to labour. However, the same link between economic development and state regulation played itself out in the domains of education, public health, urban planning, family policy, etc. In general, the whole energy of salarial society seemed focussed on absorbing the *deficit of integration* that distinguished the beginnings of industrial society. This was to be accomplished by increasing consumption, access to property or decent housing, increased participation in culture and recreation, advances towards achieving a greater equality of opportunity, consolidation of the right to work, the extension of social services, the amelioration of pockets of poverty, etc. For a brief and happy moment the social question seemed to have been resolved by the faith in unlimited progress.

It is this trajectory of unlimited economic growth that was so rudely shattered. Who today could imagine that we are all moving toward an open and more welcoming society, or working to reduce inequalities and maximize social protections? The very idea of progress itself has seemingly been abandoned.[6]

Twenty-five years ago, Castel already saw what everyone now has standing right in front of them: 'The crumbling (*effritement*) of wage-labour society'. Indeed, today, unlike a century ago, the most widespread fear is not a matter of *falling into* wage labour but rather that of *falling out of* it – to be a young NEET (Not in Education, Employment or Training), to be redundant, surplus to requirements. And even when a person does find work, they are ever more likely to exercise it in the form of providing a service from the outside. Increasingly, the employer tends to impose a relation based on such external provision (however fictitious it may be), along with its practices of invoicing and self-employment, even when this concerns a monthly pay of a few hundred euros. It is as if the shopgirl or the waiter were 'entrepreneurs', or rather, pathetic parodies of 'small businessmen'. And they are thus left without employment, a work contract, social protections, holidays, pensions, and so on.

Most importantly, the patterning of working time and free time has itself been undermined. In the wage-labour era, the great question at stake was time: the sharpest minds on the left like André Gorz reflected on precisely this, and how to move from free time to liberated time.[7] The great 'conquests' concerned the reduction of working time. This reduction could be at the level of one's whole working career, for instance by lowering the pension age or delaying entry into the labour market by extending the period spent in education. Or it could be at an annual level, by increasing the number of weeks of paid holiday. In France in 1936, for instance, the Popular Front introduced two weeks' *congés payés*, which became three weeks in 1956, four in 1969 (after May '68) and five in 1982 with François Mitterrand. Or it can be seen at the weekly level in the conquest of the forty-hour work week, which was shortened to thirty-five in France. And finally it can be seen at the daily level in the conquest of the eight-hour day, which came after epic workers' struggles.

At one time, when we spoke of a 'reform', it meant a lengthening of one's free time: today, in the new neoliberal jargon, 'reform' means 'the reintroduction of the indispensable elements of flexibility that the markets require'.

Put in other terms, paid free time was one of the clauses of the capital–labour compromise necessitated by the Soviet threat. In one of the most paradoxical examples of unintended consequences, the Soviet regime oppressed its own subjects unbearably (as well as those of the 'people's democracies' in the 'brother countries') yet at the same time, indirectly and through its mere existence lay the basis for the liberation of its enemies' subjects. The USSR's collapse in 1991 made this compromise superfluous in the countries of the bloc that had emerged victorious from the Cold War: hence the unravelling of wage-labour society, as described by Castel just four years later.

But thus also began to vanish the whole temporal architecture of wage labour to which mass tourism, as a universal phenomenon, was and remains indissolubly linked. And it is almost impossible to think that in any reasonably likely future the configuration of society that gave rise to this temporal architecture can be reconstituted.

What changes is not only our temporal horizon, but our horizon itself – which is to say, our relationship with space is transformed. Over the last century, we have passed from a three-dimensional space to a multidimensional one. Indeed, it is ever more common for two people sitting side by side to be very remote from each other, because there are other dimensions which separate them. For example, one person is listening to a football match, while the person next to her is immersed in a Brandenburg Concerto and the third is on the phone with someone in Australia. Indeed, it is extraordinary, unprecedented in human history, that when you ask someone on the street for information, they have to remove their headphones in order to hear what you are saying. In a Darwinian world, no animal would ever isolate itself from its aural environment, at the risk of being killed off by some danger that it had not heard or sensed. For each person to walk along closed off in their own universe relies on an assumed prior confidence that nothing unforeseen will happen.

Various radio and TV channels can be seen as running along different and extra dimensions, just as web navigation can. Two people can find themselves in the same dimension of the web, 'in contact' on the Internet, even when they are at opposite ends of a physical space. Or vice versa. This multidimensionality brings closer together what was hitherto far apart, allowing us, ever since the invention of the telephone, to 'speak with the absent'. But just like anything that brings things together and unites them, it separates and distances something else.

This was clearly apparent with the introduction of trams and metro services in cities of the nineteenth century. These means of transport had brought together distant neighbourhoods but separated the classes: indeed, before then service staff had to live near to (or even in) the boss's mansion. But thanks to the much lower fares on trams and the underground, it became convenient for servants, traders, shop staff and artisans to go and live in their own cheaper neighbourhoods, far from where their bosses lived. From then on, the masters lost contact with their servants – and the dialogue between the fatalist servant Jacques and his master was now no longer possible.

Similarly, telecommunications networks bring together the distant, but only those who are, so to speak, 'convergent'. The web selects people in concentric circles of congruity: each person connects with those who think like them, or have shared patterns of consumption, similar musical, literary or erotic tastes. Thus, the potentially boundless capacity for new acquaintances and friends and dialogue in fact concretises as a reflected monologue – the incessant reaffirmation of one's own convictions by others who have been selected exactly for this self-confirmatory purpose. Filtering contacts for taste and opinion, the web operates a fresh process of segregation, but on a social rather than spatial basis. Now it is much more likely that a Milanese architect will communicate with a Brazilian designer or a Pakistani engineer than with a Milanese postie. In this new multidimensional space, groups aggregate in clusters, of significant social, cultural and ideological homogeneity. This multidimensional space thus takes the shape of a discontinuous set of bubbles of contiguous social and cultural practices.

But a similar break was also brought about by the physical revolution in transport. Until the nineteenth century, the difficulty in reaching a destination was largely proportional to your distance from it (though also taking account of obstacles like deserts and mountains). This concentric propagation (like the ripples caused by a pebble falling into water) was homologous to the first epistemological model used for science, a model which was, altogether, a rustic, agricultural one, seeing as it was founded on the notion of the 'field'. Each scholar knew very well his own 'field', his bedrock. His understanding, however, would decline the further away he got from his own yard, his valley, his region, until he became a perfect stranger, ignorant of what was in front of him.

Today, conversely, our material understanding of the world around us is no longer structured in terms of gradual, smooth decrease, just as a physicist working on spin class can know much more about neural networks, that is, biology, than of the theory of elasticity, a contiguous but separate discipline of physics. Transport has brought closer much more of what was distant than of what was already close. Between the late nineteenth century and today, the time taken to get from Rome to New York has reduced twentyfold, whereas the time to get from Rome to Milan has only halved. If, as well as purely technological factors, we also add in economic ones – that is, the rationality of the fixed costs that make high-traffic routes cheaper and less-travelled ones more expensive – then we arrive at the fact that a flight between Milan and New York can cost less than a flight between Milan and Palermo, even though it is seven times farther in distance. The result is that our knowledge of the world, geographically speaking, is patterned like a leopard skin, with islands of familiarity amid seas of ignorance. I remember when my son was sixteen years old, we realised that he had visited Maputo, New York and Beijing but never been to Lucca, Siena or Pistoia. The same goes for our familiarity with cities: personally I know some neighbourhoods of Chicago, Paris, New York or London far better than whole chunks of Rome, which are largely unknown to me even though I have spent a good part of my life there.

We live in a world where the three spatial dimensions have shrunk, but at the same time we have developed other dimensions in which to move. It is because of this simultaneous spatial rapprochement and estrangement into the other dimensions that our knowledge of the world is spotted like a leopard.

The great difference between today and the 1960s and '70s, in which many of these extra dimensions had already appeared, is that back then access to them was rooted in a specific place. Rather, it pinned you to physical space: there were landline telephones, fixed to the wall; you could listen to music but only on a record player; and you could watch TV but only on a television. Then, communications technologies drove you to shut yourself in at home, in your *banlieue* or in your suburb – it was right there that you travelled the world by watching a film, listening to an opera or speaking on the phone to distant friends. Today, the technologies are essentially the same (with the notable exception of the Internet), but they are nomadic, from phones to TV and music. You can then add on to them all the other dimensions, moving in the three dimensions of physical space. It is this nomadism that allows multi-citizenship: it is no longer necessary to 'move house' in order to live in two different cities at once.

The implicit nomadism that now permeates our lives introduces an element of indiscipline, restlessness and social disorder. It is no coincidence that in 2020 all over the world the ruling classes used the Covid-19 emergency to try to restrain the technologies that had become nomadic: the whole hymn to teleworking sung in the media is actually a compulsion to become sedentary, to stay at home again, to reduce our opportunities for socialising, to finally isolate ourselves in a literal sense.

But no remote working, no containment, no social distancing can undo the world we have created, which is simultaneously made of multidimensional cities and spatial multi-citizenship. The multidimensional city, the multidimensional place of contact, crossed paths and encounters is no longer possible to conceive, weighed down as we are by the old categories. In politics we continue to think using literally anachronistic concepts: democracy was invented when people travelled in litters, capitalism was born with the wind in its sails and socialism was dreamt up under steam power. But we continue to use these ideas without noticing it, even in a world without litters or sails or steam. 'Our mental categories and our technological process are two conveyor belts running at different speeds, and we try and walk with one leg on each of them.'[8] We still need to conceive of an idea of urbanity that involves all dimensions contemporaneously: and not only the spatial dimensions, now that we can slot each of them in next to the others in the same place, even while moving through different spaces.

Under the double pressure of the crumbling of wage-labour society and the multidimensionality bursting into our lives, the traditional figure of the tourist assumes a rather old-fashioned aura. It may even have a certain quaint charm, like the night train with a sleeper car or a steamboat crossing – once-striking novelties that are now archaic and will soon be forgotten.

A spectre is circling, avoided by all the discourses on tourism: the migrant. This is relevant not only because, in the first instance, the migrant and the tourist are the two complementary, symmetrical faces of modern travel; the tourist is the foreigner that the native serves, while the migrant is the foreigner who comes to serve the natives. Here, one might add, are two reviled incarnations of otherness, each hated by one side of the political spectrum. For the Right, the Other whom it is legitimate to hate is the immigrant; for the Left, racism against the Other manifests itself as the derision of tourists.

But it is also relevant because a good part of modern migration takes place under the guise of tourism – tourists who exceed their tourist visa and stay, working in the country they are ostensibly visiting. And lastly, it is relevant because a good part of the flow of tourists is made up of migrants who return home for their holidays. In the 1960s the new motorways in Italy were packed with Southerners returning home from Switzerland or Belgium for the holidays. Each July the island of Karpathos is filled with first- or second-generation Greek Americans who buy all the villas that come up for sale. The horrible sites on the coasts of Turkey were built by speculators precisely for the *almanci* (Turks who had emigrated to Germany), milking (and profiting from) their homesickness, their *mal du pays*. These are rather particular tourists, like the Filipino family that returns to its own island every three years to see the kids who are being brought up by the grandmother while the parents send back money from Europe. These are tourists who are not tourists.

But there is now a subtler connection between tourist and migrant, owing to the revolution in our relationship with space.

Once, when he set off, the emigrant abandoned his homeland perhaps forever. He was compelled to integrate: a homeward return was a rarity and often came soon before death. Through schooling, his children learned the host language. The links with the original homeland weakened. He supported the sports teams of his newfound country, watched its TV and listened to its music. But now, multidimensionality has put an end to all this. Migrants can spend their whole adult life abroad and yet continue to watch the films, take in the music and listen to the sermons of their own native country, support the same team they did as teenagers, send their kids to school in their homeland, make frequent return trips there with low-cost flights and dine together with loved ones on the other side of the planet via Skype or Zoom. They can literally live in two places at once, residing in the land where they work without ever having really abandoned their homeland, without really having to master the new language or learn new social codes. Integration is no longer at the top of the agenda, or even desired: it may happen, but also may not. This is one reason why different ethnicities are no longer fusing in the same melting pot.

Once again, what allows us to communicate also isolates us – a connection also disconnects. It is this disconnected connection that multiculturalism has acknowledged and awkwardly sought to manage.

Society has found a new way of 'isolating us together', as Debord put it, of diluting the tourist experience in everyday life. And in the long run it will make tourists disappear from the everyday landscape. It makes us touch without ever interacting, observe without seeing, listen without hearing. It makes us go in search of markers that give us some meaning.

Postscript

A Valediction

As the reader who has been patient enough to follow me this far will have realised, my plans changed even while I was working on this book. Indeed, my topic changed. I had undertaken to study the tourist *city*, as an urban aggregation unique to our time. Gradually I came to understand that I was studying not the tourist city but rather the tourist *civilisation*. And, having gone that far, I understood that what was taking shape was the *age* of tourism, which I would have to define – and do so in terms of its foreseeable end as well as its birth and development.

Even that does not suffice: for what changed was not just my topic, but my perspective and, lastly, the judgement I drew. Only while I was already on my way did I realise that I, too, had fallen into the Hegelian trap and had allowed myself to become wrapped up in the cruel and childish game of making tourism the easy scapegoat for all the wrongdoings of the modern. Only gradually did I begin to find intolerable the classist – sometimes outright reactionary – undertones winding their way through the most radical left-wing and anti-capitalist critiques. Only by going further in my studies did I come to understand that standing behind the critique of tourism there was nothing but a refusal to look at oneself in the mirror and recognise that this tourist is simply our society's peculiar perception of the world. It is because of this groping forward, revising my outlook and reinterpreting what I had already seen, that my writing sways back and forth, full of imperfections and rollercoasters in its stylistic register. I can only apologise for not going back and correcting it, but I think that ultimately this, too, has its uses.

Through all my research and writing, two points disturbed (and continue to disturb) me: namely the question of number (singular or plural) and, even more importantly, that of gender (masculine or feminine).

By tradition (and habit) Anglophone sociology always uses the singular to indicate some social figure: thus in the classics of US sociology we find *The Polish Peasant*, *The Hobo*, *The Young Delinquent*, *The Unadjusted Girl* and *Marginal Man*, but never *Hobos*, *Polish Peasants* or still less *Unadjusted Girls*. The subtle operation at work behind this use of the singular is more noticeable if we write, for example, *Marginal Men*: for here, the solitude so striking in the singular title becomes problematic in the plural. In its singular inflection, a social group becomes a human type, a kind of Theophrastus character (the miser, the adulator, the jealous). Similarly, *The Tourist* is always inflected in the singular, as in MacCannell's book. It is this singular which allows for the tourist to be contrasted with the traveller. But therein lies the point. Whereas the traveller is singular, which is to say, she can be thought of in the singular (in a 'Robinsonade', as Marx would say) the very word tourist cannot even be conceived of, except in the plural. If there were only one tourist, she would not be a tourist. Without the plural, the essential point is completely lost, namely the fact that tourism is a social phenomenon (as Émile Durkheim taught us when he observed that each suicide is the most individual act there can be, yet its social nature is revealed by the fact that the statistics for each country exhibit an extraordinary regularity year on year). It is the singular that lies at the foundation of the widespread hack psychologism that marks the greater part of research on tourism, as if it were necessary to explain the individual mental mechanism that drives someone to set off on a trip rather than observe its quintessentially collective dimension. It is as if one studied car use by billions of human beings by devoting oneself to observing the psychological motivations of the *motorist*. It is very difficult not to fall into this trap – I did not always manage to avoid it.

Even more of a problem is the aporia of gender. In Italian we are forced to speak of *il turista* and *il migrante* – to inflect the universe with the masculine, something that has become ever more intolerable to me. In this English-language translation we have used the plural 'they' or, when impossible, opted for a feminine singular whenever it came of speaking of what *she*, the tourist, does. But perhaps we ought to ask for a reform of the language (not only the Italian one) – not so much a reintroduction of the neuter, but rather the coining of a bisex gender, a syntactical-grammatical equivalent of blue jeans, which does not cut out half the human race.

This journey – a strenuous but incredibly stimulating one (I learned a lot and thought new thoughts) – was not made alone. Along stretches of the way I had my tender comrades, to whom I am grateful: Enrico Alleva, Daniella Ambrosino, Perry Anderson, Paola Bellusci, Rita Capezzuto, Francesco Cataluccio, Giulio d'Eramo, Alessandro Fallavollita, Andrea Forti, Marina Forti, Tom Hazeldine, Corinne Lucas Fiorato, Anna Nadotti, the Nnoberavez family, Lea Nocera, Marc Saint-Upéry, Anna Maria Testa, Ambros Waibel and Susan Watkins.

Gratitude is tinged with melancholy when it is directed toward people who were friends and teachers of mine but are no longer with us. I cited some of them (Benedict Anderson, Roland Barthes, Pierre Bourdieu, Robert Castel, Michel Foucault); others, like Marshall Berman, were present even if I did not explicitly name them. But there is one person – Claude Lévi-Strauss, both friend and teacher to me – who was a constant point of reference, even if an implicit one. It is only right to conclude this volume with an extraordinary passage of his, referring to his stays in Brazil. It synthesises how our experience of the world is both unique and temporary.

I should have liked to live in the age of *real* travel, when the spectacle on offer had not yet been blemished, contaminated, and confounded; then I could have seen Lahore not as I saw it, but as it appeared to Bernier, Tavernier, Manucci ... There's no end, of course, to such conjectures. When was the right moment to see

India? At what period would the study of the Brazilian savage have yielded the purest satisfaction and the savage himself been at his peak? Would it have been better to have arrived at Rio in the eighteenth century, with Bougainville, or in the sixteenth, with Léry and Thevet? With every decade that we travelled further back in time, I could have saved another costume, witnessed another festivity, and come to understand another system of belief. But I am too familiar with the texts not to know that this backward movement would deprive me of much information, many curious facts and objects, that would enrich my meditations. The paradox is irresoluble: the less one culture communicates with another, the less likely they are to be corrupted, one by the other; but on the other hand, the less likely it is, in such conditions, that the respective emissaries of these cultures will be able to seize the richness and the significance of their diversity. The alternative is inescapable: either I am a traveller in ancient times, and faced with a prodigious spectacle which would be almost entirely unintelligible to me and might, indeed, provoke me to mockery or disgust; or I am a traveller of our own day, hastening in search of a reality. In either case I am the loser – and more heavily than one might suppose; for today, as I go groaning among the shadows, I miss, inevitably, the spectacle that is now taking shape. My eyes, or perhaps my degree of humanity, do not equip me to witness that spectacle; and in the centuries to come, when another traveller revisits this same place, he too may groan aloud at the disappearance of much that I should have set down, but cannot. I am the victim of a double infirmity: what I see is an affliction to me; what I do not see, a reproach.[1]

Notes

1. Tourism in a Time of Cholera

1 'Travel and Tourism Economic Impact 2019', World Travel & Tourism Council, March 2019, wttc.org.
2 See the 'Research' page at nycgo.com.
3 See Ministère de l'économie, des finances, et de la relance, entreprises. gouv.fr. In 2016, arrivals in France were falling by 2.3 per cent compared to 2015, because of the terror attacks in Paris in November 2015 and in Nice in July 2016.
4 Stephen Britton, 'Tourism, Capital and Place: Towards a Critical Geography of Tourism', in *Environment and Planning D: Society and Space*, 1991, vol. 9, p. 455.
5 'Airline Profitability Strengthens Further', press release 26, 8 June 2015, iata.org.
6 David Smith, 'Trump Gives Up on Virus Fight to Focus on Economic Recovery – and Reelection', *Guardian*, 5 May 2020.
7 Manfred Lenzen, et al., 'The Carbon Footprint of Global Tourism', in *Nature Climate Change*, vol. 8, 7 May 2018.

2. The Leisure Revolution

1 Piers Brendon, *Thomas Cook: 150 Years of Popular Tourism*, London: Secker & Warburg, 1991.
2 James Buzard, *The Beaten Track: European Tourism, Literature, and the Ways to 'Culture' (1800–1918)*, Oxford: Clarendon Press, 1993, in particular pp. 65–77.
3 'Modern Tourism', *Blackwood's Edinburgh Magazine*, August 1848, no. 64, p. 185. The untitled article was a review of Harriet Martineau's *Eastern Life, Past and Present*, an account of her travels in Egypt.
4 Cited by Wolfgang Schivelbusch in *The Railway Journey: The Industrialization and Perception of Time and Space*, Berkeley: University of California Press, 1986, p. 55.
5 James Buzard, *The Beaten Track*, cit., pp. 1–2. According to the Oxford English Dictionary, the term 'tourist' emerged in 1780.

6 Joseph Arthur de Gobineau, 'La vie de voyage', in *Nouvelles Asiatiques* (1876), Pauvert, Paris 1960, vol. II, p. 332.

7 Daniel Boorstin, *The Image: A Guide to Pseudo-Events in America*, New York: Harper & Row, 1961, p. 88.

8 Buzard, *The Beaten Track*, p. 1.

9 See, for example, Pierre Bourdieu, *Distinction: A Social Critique of the Judgment of Taste* (1979), translated by Richard Nice. Cambridge MA: Harvard University Press, 1984.

10 Ibid., p. 163.

11 Alexander Innes Shand, *Old-Time Travel: Personal Reminiscences of the Continent Forty Years Ago Compared with Experiences of the Present Day*, London: John Murray, 1903, pp. 5 and 139.

12 Francis Bacon, Lord Verulam Viscount St. Albans, 'Of Travel', in *The Essays or Counsels, Civil and Moral* (1625), London: J. M. Dent & Sons Ltd, (1907) 1968, p. 54, available at gutenberg.org.

13 Vittorio Alfieri, *Vita* (1803), Einaudi, Torino, 1974, see the whole part about the 'third age: Youth. It includes about ten years of travel, and debauchery'. The life of Vittorio Alfieri was translated into French, English, German and Swedish.

14 Adam Smith, *An Inquiry into the Nature and Causes of the Wealth of Nations*, Methuen & Co. Ltd, London, 1961, Book V: 'Of the Revenue of the Sovereign or Commonwealth', Part III: 'Of the Expense of public Works and public Institutions'.

15 Cited by Orvar Löfgren, *On Holiday: A History of Vacationing*, Berkeley: University of California Press, 1999.

16 The list is taken from Judith Adler, 'Origins of Sightseeing', in *Annals of Tourism*, vol. 16, no. 1, 1989, p. 16.

17 Mike Crang, 'Cultural Geographies of Tourism', in Alan A. Lew, C. Michael Hall, Allan M. Williams (eds), *A Companion to Tourism*, Malden, MA: Blackwell, 2004, p. 80.

18 Jean-Claude Richez, Léon Strauss, 'Un tempo nuovo per gli operai: le ferie pagate (1930–1960)', in *L'invenzione del tempo libero (1850–1960)*, edited by Alain Corbin, Bari: Laterza, 1996, especially pp. 404–5.

19 Norbert Elias, *The Civilizing Process* (1939), Oxford: Oxford University Press, 2000, p. 128, cited by Franco Moretti in *The Bourgeois: Between History and Literature*, London: Verso, 2013, p. 30.

20 Data taken from Eurostat: numbers of campsites and of overnight bookings by accommodation type can be found under the subheading of camping.

21 Susan S. Fainstein, Dennis R. Judd, 'Global Forces, Local Strategies and Urban Tourism', in Dennis R. Judd, Susan S. Fainstein (eds), *The Tourist City*, New Haven: Yale University Press, 1999, p. 2.

22 Löfgren, *On Holiday*, p. 181.

23 Data from the World Tourism Organisation.

24 flightradar24.com (accessed 25 May 2020).

3. The World's Finest Sewer

1 Cited by David L. Pike in *Subterranean Cities: The World beneath Paris and London*, 1800–1945, Ithaca, NY: Cornell University Press, 2005, p. 244.

2 Louis Veuillot, *Les odeurs de Paris*, Paris: Palmé, 1867 (available in French at gallica.bnf.fr), p. vi.

3 In Jacques-Pierre Brissot's *Théorie des lois criminelles*, cited by Michel Foucault in *Discipline and Punish: The Birth of the Prison* (1975), translated by Alan Sheridan, Vintage Books Random House, New York, 1995, pp. 111–12.

4 Ibid., p. 233.

5 Michel de Montaigne, *Essais* (1588), 3 vols., Paris: Gallimard, 1965, vol. I, chapter XXX, p. 262. English Translation by Charles Cotton, *The Essays of Michel de Montaigne* (1877), available on gutenberg. org.

6 Stephen Jay Gould, 'The Hottentot Venus', see chapter 19; *The Flamingo's Smile: Reflections in Natural History*, Norton Press, New York, 1985.

7 Nicolas Bancel, Pascal Blanchard, Sandrine Lemaire, 'Ces zoos humains de la République coloniale', *Le Monde diplomatique*, August 2000. The three authors of this article also edited a book on the topic, with Gilles Boëtsch and Éric Deroo, titled *Zoos humains: De la Vénus hottentote aux reality shows*, Paris: La Decouverte, 2002.

8 Guido Abbattista, *Umanità in mostra: Esposizioni etniche e invenzioni esotiche in Italia (1880–1940)*, Trieste: EUT (Università degli Studi di Trieste), 2013. Available to download at units.it.

9 Jeffrey A. Melton, *Mark Twain, Travel Books and Tourism: The Tide of a Great Popular Movement*, Tuscaloosa: University of Alabama Press, 2002, pp. 1–2.

10 James M. Cox, *Mark Twain: The Fate of Humor*, Princeton, NJ: Princeton University Press, 1966, p. 37.

11 Melton, *Mark Twain, Travel Books and Tourism*, p. 5 (emphases added).

12 Malcolm Bradbury, *Dangerous Pilgrimages: Transatlantic Mythologies and the Novel*, New York: Viking, 1996, p. 159 (emphasis added).

13 Bruce Michelson, 'Mark Twain the Tourist: The Form of *The Innocents Abroad*', *American Literature*, November 1977, vol. 49, no. 3, pp. 391–2.

14 Mark Twain, *Innocents Abroad*, London: Wordsworth Classics, 2010, pp. 83–4.

15 Dean MacCannell, *The Tourist: A New Theory of the Leisure Class* (1976), Berkeley, CA: University of California Press, 1999, p. 57.

16 Bernice M. Goetz, 'Jungle Haunt on Amazon Headwaters: Foaming River Led a Lone White Woman to Remote Clearings Where Primitive Indians Peered at Her in Wonder', *National Geographic*, September 1952, vol. 102.

17 Baucel et al., *Zoos humains*, pp. 423 et seq.

18 The travelling show *Body Worlds* was created by the German Gunther von Hagens, who founded the Heidelberg institute for plastination. See bodyworlds.com.

19 John Urry, *The Tourist Gaze* (1990), Sage, London, 2002.

20 John Urry, 'The Tourist Gaze "Revisited"', in *American Behavioral Scientist*, vol. 36, no. 2, November 1992, in which Urry revisits the Foucauldian theme of the perception of the crowd and of the criminal.

21 Marco d'Eramo, 'Turismo, metafora dei tempi moderni. Intervista a John Urry,' *il manifesto*, 6 December 1996.

22 Mark Neumann, 'Making the Scene: The Poetics and Performances of Displacement at the Grand Canyon', in Simon Coleman and Mike Crang (eds), *Tourism: Between Place and Performance*, New York: Berghahn, 2002, p. 39.

4. Mark Twain's TripAdvisor

1 Twain, *Innocents Abroad*, p. 71.

2 Ibid, p. 82 (emphasis added).

3 Letter to Hester Thrale, 21 September 1773, cited in Richard B. Schwartz, *Samuel Johnson and the New Science*, Madison, WI: University of Wisconsin Press, 1971, p. 49.

4 Olivier Burgelin, 'Le tourisme jugé', *Communications*, 10, 1967.

5 G. Harry Stine, 'Travel and Tourism', *Analog Science Fiction / Science Fact*, vol. 111, no. 1–2, January 1991, p. 185.

6 Daniel Boorstin, *The Image: A Guide to Pseudo-Events in America*, New York: Harper & Row, 1961, p. 106.

7 Quoted by Martin Heidegger in 'Wozu Dichter' ('What are poets for?'), in *Holzwege*, Vittorio Klostermann, Frankfurt, 1950. English translation by Albert Hofstadter, *Poetry, Language, Thought*, Harper Perennial Modern Classics, New York, 2001, pp. 110–11.

8 Hans Magnus Enzensberger, 'A Theory of Tourism', in *Einzelheiten*, Frankfurt: Suhrkamp Verlag, 1962, English translation by Gerd Gemünden and Kenn Johnson, 'A Theory of Tourism', *New German Critique*, No. 68, Spring/Summer 1996.

9 Max Horkheimer and Theodor W. Adorno, *Dialectic of Enlightenment* (1947), translated by John Cummings, London: Verso, 1997, p. 161.

10 Enzensberger, 'A Theory of Tourism', p. 131.

11 Ibid. p. 129.

12 Horkheimer and Adorno, *Dialectic of Enlightenment*, p. 111.

13 Enzensberger, 'A Theory of Tourism', p. 131.

14 Horkheimer and Adorno, *Dialectic of Enlightenment*, p. 178.

15 Boorstin, *The Image*, p. 106.

16 Roland Barthes, 'Le Guide Bleu', in *Mythologies* (1957), translated

by Richard Howard and Annette Lavers, New York: Hill and Wang, 2012.

17 Roland Barthes, 'Éléments de sémiologie', *Communications*, 1964, no. 4, p. 106.

18 MacCannell, *The Tourist*, p. 57 and p. 110.

19 Ibid., pp. 111–12.

20 John Frow, 'Tourism and the Semiotics of Nostalgia', *October*, vol. 57, 1991, p. 144.

21 Tom Vanderbilt, 'Inside the Mad, Mad World of TripAdvisor', *Outside*, 13 March 2015. See outsideonline.com.

22 Horkheimer and Adorno, *Dialectic of Enlightenment*, p. 214.

23 Enzensberger, 'A Theory of Tourism', p. 134.

24 Urry, *The Tourist Gaze*, pp. 138–40.

25 MacCannell, *The Tourist*, p. 49.

26 Jonathan Culler, 'Semiotics of Tourism', in *The American Journal of Semiotics*, vol. 1, no. 1/2, 1981. The version I have used, however, is an extended version titled 'The Semiotics of Tourism', published in *Framing the Sign, Criticism and Its Institutions,* Norman: University of Oklahoma Press, 1988, p. 5. Available online at mit.edu.

27 MacCannell, *The Tourist*, p. 155.

28 Culler, 'Semiotics of Tourism', p. 4.

29 Twain, *Innocents Abroad*, pp. 119–20.

30 Ibid. p. 352 (emphasis added).

31 Ibid., pp. 78–9 (emphasis in original).

32 John Urry, *Consuming Places,* London: Routledge, 1995, p. 138.

33 Urry, *The Tourist Gaze*, pp. 126–7.

34 Susan Sontag, *On Photography*, New York: Farrar, Straus and Giroux, 1977, p. 55.

5. Tourism à la Carte

1 Office du Tourisme et des Congrès de Paris, *Le tourisme à Paris*, Edition 2009, p. 27.

2 Data taken from choosechicago.com.

3 Condor Ferries, 'US Tourism and Travel Statistics 2020', condorferries. co.uk (last accessed 9 June 2020).

4 Paris Région, Comité régional du tourisme, pro.visitparisregion.com (last accessed on 30 January 2019).

5 Las Vegas Convention Center, lvcva.com/stats-and-facts/economic-impact/ (last accessed on 23 July 2020).

6 Guido Guerzoni, *Effetto festival. L'impatto economico dei festival di approfondimento culturale*, La Spezia: Fondazione Carispe, 2008, p. 5.

7 Ibid., pp. 18–19.

8 Emmanuel Botta, 'Lourdes, sanctuaire en quête de miracle économique', *L'Express*, 23 April 2017.

9 Krzysztof Pomian, *Des saintes reliques à l'art moderne. Venice-Chicago XIIIe-XXe siècle*, Paris: Gallimard, 2003. The quotations are taken from pp. 8 and 12–13 respectively.

10 Victor Turner and Edith Turner, *Image and Pilgrimage in Christian Culture: Anthropological Perspectives*, New York: Columbia University Press, 1978, p. 20.

11 *Historia Hierosolymitana* (a history of the Holy Land from the advent of Islam until the crusades of his own day, written in 1219), I, 82 as cited by Jonathan Sumption, *Pilgrimage: An Image of Medieval Religion*, Totowa, NJ: Bowman & Littlefield, 1975, p. 257.

12 MacCannell, *The Tourist*, pp. 42–3.

13 Turner and Turner, *Image and Pilgrimage in Christian Culture*, p. 20.

14 Ibid., p. 241.

15 factsanddetails.com (last accessed on 30 January 2019).

16 Tobias Smollett, *The Expedition of Humphrey Clinker* (1771), letter to Miss Laetitia Willis (6 April) and to Dr Lewis (23 April), online edition: gasl.org/refbib/Smollett_Humphry_Clinker.pdf.

17 'Rubeln und Roulette: Russen in Baden Baden', in *Berliner Zeitung*, 23 August 2008. The article cites notes made by Tolstoy while in Baden-Baden.

18 Patti Waldmeir, 'Shanghai Notebook: Bronchial Set Seek Blue Sky Breathing in China', *Financial Times*, 24 November 2014.

19 Patricia Marx, 'About Face: Why Is South Korea the World's Plastic Surgery Capital?', *New Yorker*, 23 March 2015.

20 Nancy Scheper-Hughes, 'The Global Traffic in Human Organs', *Current Anthropology*, vol. 41, no 2, 2000: 191–211. See also Nancy Scheper-Hughes and Loïc Wacquant (eds), *Commodifying Bodies*, Sage, London, 2002.

21 Saskia Gauthier, Julian Mausbach, Thomas Reisch and Christine Bartsch, 'Suicide Tourism: A Pilot Study of the Swiss Phenomenon', *Journal of Medical Ethics*, 2015, vol. 41, no. 8, pp. 611–17.

6. A Brief Intrusion by an Earthologist Friend

1 Cited by Eric J. Leed in *The Mind of the Traveler: From Gilgamesh to Global Tourism*, New York: Basic Books, New York, 1991.

2 Louis-Antoine de Bougainville, *A Voyage Round the World*, trans. John Reinhold Forster, Dublin: printed for J. Exshaw et al., 1772, pp. 230–1, 251, 260.

3 Denis Diderot, *Supplément au voyage de Monsieur de Bougainville* (1772), Paris: Presses Pocket, 1992, p. 85 (emphasis added).

4 My knowledge of the history of naturism comes from an essay by Francine Barche-Deloizy titled 'Le naturisme: des cures atmosphériques au tourisme durable' in *Communications*, no. 74, 2003.

5 Heinrich Heine, *Lutetia* (1854), English translation in *The Works*

of Heinrich Heine, vol. 8, London: William Heidemann, 1893, pp. 368–9.

6 Hans Magnus Enzensberger, 'A Theory of Tourism', cit., p. 126.

7 David Cassidy, *Uncertainty: The Life and Science of Werner Heisenberg*, New York: W.H. Freeman and Co., 1992.

8 Barche-Deloizy, 'Le naturisme'.

9 Fred Hirsch, *Social Limits to Growth*, Cambridge, MA: Harvard University Press, 1976, p. 167.

10 Coleman and Crang, 'Grounded Tourists, Travelling Theory', in Coleman and Crang (eds), *Tourism*, pp. 2–3.

7. The Tourist City

1 Introduction to D. MacCannell, *The Tourist*, cit., p, X.

2 Dennis R. Judd (ed.), *The Infrastructure of Play: Building the Tourist City*, Armonk, NY: M.E. Sharpe, 2003 (sponsored by the Urban Center, Levin College of Urban Affairs, Cleveland State University), p. 5.

3 Peter E. Murphy, 'Urban Tourism and Visitor Behavior', in *American Behavioral Scientist*, 36, no. 2, November 1991, pp. 200–11.

4 MacCannell, *The Tourist*, p. 43.

5 Fainstein and Gladstone, 'Evaluating Urban Tourism', in Judd and Fainstein (eds), *The Tourist City*, p. 23.

6 Stefano Picascia, Antonello Romano and Capineri Cristina, 'The airification of cities: Making sense of the impact of peer to peer short term letting on urban functions and economy', in the proceedings of the Annual Congress of the Association of European School of Planning, Lisbon, 11–14 July 2017. For world data see '105 Airbnb Statistics and Facts (2002)' at expandedramblings.com.

7 Robert Hewison, *The Heritage Industry: Britain in a Climate of Decline*, London: Methuen, 1987, p. 24.

8 Gilles Bertrand, *Histoire du carnaval de Venise, XIe–XXIe siècle*, Paris: Pygmalion, 2013, p. 15.

9 Pomian, *Des saintes reliques à l'art moderne*, p. 26.

10 Fainstein and Gladstone, 'Evaluating Urban Tourism', in Judd and Fainstein (eds), *The Tourist City*, p. 5.

11 Françoise Choay, *L'Allégorie du patrimoine*, Paris: Seuil, 1992, p. 175.

12 MacCannell, *The Tourist*, pp. 91–107.

13 Erving Goffman, *The Presentation of Self in Everyday Life*, New York: Doubleday & Company, 1959.

14 Eric Hobsbawm and Terence Ranger, *The Invention of Tradition*, Cambridge: Cambridge University Press, 1983. The story of the kilt is told in the chapter by Hugh Trevor-Roper, 'The Highland Tradition of Scotland'.

15 Richard Handler and Jocelyn Linnekin, 'Tradition, Genuine or

Spurious', in *Journal of American Folklore*, vol. 97, no. 385, 1984, p. 288.

16 Valene L. Smith (ed.), *Hosts and Guests: The Anthropology of Tourism*, Philadelphia: University of Pennsylvania Press, 1989.

17 Ibid., from the chapter by Theron Nuñez: 'Touristic Studies in Anthropological Perspective', p. 209.

18 Britton, 'Tourism, Capital and Place', p. 458.

19 Goffman, *The Presentation of Self in Everyday Life*, p. 121.

8. UNESCO's Urbicide

1 Eugène-Emmanuel Viollet-le-Duc, 'Restauration', in *Dictionnaire raisonné de l'architecture française du XIe au XVIe siècle*, 10 vol., Morel et Co., Paris 1854–1868, vol. VIII, p. 14 (emphasis added). The entry 'Restauration' can be easily found on the web, see for example: fr.wikisource.org.

2 John Ruskin, *The Seven Lamps of Architecture*, Boston: Dana Estes & Co, [1849] (no date for this edition), p. 184. The quote 'hating restoration of any kind' is from p. 139. The book can be found online at gutenberg.org.

3 Guerzoni, *Effetto festival*, p. 15.

4 See the website for the Salzburg Festival Archive at: salzburger festspiele.at.

5 Choay, *L'allégorie du patrimoine*, p. 175.

6 Viollet-le-Duc, 'Restauration', p. 32.

7 Gregory J. Ashworth and John E. Tunbridge, *The Tourist-Historic City*, London: Behalven Press, 2000, p. 28.

8 Françoise Choay, *Le patrimoine en question: Anthologie pour un combat*, Paris: Seuil, 2009, p. XL.

9 David Lowenthal, *The Heritage Crusade and the Spoils of History* (1996), London: Viking, 1997, p. 3.

10 Ashworth and Tunbridge, *The Tourist-Historic City*, pp. 24–5.

11 Eric Hobsbawm, 'Identity Politics and the Left', *New Left Review*, no. 217, May–June 1996, p. 38.

12 Marco d'Eramo, 'Localismo e globalizzazione', in *Iter* (journal published by the Italian *Enciclopedia Treccani*), no. 10, January–March 2001.

13 Lowenthal, *The Heritage Crusade and the Spoils of History*, pp. IX–X.

14 Hewison, *The Heritage Industry*, p. 31.

15 'Lo Zibibbo di Pantelleria patrimonio dell'Unesco', *La Repubblica*, 26 November 2014.

16 Choay, *Le patrimoine en question*, p. XLI (emphasis in original).

17 John Langshaw Austin, *How to Do Things with Words*, Oxtord: Oxford Clarendon Press, 1962.

18 Lowenthal, *The Heritage Crusade and the Spoils of History*, pp. 26–7.

19 Choay, *Le patrimoine en question*, p. LXI.
20 Jean de La Bruyère, 'Discours sur Théphraste', in *Charactères* (1688), Paris: Garnier Flammarion, 1965, p. 34.
21 Giacomo Leopardi, *Zibaldone: The Notebooks of Leopardi*, ed. Michael Caesar and Franco D'Intino, London: Penguin, 2013, p. 1896.
22 An English translation of the *Futurist Manifesto*, taken from the appendix to James Bysse Joll's *Three Intellectuals in Politics*, London: Weidenfeld & Nicolson, 1960, can be found at sites.google.com.
23 Lowenthal, *The Heritage Crusade and the Spoils of History*, p. 155; Viollet-le-Duc, *Restauration*, p. 31.
24 Ashworth and Tunbridge, *The Tourist-Historic City*, pp. 30–1. Or *The Tourist-History City: Retrospect and Prospect of Managing the Heritage City*, Oxford: Pergamon, 2000, pp. 30–1.

9. Lijiang: Inventing Authenticity

1   Choay, *Le patrimoine en question*, p. XLI.
2   Fan Li, *Tourism and urban conservation: Heritage management in the old town of Lijiang, China, 1994–2004, and future directions*, Master's dissertation presented in 2004 to the faculty of Architecture, Civil Engineering and Urban Planning at the Brandenburg University of Technology Cottbus-Senftenberg, p. 34.
3   Geoffrey Read and Katrinka Ebbe, 'Post-Earthquake Reconstruction and Urban Heritage Conservation in Lijiang', in Ismail Serageldin, Ephim Shluger and Joan Martin-Brown (eds), *Historic Cities and Sacred Sites: Cultural Roots for Urban Futures*, Washington: World Bank, 2000, pp. 105 and 106.
4   Photos of now-demolished authentic traditional houses and new faux-traditional houses under construction can be found on p. 114 of Fan Li's dissertation, *Tourism and urban conservation*.
5   Read and Ebbe, 'Post-Earthquake Reconstruction and Urban Heritage Conservation in Lijiang', pp. 110 and 111.
6   Xiaobo Su and Peggy Teo, *The Politics of Heritage Tourism in China: A View from Lijiang*, London and New York: Routledge, 2011, p. 82.
7   Data for 1990 to 2002 taken from Fan Li, *Tourism and urban conservation*, p. 35; data for 2007 from Xiaobo Su, P. Teo, *The Politics of Heritage Tourism in China*, p. 96; for 2009 from Yujie Zhu, 'When the Global Meets the Local in Tourism-Cultural Performances in Lijiang as Case Studies', *Journal of China Tourism Research*, 2012, vol. 8, no. 3, p. 307; for 2012 and 2013 from the website China Knowledge: chinaknowledge.com. Consulted 12 March 2015. A different source cited 16 million tourists in 2015.
8   Xiabo Su, 'Tourism, Migration and the Politics of Built Heritage in Lijiang China', in Tami Blumenfield and Helaine Silverman (eds),

Cultural Heritage Politics in China, New York: Springer Science, 2013, p. 108.

9 UNESCO, 'WHC-ICOMOS Reactive Monitoring Mission to the Old Town of Lijiang (China), 10–19 January 2008'. The report was presented in Paris on 19 May 2008 and can be viewed online at whc. unesco.org. Quotes are from pp. 7, 13–14 and 18.

10 Denis Diderot and Jean Baptiste Le Rond d'Alembert, *Encyclopédie, ou Dictionnaire raisonné des sciences, des arts et des métiers* (1751–1772), Stuttgart and Bad Cannstadt: Friedrich Frommann Verlag, 1966, vol. 13, p. 433.

11 Denis Diderot, *Salons,* vol. 2, J.L.J. Brière Libraire, rue Saint-André-des-Arts n° 68, Paris, 1821, pp. 367–8 (emphasis added).

12 Katalin Bartha-Kovács, 'L'Écriture des Ruines au XVIII Siècle: Vestige et Vertige', in *Verbum Analecta Neolatina,* 2010, vol. XII, issue 2, p. 278.

13 Ibid., p. 371.

14 Ibid., p. 386.

15 Carlo Carena, 'La cultura delle rovine', in *Rivista di estetica,* vol. 8, 1981, monographic edition dedicated to 'the aesthetics and rhetoric of ruins', p. 156.

16 In the fourth book (titled *Harmonies de la religion chrétienne avec les scènes de la nature et les passions du coeur humain*) of the third part ('Beaux arts et littérature') of his *Génie du christianisme,* Chateaubriand dedicated three whole chapters to ruins. The passage quoted here is from the first of the three, titled 'Des ruines en général'. The French text is available on fr.wikisource, English translation *The Genius of Christianity: The Spirit and Beauty of the Christian Religion,* Baltimore, MD: Murphy, Baltimore, 1871, available on openlibrary. org.

17 From the poem 'Den Vereinigten Staaten', in *Goethes Werke,* book 1, Munich: Verlag C.H. Beck, 1981 (emphasis added).

18 William Cronon, *Nature's Metropolis: Chicago and the Great West,* New York: Norton & Co., 1991, p. 43.

19 Marco Bascetta, 'L'esteta e il pecoraio', *il manifesto,* 30 August 1989, p. 10.

20 Diderot, *Salons,* p. 372 (emphasis added).

21 See Arthur Waldron, *The Great Wall of China: From History to Myth,* Cambridge: Cambridge University Press, 1990.

10. Relearning from Las Vegas

1 MacCannell, *The Tourist,* p. 196.

2 Maxine Feifer, *Going Places: The Ways of the Tourist from Imperial Rome to the Present Day,* London: MacMillan, 1985, p. 271.

3 Aside from Bruce Michelson's 'Mark Twain the Tourist: The Form

of *The Innocents Abroad*', from *American Literature*, November 1977, there is also, for instance, Johanna Dybiec, 'Mark Twain's *The Innocents Abroad* as a Post-Tourist Travelogue', in *Metamorphoses of Travel Writing: Across Theories, Genres, Centuries and Literary Traditions*, Grzegorz Moroz and Jolanta Sztachelska (eds), Newcastle upon Tyne: Cambridge Scholars, 2010.

4 Graham Huggan, *The Postcolonial Exotic: Marketing the Margins*, New York: Routledge, New York, 2001, p. 200.

5 Robert Parker, 'Las Vegas Casino Gambling and Local Culture', in Judd and Fainstein (eds), *The Tourist City*, pp. 109–10.

6 Robert Venturi, Denise Scott Brown and Steven Izenour, *Learning From Las Vegas: The Forgotten Symbolism of Architectural Form*, Cambridge, MA: MIT Press, 1977.

7 Ibid., p. 134 and image no. 118 on p. 143.

8 Ibid., p. 135.

9 Ibid., p. 117.

10 Ibid., p. 105.

11 'La post-città', interview with Robert Venturi and Denise Scott Brown by Francesco Erbani, *La Repubblica*, 2 February 2011.

12 Venturi, Scott Brown, and Izenour, *Learning from Las Vegas*, p. 52.

13 The overall figures are taken from www.lvca.com on the page titled 'Economic Impacts of Southern Nevada's Tourism Industry and Convention Sector', April 2018. While the figures for the Strip are processed by the Center for Gaming Research at the University of Nevada at Las Vegas: gaming.unlv.edu. Both sites visited 28 November 2018.

14 The source for this is by Abby Messick, 'Top 10 casinos in the US by number of employees', *Casino City Times*, 14 April 2017, casinocity times.com, last accessed 18 November 2018.

15 Sabrina Tavernise, 'How Las Vegas Became Ground Zero for the American Job Crisis', *New York Times*, 26 April 2020.

16 Richard N. Velotta, '10 Las Vegas Hotels Set to Host Tourists Sick With Coronavirus', *Las Vegas Review Journal*, 26 May 2020.

17 lakemead.water-data.com, last accessed 28 January 2019.

18 Eric Holthaus, 'Lake Mead before and after the Epic Drought: A New Study Shows the Colorado River Basin Is Losing Water at a "Shocking" Rate', *Slate*, 25 July 2014, slate.com.

11. The Zoning of the Soul

1 Citations from Marina Moskowitz, 'Zoning the Industrial City: Planners, Commissioners, and Boosters in the 1920s', *Business and Economic History*, vol. XXVII, no. 2, winter 1998, p. 307.

2 Le Corbusier, *The Athens Charter* (1957), translated by Anthony Eardley, New York: Grossman Publishers, 1973, p. 57.

3   'Formulaire pour un urbanisme nouveau'. This text, written by Ivan Chtcheglov in 1953 and then published in the first *Internationale situationniste* bulletin in 1958 under the pseudonym Gilles Ivain, was republished in *Internationale situationniste (1958–1969)*, Paris: Fayard, 1997, pp. 16–17.

4   Pierre Bourdieu, 'Effets de lieu' in Pierre Bourdieu et al., *La Misère du monde*, collective research project directed by Pierre Bourdieu, Paris: Seuil, 1993, p. 163. The 2018 English translation by Loïc Wacquant 'Social Space and the Genesis of Appropriated Physical Space', *International Journal of Urban and Regional Research*, vol. 2, issue 1, January 2018, can be found at onlinelibrary.wiley.com.

5   I have adopted these citations from Xavier de Jarcy, *Le Corbusier, un fascisme français*, Albin Michel, Paris, 2015, pp. 86, 175, 19 and 79; the citations from Le Corbusier are taken, respectively, from *La ville radieuse* (1937), *Urbanisme* (1924), *Quand les cathédrales étaient blanches* (1935), 'L'esthétique mecanique' (in *L'Esprit nouveau*, no. 1, October, 1920) and *L'art décoratif d'aujourd'hui* (1925).

6   Kenneth T. Jackson, *The Crabgrass Frontier: The Suburbanization of the United States*, Oxford: Oxford University Press, 1985, p. 242.

7   Bourdieu, 'Effets de lieu', p. 167.

8   Pierre Bourdieu, *Masculine Domination* (1998), translated by Richard Nice, Palo Alto, CA: Stanford University Press, 2002, p. 35.

9   Guy Debord, *The Society of the Spectacle* (1967), translated by Donald Nicholson-Smith, Zone Books, New York, 1995, paragraph 172.

10 Robert E. Park, 'The City: Suggestions for Investigation of Human Behavior in the Urban Environment', in Robert E. Park, Ernest W. Burgess and Roderick D. McKenzie, *The City*, Chicago: University of Chicago Press, (1925) 1967, p. 40.

11 Arthur Rimbaud, 'Les poètes de sept ans', in *Oeuvres*, Paris: Garnier, Paris, 1979, pp. 95–7.

12 Park, 'The City', p. 40.

13 Georg Simmel, *Die Großstädte und das Geistesleben* (1903), available in English translation, *The Metropolis and the Mental Life*, at hu-berlin.de, (unpaginated), adapted by D. Weinstein from Kurt Wolff (trans.), *The Sociology of Georg Simmel*, New York: Free Press, 1950, pp. 409–24.

14 Max Weber, *Economy and Society: An Outline of Interpretive Sociology*, ed. Guenther Roth and Claus Wittich, translated by Ephraim Fischoff et al., Berkeley: University of California Press, 1978, vol. 2, p. 1239.

15 Niccolò Machiavelli, *The Prince* (1513), translated by W. K. Marriott, J.M. Dent & Sons, Ltd., London, 1908, p. 8.

16 Debord, *The Society of the Spectacle*, paragraph 174.

17 Ernst Cassirer, 'Das Problem Jean-Jacques Rousseau', in *Archiv für Geschichte der Philosophie*, XLI, 1932, pp. 177–213.

18 Henri Lefebvre, *Critique de la vie quotidienne*, Paris: L'Arche, 1958.
19 Debord, *The Society of the Spectacle*, paragraph 172.
20 Henri Lefebvre, 'The Right to the City' (1967), translated by Eleonore Kofman and Elizabeth Lebas in *Writings on Cities*, London: Blackwell, 1996, pp. 149, 148.

12. Long Live Alienation! Or, Peeling the Hegelian Onion

1 Jonathan Culler, 'Semiotics of Tourism', in *American Journal of Semiotics*, vol. 1, no. 1/2, 1981 pp. 156–7.
2 Jean-Paul Sartre, *Being and Nothingness: An Essay on Phenomenological Ontology*, translated by Hazel E. Barnes, London and New York: Routledge, 2003, p. 82.
3 Britton, 'Tourism, Capital and Place', pp. 452–3.
4 Karl Marx, *Das Kapital. Kritik der politischen Ökonomie* (1867); English translation by Eden and Cedar Paul, *Capital*, London: J. M. Dent & Sons, 1930; vol. 1, chapter 1, 'Section 4: The Fetishism of Commodities and the Secret Thereof', text from marxists.org.
5 David Lowenthal, *The Heritage Crusade and the Spoils of History* (1996), London: Viking, 1997, p. 101.
6 Stuart Plattner, 'A Most Ingenious Paradox: The Market for Contemporary Fine Art', in *American Anthropologist*, vol. 100, no. 2, 1998, p. 482.
7 Deloitte ArtTactic, *Art and Finance Report 2014*, deloitte.com, p. 29.
8 Ibid., p. 20.
9 Debord, *The Society of the Spectacle*, paragraph 168.
10 Coleman and Crang, *Tourism*, p. 3.
11 Ibid., pp. 2–3.
12 G.W.F. Hegel, *Phenomenology of Spirit* (1807), translated by Terry Pinkard, Cambridge: Cambridge University Press, 2018, p. 128.
13 Ibid., pp. 131–2.
14 Frow, 'Tourism and the Semiotics of Nostalgia', pp. 136, 135.
15 Ibid., p. 136.
16 Jean-Jacques Rousseau, *Of the Social Contract and Other Political Writings*, ed. Christopher Bertram, translated by Quintin Hoare, London: Penguin, 2012, pp. 19–20.
17 Max Hortheimer and Theodor Adorno, *Dialectic of Enlightenment*, translated by Edmund Jephcott, Stanford: Stanford University Press, 2002, p. 106.
18 Paul Ricoeur, the entry "Aliénation" in *Encyclopaedia Universalis*, vol. 1, Paris 1969.
19 Debord, *Society of the Spectacle*, paragraph 161.
20 Karl Marx, Friedrich Engels, *Die Deutsche Ideologie* (1846); *The German Ideology*, available on marxists.org.

13. Yearning for the Other

1 Oliver Sacks, 'An Anthropologist on Mars', *New Yorker*, 27 December 1993; republished in Sacks, *An Anthropologist on Mars: Seven Paradoxical Tales*, Knopf, New York, 1995, p. 295.
2 Ian Hacking, 'Humans, Aliens & Autism', *Daedalus*, vol. 138, no. 3, summer 2009, p. 57.
3 R. Barthes, 'Martiens' in *Mythologies*, cit., p. 44.
4 Fredric Brown, *Sentry* (1954), available online at lupinworks.com. Originally published in *Focus*, Walter R. Bremner (ed.), Thomas Nelson & Sons, Toronto, 1970, p. 177.
5 Stanislaw Lem, *Solaris* (1961), translated by Joanna Kilmartin and Steve Cox, Faber & Faber, London, 1971.
6 Fred Hoyle, *The Black Cloud*, Harper, New York, 1957.
7 Helene Cooper, Ralph Blumenthal, and Leslie Kean, '"Wow, What Is That?" Navy Pilots Report Unexplained Flying Objects', *New York Times*, 26 May 2019.
8 Cesare Lombroso, 'I nuovi orizzonti della psichiatria', in *Rivista d'Italia*, January, 1904, VII, vol. 1, no. 1, p. 17, reprinted in Cesare Lombroso, *Delitto, genio, follia: Scritti scelti*, Bollati Boringhieri, Turin, 1995, p. 315.
9 Ian Hacking, 'On Sympathy: With Other Creatures', in *Tijdschrift voor Filosofie*, 2001, vol. 63, citations from pp. 700, 714 and 715.
10 Wiktor Stoczkowski, *Des hommes, des dieux et des extraterrestres. Ethnologie d'une croyance moderne*, Flammarion, Paris, 1999.
11 Translated into English by Rollo Myers as *The Morning of the Magicians*, Avon, New York 1968.
12 W. Stoczkowski, *Des hommes, des dieux et des extraterrestres*, p. 67.
13 Erich von Däniken, *Erinnerungen an die Zukunft*, Econ Verlag, Düsseldorf-Wien, 1968.

14. The World at Our Disposal

1 Ian Hacking, *Mad Travellers: Reflections on the Reality of Transient Mental Illnesses*, Free Association, London, 1999, p. 7.
2 Henry Meige, *Études sur certains névropathes voyageurs: le juif-errant à la Salpêtrière* (1893), reprinted as *Le Juif-Errant à la Salpêtrière*, Editions du Nouvel Objet, Paris, 1993.
3 Britton, 'Tourism, Capital, and Place', p. 453.
4 Henri Lefebvre, *La vie quotidienne dans le monde moderne*, Gallimard, Paris 1968. These words are the title of the second chapter, pp. 133–207.
5 Amitav Ghosh, *The Imam and the Indian* (1986), in *Incendiary Circumstances: A Chronicle of the Turmoil of Our Times*, Houghton Mifflin Company, New York, 2005, pp. 291–2.

6 Walker Percy, *The Message in the Bottle: How Queer Man Is, How Queer Language Is, and What One Has to Do With the Other* (Farrar Strauss, New York, 1975), p. 53, cited by J. Culler, 'Semiotic of Tourism', in *The American Journal of Semiotics*, vol, 1, nos. 1/2, 1981.

7 Simon Coleman, Mike Grang, 'Grounded Tourists, Travelling Theory', in Simon Coleman, Mike Crang (eds), *Tourism: Between Place and Performance*, Berghahn, New York, 2002, p. 9.

8 Walter Benjamin, *Das Passagenwerk*, Suhrkamp, Frankfurt am Main 1982; *The Arcades Project*, Cambridge, MA: Belknap Press, 1999, pp. 446 and 442.

9 Giacomo Leopardi, *Discorso sopra lo stato presente dei costumi degl'italiani* (1824/1826), Rome: Delotti, 1988, p. 7.

10 Ibid.

11 Here I pick up on the theme I expounded at greater depth in *Lo sciamano in elicottero. Per una storia del presente*, Milan: Feltrinelli, 1999. See the chapter 'A Parigi scroscia il Mare del Nord', pp. 153–71.

12 Heine, *Lutetia*, pp. 368–9.

13 Henry T. Tuckerman, 'Philosophy of Travel', in *The United States Democratic Review*, no. 41, 1844, p. 527.

14 Karl Marx, *Grundrisse. Foundations of the Critique of Political Economy*, London: Penguin, 1973, p. 539.

15 Benedict Anderson uses the term 'Early Globalization' in *Under Three Flags: Anarchism and the Anti-Colonial Imagination*, London and New York: Verso, 2005, p. 3.

16 Armand Mattelart, *L'invention de la communication*, Paris: La Découverte, (1994) 2011, p. 189.

17 Anderson, *Under Three Flags*, p. 3.

18 '...---... .-. .. .--. (SOS, RIP)', *Economist*, 21 January 1999.

19 H.T. Tuckerman, 'Philosophy of Travel', cit., p. 527 (emphasis added).

20 Henry T. Tuckerman, 'Going Abroad', in *Putnam's Monthly Magazine*, vol. 11, May 1868, pp. 530–1.

21 Siegfried Kracauer, 'Travel and Dance' in *The Mass Ornament, Weimar Essays*, Harvard University Press, Cambridge, MA, 1995, p. 73.

22 Voltaire, *De l'horrible danger de la lecture* (1765), Folio, Paris, 2015. This pamphlet is little more than a page long. The English version, 'On the Horrible Danger of Reading' is available online at openedition.org.

23 '$11 Billion Self-Improvement Market Is Growing, But Has Its Critics', *Webwire*, 15 October 2019.

15. Life's Menu

1 OECD, *Food and the Tourism Experience*, the OECD-Korea Workshop, 2012, p. 9.

2   Food as an obstacle is examined in particular by Erik Cohen and Nir Avieli in 'Tourism: Attraction and Impediment', in *Annals of Tourism Research*, 2004, vol. 31, no. 4, pp. 755–78, in which the authors use the notions of 'neophobia' or 'neophilia' regarding foreign food.

3   First used by John Honigmann in 1948, with reference to the food-related customs of the Attawapiskat First Nation in Canada: John J. Honigmann's book: *Foodways in a Muskeg Community: An Anthropological Report on the Attawapiskat Indians*, Northern Co-ordination and Research Centre, Department of Northern Affairs and National Resources, Ottawa, Canada, 1961.

4   Lucy M. Long, 'A Folkloristic Perspective on Eating and Otherness', in *Culinary Tourism*, edited by Lucy M. Long, University Press of Kentucky, Lexington, KY, 2003, pp. 20–1.

5   Julia Csergo, 'La gastronomie dans les guides de voyage: de la richesse industrielle au patrimoine culturel, France XIXe–début XXe siècle', *In Situ: Revue des patrimoines*, 15, 2011 (pp. 3–12, quote is from p. 4), available online at: openedition.org and insitu.revues.org. Consulted 14 June 2020.

6   Jean-Anthelme Brillat-Savarin, *Physiologie du gout, ou méditations de gastronomie transcendante* (1825). This is the fourth of twenty aphorisms which the author sets before his text, and it also appears on the cover of the 1842 edition (Librairie Charpentier, Paris). Text is available in English at gutenberg.org.

7   Pierre Bourdieu. *Distinction: A Social Critique of the Judgement of Taste,* Harvard University Press, Cambridge, MA, 1984, p. 79.

8   Jack Goody, *Cooking, Cuisine and Class: A Study in Comparative Sociology*, Cambridge University Press, Cambridge, 1982, p. 108.

9   Gaëlle van Ingelgem, 'Voyage en terre inconnue: Le tourisme culinaire comme objet de distinction sociale', article presented at the University of Barcelona as part of the 2013 'European Food History and Culture' programme and communicated personally to the author. The French version of this article can be found at tenzo.fr.

10 The caterpillars in question are of the *Gonimbrasia belina* moths and called mopane worms (since they live on the mopane tree).

11 This and other insect ingredients are listed by Jeremy MacClancy in *Consuming Culture: Why You Eat What You Eat*, Chapmans, London, 1992, p. 38.

12 David Bell and Gill Valentine, *Consuming Geographies: We Are What We Eat*, Routledge, London, 1997, p. 18.

13 Howard Lyons and Liz Sharples, 'Beer Festivals: A Case Study Approach' in Michael Hall and Liz Sharples (eds) *Food and Wine Festivals and Events Around the World: Development, Management and Markets*, Elsevier, Oxford, 2008, p. 174.

14 Ibid., pp. 175–7.

15 M. Hall and L. Sharples (eds), *Food and Wine Festivals and Events Around the World. Development*, 'Introduction', p. 13.

16 bell hooks, 'Eating the Other', in *Black Looks: Race and Representation*, South End Press, Boston 1992, p. 21, my italics.

17 Salla Tuori, 'Cooking Nation: Gender Equality and Multiculturalism as Nation-Building Discourses', *European Journal of Women's Studies*, February 2007, vol. 14, no. 1, (pp. 21–35), p. 25.

18 Ibid., p. 27.

19 Yasmin Alibhai-Brown, *Imagining the New Britain*, Routledge, New York, 2001, p. 9.

20 Angela Y. Davis, 'Gender, Class and Multiculturalism', in Avery F. Gordon and Christopher Newfield (eds), *Mapping Multiculturalism*, University of Minnesota Press, Minneapolis, 1996, p. 45.

21 Cited in Christian Joppke and Steven Lukes (eds), *Multicultural Questions*, Oxford University Press, Oxford, 1999, p. 8.

22 Amartya Sen, 'The Uses and Abuses of Multiculturalism: Chili and Liberty', in *New Republic*, 27 February 2006.

23 Salman Rushdie, *Imaginary Homelands: Essays and Criticism 1981–1991*, London: Granta Books, 1991, p. 394.

24 Ibid.

25 On this, see Amartya Sen's fine article in the 22 August 2006 *Financial Times*, 'Multiculturalism: an unfolding tragedy of two confusions'.

26 Brent L. Pickett, 'Multiculturalism, Liberalism and Philosophy', in *Polity*, January 2006, vol. 38, no. 1, p. 142.

27 Katha Pollitt, 'Whose Culture?', in Susan Moller Okin with respondents (eds Joshua Cohen, Matthew Howard and Martha C. Nussbaum), *Is Multiculturalism Bad for Women?*, Princeton University Press, Princeton, New Jersey, 1999, pp. 27–30.

28 B.L. Pickett, *Multiculturalism, Liberalism and Philosophy*, cit., pp. 143–4.

29 Slavoj Žižek, 'Multiculturalism, or the Cultural Logic of Multinational Capitalism', *New Left Review*, September–October 1997, no. 225, p. 44.

30 Martin Hollis, 'Is Universalism Ethnocentric?', in C. Joppke, S. Lukes (eds), *Multicultural Questions*, cit., p. 36.

16. Maybe One Day

1 Marco d'Eramo, *Il maiale e il grattacielo. Per una storia del nostro futuro*, Milan: Feltrinelli, (1995) 2009, translated by Graeme Thompson, *The Pig and the Skyscraper, Chicago: A History of Our Future*, London: Verso, 2002, p. 104.

2 This disciplinary power is the subject of Foucault's *Discipline and Punish*, but the formulation I am giving of it here is taken from the course at the Collège de France in the 1971–2 academic year, such as it is reflected in my own notes rather than from the official version.

3 I cannot recommend this underestimated classic of political thought

enough: Albert O. Hirschman, *Exit, Voice, and Loyalty: Responses to Decline in Firms, Organizations, and States*, Cambridge, MA: Harvard University Press, Cambridge, 1970.

4 Author interview with Kenneth Jackson, '*Il cuore metropolitano dell'America*' ('*The Metropolitan Heart of America*'), *il manifesto*, 31 January 2002.

5 Robert Castel, *From Manual Workers to Wage Labourers: Transformation of the Social Question*, translated by Richard Boyd, New Brunswick, NJ: Transaction Publishers, 2003, pp. 351–2.

6 Ibid., pp. 11–12.

7 André Gorz, *Les chemins du paradis: L'agonie du capital*, Paris: Éditions Galilée, Paris, 1983.

8 D'Eramo, *Lo sciamano in elicottero*, p. 215.

Postscript

1 Claude Lévi-Strauss, *Tristes tropiques*, Paris: Plon, 1955, pp. 44–5.

Bibliography

Abbattista, Guido, *Umanità in mostra: Esposizioni etniche e invenzioni esotiche in Italia (1880–1940)*, Trieste: EUT (Università Degli Studi di Trieste), 2013, available at units.it.

Adams, Douglas, *The Hitchhiker's Guide to the Galaxy*, London: Picador, 1979.

Adler, Judith, 'Origins of Sightseeing', *Annals of Tourism Research*, vol. 16, no. 1, 1989.

Alfieri, Vittorio, *Vita* (1803), English translation, *Memoirs of the Life and Writings of Vittorio Alfieri; written by himself. Translated from the Italian*, London: Henry Colburn, 1810.

Alibhai-Brown, Yasmin, *Imagining the New Britain*, New York: Routledge, 2001.

Anderson, Benedict, *Under Three Flags: Anarchism and the Anti-Colonial Imagination*, London and New York: Verso, 2005.

Appadurai, Arjun, 'On Culinary Authenticity' (letter), *Anthropology Today*, vol. 2, no. 4, 1986.

——, 'How to Make a National Cuisine: Cookbooks in Contemporary India', *Comparative Studies in Society and History*, vol. 30, no. 1, January 1988.

Aristotle, *Politics*, translated by Carnes Lord, Chicago: University of Chicago Press, 2013.

Ashworth, Gregory J., John E. Tunbridge, *The Tourist-Historic City*, London: Belhaven Press, 2000.

Austin, John Langshaw, *How to Do Things With Words*, Oxford: Oxford Clarendon Press, 1962.

Bacon, Francis, Lord Verulam Viscount St Albans, 'Of Travel', in *The Essays or Counsels, Civil and Moral* (1625), London: J. M. Dent & Sons Ltd, (1907) 1968, available at gutenberg.org.

Bancel, Nicolas, Pascal Blanchard, Gilles Boëtsch, Éric Deroo, Sandrine Lemaire, *Zoos humains: De la Vénus hottentotte aux reality shows*, Paris: La Decouverte, 2002.

Barche-Deloizy, Francine, 'Le naturisme: des cures atmosphériques au tourisme durable', *Communications*, no. 74, 2003.

Bartha-Kovács, Katalin, 'L'Écriture des Ruines au XVIII Siècle: Vestige et Vertige', *Verbum Analecta Neolatina*, vol. 12, no. 2, 2010.

Barthes, Roland, 'Martiens' and 'Le Guide Bleu', *Mythologies* (1957), English translation by Richard Howard and Annette Lavers, *Mythologies*, New York: Hill and Wang, 2012.

——, 'Éléments de sémiologie', *Communications*, no. 4, 1964.

Bell, David, Gill Valentine, *Consuming Geographies: We Are What We Eat*, London: Routledge, 1997.

Benjamin, Walter, *Das Kunstwerk im Zeitalter seiner technischen Reproduzierarbeit* (1936), English translation by J. A. Underwood, *The Work of Art in the Age of Mechanical Reproduction*, London: Penguin, 2008.

——, *Das Passagenwerk*, Frankfurt am Main: Suhrkamp, 1982, English translation by Howard Eiland and Kevin McLaughlin, *The Arcades Project*, Cambridge, MA: Belknap Press, 1999.

Bertrand, Gilles, *Histoire du carnaval de Venise, XIe-XXIe siècle*, Paris: Pygmalion, 2013.

Boorstin, Daniel, *The Image: A Guide to Pseudo-Events in America*, New York: Harper & Row, 1961.

de Bougainville, Louis-Antoine, *Voyage autour du monde par la frégate Boudeuse et la flûte l'Étoile; en 1766, 1767, 1768 et 1769* (1771), English translation by John Dunmore *The Pacific Journal of Louis-Antoine de Bougainville 1767–1768*, London: Hakluyt Society, 2002.

Bourdieu, Pierre, *La distinction: Critique sociale du jugement* (1979), English translation by Richard Nice, *Distinction: A Social Critique of the Judgment of Taste*, Cambridge, MA: Harvard University Press: 1984.

——, 'Effets de lieu', in Pierre Bourdieu et al., *La Misère du monde* (1993), collective research project directed by Pierre Bourdieu, English translation by Loïc Wacquant, 'Social Space and the Genesis of the Appropriated Physical Space', *International Journal of Urban Research*, vol. 2, no. 1, January 2018.

——, *La domination masculine* (1998), English translation by Richard Nice, *Masculine Domination*, Palo Alto, California: Stanford University Press, 2002.

Bradbury, Malcolm, *Dangerous Pilgrimages: Transatlantic Mythologies and the Novel*, New York: Viking, 1996.

Brendon, Piers, *Thomas Cook: 150 Years of Popular Tourism*, London: Secker and Warburg, 1991.

Brillat-Savarin, Jean-Anthelme, *Physiologie du goût, ou méditations de gastronomie transcendante* (1825), Paris: Charpentier Libraire éditeur, 1842. Text available in English at gutenberg.org.

Britton, Stephen, 'Tourism, Capital and Place: Towards a Critical Geography of Tourism', *Environment and Planning D: Society and Space*, vol. 9, no. 4, 1991.

Brown, Fredric, 'Sentry' (1954), available at lupinworks.com. Originally published in *Focus*, Walter R. Bremner (ed.), Toronto: Thomas Nelson & Sons, 1970.

Burgelin, Olivier, 'Le tourisme jugé', *Communications*, no. 10, 1967.

Buzard, James, *The Beaten Track: European Tourism, Literature, and the Ways to 'Culture' (1800–1918)*, Oxford: Clarendon Press, 1993.

Carena, Carlo, 'La cultura delle rovine', *Rivista di estetica*, vol. 8, 1981, monographic issue on 'aesthetics and rhetoric of ruins'.

Cassidy, David, *Uncertainty: The Life and Science of Werner Heisenberg*, New York: W.H. Freeman and Co., 1992.

Cassirer, Ernst, 'Das Problem Jean-Jacques Rousseau', *Archiv für Geschichte der Philosophie*, vol. 41, no. 3, 1932, English translation by Peter Gay, *The Question of Jean-Jacques Rousseau*, New York: Columbia University Press, 1954.

Castel, Robert, *Les métamorphoses de la question sociale: Une cronique du salariat* (1995), English translation by Richard Boyd, *From Manual Workers to Wage Labourers: Transformation of the Social Question*, New Brunswick, New Jersey: Transaction Publishers, 2002.

de Chateaubriand, François-René, *Génie du christianisme* (1802), French text available at fr.wikisource.org. The English translation, *The Genius of Christianity: The Spirit and Beauty of the Christian Religion*, Baltimore, Maryland: John Murphy & Co., 1871, is available at open library.org.

Choay, Françoise, *L'allégorie du patrimoine*, Paris: Seuil, 1992.

———, *Le patrimoine en question: Anthologie pour un combat*, Paris: Seuil, 2009.

Cohen, Erik e Nir Avieli, 'Food in Tourism: Attraction and Impediment', in *Annals of Tourism Research*, vol. 31, no. 4, 2004, pp. 755–778.

Coleman, Simon, Mike Crang, 'Grounded Tourists, Travelling Theory', in Simon Coleman, Mike Crang (eds), *Tourism: Between Place and Performance*, New York: Berghahn, 2002.

Cox, James M., *Mark Twain: The Fate of Humor*, Princeton, New Jersey: Princeton University Press, 1966.

Crang, Mike, 'Cultural Geographies of Tourism', in Alan A. Lew, C. Michael Halland, Allan M. Williams (eds), *A Companion to Tourism*, Malden, Massachusetts: Blackwell, 2004.

Cronon, William, *Nature's Metropolis: Chicago and the Great West*, New York: Norton & Co., 1991.

Csergo, Julia, 'La gastronomie dans les guides de voyage: de la richesse industrielle au patrimoine culturel, France XIXe-début XXe siècle', *In Situ: Revue des patrimoines*, no. 15, 2011, available at openedition.org and instu.revues.org.

Culler, Jonathan, 'The Semiotics of Tourism', *The American Journal of Semiotics*, vol. 1, no. 1/2, 1981. An enlarged version, 'The Semiotics of Tourism', in *Framing the Sign, Criticism and Its Institutions*, Norman, Oklahoma: University of Oklahoma Press, 1988, available at mit.edu.

von Däniken, Erich, *Erinnerungen an die Zukunft*, Düsseldorf-Wienn: Econ Verlag, 1968.

Davis, Angela Y., 'Gender, Class and Multiculturalism', in Avery F. Gordon and Christopher Newfield (eds), *Mapping Multiculturalism*, Minneapolis: University of Minnesota Press, 1996.

Debord, Guy, *La société du spectacle* (1967), English translation by Donald Nicholson-Smith, *The Society of the Spectacle*, New York: Zone Books, 1995.

Deloitte ArtTactic, *Art & Finance Report 2014*, at deloitte.com.

d'Eramo, Marco, *Il maiale e il grattacielo: Per una storia del nostro futuro* (1995), English translation by Graeme Thompson, *The Pig and the Skyscraper. Chicago: A History of Our Furure*, London: Verso, 2002.

———, *Lo sciamano in elicottero: Per una storia del presente*, Milan: Feltrinelli, 1999.

———, 'Localismo e globalizzazione', *Iter* (journal published by the Italian Enciclopedia Treccani), no. 10, January–March 2001.

———, *Via dal vento: Viaggio nel profondo sud degli Stati Uniti*, Rome: manifestolibri, 2004.

Diderot, Denis, *Supplément au voyage de Monsieur de Bougainville* (1772), English translation by Wilfrid Jackson, *A Supplement to Bougainville's Voyage* in *Rameau's Nephew, and Other Works*, London: Chapman & Hall, 1926.

———, *Salons*, vol. 2, Paris: J. L. J. Brière Libraire, 1821.

Diderot, Denis, Jean Baptiste Le Rond d'Alembert (eds), *Encyclopédie, ou Dictionnaire raisonné des sciences, des arts et des métiers (1751–1772)*, Stuttgart & Bad Cannstadt: Friedrich Frommann Verlag, 1966, available at fr.wikisource or gallica.bnf.fr of the Bibliothèque Nationale de France.

Dybiec, Johanna, 'Mark Twain's *The Innocents Abroad* as a Post-Tourist Travelogue', in *Metamorphoses of Travel Writing: Across Theories, Genres, Centuries and Literary Traditions*, Grzegorz Moroz, Jolanta Sztachelska (eds), Newcastle upon Tyne: Cambridge Scholars, 2010.

Elias, Norbert, *The Civilizing Process* (1939), Oxford: Oxford University Press, 2000.

Enzensberger, Hans Magnus, 'Eine Theorie des Tourismus', in *Einzelheiten* (1962), English translation by Gerd Gemünden and Kenn Johnson 'A Theory of Tourism', *New German Critique*, no. 68, Spring/Summer 1996.

Fainstein, Susan S. and David Gladstone, 'Evaluating Urban Tourism', in Dennis R. Judd and Susan S. Fainstein (eds), *The Tourist City*, New Haven, CT: Yale University Press, 1999.

Fan Li, *Tourism and Urban Conservation: Heritage Management in the Old Town of Lijiang, China, 1994–2004, and Future Directions*, dissertation presented in 2004 to the faculty of Architecture, Civil Engineering and Urban Planning at the Brandenburg University of Technology Cottbus-Senftenberg.

Feifer, Maxine, *Going Places: The Ways of the Tourist From the Imperial Rome to the Present Day*, London: MacMillan, 1985.

de Fontenelle, Bernard le Bouyer, *Digression sur les anciens et les modernes* (1688), available at fr.wikisource.org.

Foucault, Michel, *Surveiller et punir: Naissance de la prison* (1975), English translation by Alan Sheridan *Discipline and Punish: The Birth of the Prison*, London: Penguin Books 2019.

Frow, John, 'Tourism and Semiotics of Nostalgia', *October*, vol. 57, Summer 1991.

Gabaccia, Donna R., *We Are What We Eat: Ethnic Food in the Making of Americans*, Cambridge, MA: Harvard University Press, 1998.

Galilei, Galileo, *Dialogo sopra i due massimi sistemi del mondo* (1630), English translation by Sillman Deake, foreword by Albert Einstein, *Dialogue Concerning the Two Chief World Systems* (1953), Berkeley: University of California Press, 1967.

Gauthier, Saskia, Julian Mausbach, Thomas Reisch, Christine Bartsch, 'Suicide Tourism: A Pilot Study of the Swiss Phenomenon', *Journal of Medical Ethics*, vol. 41, no. 8, 2015.

de Gérando, Joseph-Marie, *Considérations sur les diverses méthodes à suivre dans l'observation des peuples sauvages*, Société des observateurs de l'homme (1800), available at gallica.bnf.fr.

Ghosh, Amitav, 'The Imam and the Indian' (1986), in *Incendiary Circumstances: A Chronicle of the Turmoil of Our Times*, New York: Houghton Mifflin Company, 2005.

de Gobineau, Joseph Arthur, 'La vie de voyage' in *Nouvelles Asiatiques* (1876), vol. II, Paris: Pauvert, 1960.

Goethe, Wolfgang, 'Den Vereinigten Staaten', in *Goethes Werke*, book 1, Munich: Verlag C.H. Beck, 1981.

Goetz, Bernice M., 'Jungle Haunt on Amazon Headwaters (Foaming River Led a Lone White Woman to Remote Clearings Where Primitive Indians Peered at Her in Wonder)', *National Geographic*, vol. 102. September 1952.

Goffman, Erving, *The Presentation of Self in Everyday Life*, New York: Doubleday & Company, 1959.

Goody, Jack, *Cooking, Cuisine and Class: A Study in Comparative Sociology*, Cambridge: Cambridge University Press, 1982.

Gorz, André, *Les chemins du paradis: L'agonie du capital* (1983), English translation by Malcom Imrie, *Paths to Paradise: On the Liberation From Work*, London: Pluto, 1985.

Gould, Stephen Jay, *The Flamingo's Smile: Reflections in Natural History*, New York: Norton Press, 1985.

Guerzoni, Guido, *Effetto festival: L'impatto economico dei festival di approfondimento culturale*, La Spezia: Fondazione Carispe, 2008.

Hacking, Ian, *Mad Travellers: Reflections on the Reality of Transient Mental Illnesses*, London: Free Association, 1999.

———, 'On Simpathy: With Other Creatures', *Tijdschrift voor Filosofie*, vol. 63, 2001.

———, 'Humans, Aliens and Autism', *Daedalus*, vol. 138, no. 3, Summer 2009.

Hall, Michael, Liz Sharples (eds), *Food and Wine Festivals and Events Around the World: Development, Management and Markets*, Oxford: Elsevier 2008.

Handler, Richard, Jocelyn Linnekin, 'Tradition, Genuine or Spurious', *Journal of American Folklore*, vol. 97, no. 385, 1984.

Hegel, Georg Wilhelm Friedrich, *Die Phänomenologie des Geistes* (1807), English translation by Terry Pinkard, *Phenomenology of Spirit*, Cambridge: Cambridge University Press, 2018.

Heidegger, Martin, 'Wozu Dichter?' ('What are poets for?'), in *Holzwege* (1950), English translation by Alfred Hofstadter, *Poetry, Language, Thought*, New York: Harper Perennial Modern Classics, 2001.

Heine, Heinrich, *Lutetia* (1854), English translation in *The Works of Heinrich Heine*, vol. 8, London: William Heinemann, 1893.

Hewison, Robert, *The Heritage Industry: Britain in a Climate of Decline*, London: Methuen, 1987.

Hirsch, Fred, *Social Limits to Growth*, Cambridge, MA: Harvard University Press, 1976.

Hirschman, Albert O., *Exit, Voice and Loyalty: Responses to Decline in Firms, Organizations, and States*, Cambridge, MA: Harvard University Press, 1970.

Hobsbawm, Eric, 'Identity Politics and the Left', *New Left Review*, no. 217, May-June 1996.

Hobsbawm, Eric, Terence Ranger, *The Invention of Tradition*, Cambridge: Cambridge University Press, 1983.

Hollis, Martin, 'Is Universalism Ethnocentric?', in Christian Joppke and Steven Lukes (eds), *Multicultural Questions*, Oxford: Oxford University Press, 1999.

Holthaus, Eric, 'Lake Mead Before and After the Epic Drought: A New Study Shows the Colorado River Basin Is Losing Water at a "Shocking" Rate', *Slate* (slate.com), 25 July 2014.

Honigmann, John J., *Foodways in a Muskeg Community: An Anthropological Report on the Attawapiskat Indians*, Northern Coordination and Research Centre, Department of Northern Affairs and National Resources, Ottawa, Canada, 1961.

hooks, bell, *Black Looks: Race and Representation*, Boston: South End Press, 1992.

Horkheimer, Max, Theodor W. Adorno, *Dialektik der Aufklärung: Philosophische Fragmente* (1947), English translation by John Cummings *The Dialectic of Enlightenment*, London and New York: Verso, 1997.

Hoyle, Fred, *The Black Cloud*, New York: Harper, 1957.

Huggan, Graham, *The Postcolonial Exotic: Marketing the Margins*, New York: Routledge, 2001.

Ingelgem, Gaëlle Van, 'Voyage en terre inconnue: Le tourisme culinaire comme objet de distincion sociale', University of Barcelona, European Food History and Culture programme, 2013, available at tenzo.fr.

Innes Shand, Alexander, *Old-Time Travel: Personal Reminiscences of the Continent Forty Years Ago Compared With Experiences of the Present Day*, London: John Murray, 1903.

Ivain, Gilles (pseudonym of Ivan Chtcheglov), 'Formulaire pour un urbanisme nouveau' (1958), in *Internationale situationniste*, Paris: Fayard, 1997.

Jackson, Kenneth T., *Crabgrass Frontier: The Suburbanization of the United States*, Oxford: Oxford University Press, 1985.

Jarcy, Xavier de, *Le Corbusier, un fascisme français*, Paris: Albin Michel, 2015.

Joppke, Christian and Steven Lukes (eds), *Multicultural Questions*, Oxford: Oxford University Press, 1999.

Judd, Dennis R. (ed), *The Infrastructure of Play: Building the Tourist City*, Armonk, New York: M.E. Sharpe Inc., 2003.

Judd, Dennis R., Susan S. Fainstein editors, *The Tourist City*, New Haven, Connecticut: Yale University Press, 1999.

Kracauer, Siegfried, 'Der Reise und die Tanze', first published in *Die Frankfurter Zeitung*, 15 March 1925, reprinted in *Das Ornament der Masse: Strassen in Berlin und Anderswo* (1963), English translation by Thomas Y. Levin *The Mass Ornament: Weimar Essays*, Cambridge, MA: Harvard University Press, 1995

Kukathas, Chandran, *The Liberal Archipelago: A Theory of Diversity and Freedom*, Oxford: Oxford University Press, 2002.

La Bruyère, Jean de, *Charactères* (1688), Paris: Garnier Flammarion, 1965.

Le Corbusier, *La Charte d'Athènes* (1942), English translation by Anthony Eardley, *The Athens Charter*, New York: Grossman Publishers, 1973.

——, 'Manières de penser l'urbanisme', in *L'architecture aujourd'hui*, Paris 1946.

Leed, Eric J., *The Mind of the Traveler: From Gilgamesh to Global Tourism*, New York: Basic Books, 1991.

Lefebvre, Henri, *Critique de la vie quotidienne* (1958), English translation by John Moore and Gregory Elliott, *Critique of Everyday Life*, London and New York: Verso, 2008.

——, 'Le Droit à la ville', *L'homme et la société*, vol. 6, no. 6, 1967, English translation by Eleonore Kofman and Elizabeth Lebas, 'The Right to the City', in *Writings on Cities*, London: Blackwell, 1996.

——, *La vie quotidienne dans le monde modern* (1968), English translation by Sasha Rabinovitch, *Everyday Life in the Modern World*, London: Athlone, 2000.

Lem, Stanislaw, *Solaris* (1961), English translation by Joanna Kilmartin and Steve Cox, *Solaris*, London: Faber & Faber, 1971.

Leopardi, Giacomo, *Zibaldone di pensieri*, Turin: Einaudi, [1977], available at letteraturaitaliana.net.

————, *Discorso sopra lo stato presente dei costumi degl'italiani* (1824 or 1826), Rome: Delotti, 1988.

Lenzen, Manfred et al., 'The Carbon Footprint of Global Tourism', *Nature Climate Change*, vol. 8, May 2018.

Lévi-Strauss, Claude, *Tristes tropiques* (1955), English translation by John Russell, *A World On the Wane*, New York: Criterion Books, 1961.

Löfgren, Orvar, *On Holiday: A History of Vacationing*, Berkeley: University of California Press, 1999.

Lombroso, Cesare, 'I nuovi orizzonti della psichiatria', *Rivista d'Italia*, January 1904, a. VII, vol. 1, no. 1, reprinted in Cesare Lombroso, *Delitto, Genio, Follia: Scritti scelti*, Turin: Bollati Boringhieri, 1995.

Long, Lucy M., 'A Folkloristic Perspective on Eating and Otherness', in *Culinary Tourism*, Lucy M. Long (ed.), Lexington, Kentucky: University Press of Kentucky, 2003.

Lowenthal, David, *The Heritage Crusade and the Spoils of History* (1996), London: Viking, 1997.

Lyons, Howard and Liz Sharples, 'Beer Festivals: A Case Study Approach', in Michael Hall and Liz Sharples (eds), *Food and Wine Festivals and Events Around the World: Development, Management and Markets*, Oxford: Elsevier, 2008.

MacCannell, Dean, *The Tourist: A New Theory of the Leisure Class* (1976), Berkeley: University of California Press, 1999.

MacClancy, Jeremy, *Consuming Culture*: *Why You Eat What You Eat*, London: Chapmans, 1992.

Machiavelli, Niccolò, *Il Principe* (1513), English translation by W. K. Marriott, *The Prince*, London, J.M. Dent & Sons, Ltd., 1908.

Marx, Karl, *Grundrisse der Kritik der politischen Ökonomie* (1857–1858), English translation by Martin Nicolaus, *Grundrisse: Foundations of the Critique of Political Economy*, London: Penguin, 1973.

————, *Das Kapital*: *Kritik der politischen Ökonomie* (1867), English translation by Eden & Cedar Paul, *Capital*, London: J. M. Dent & Sons, 1930; available at Marxists.org.

Marx, Karl and Friedrich Engels, *Die Deutsche Ideologie* (1846), English translation *The German Ideology*, available at Marxists.org.

Martineau, Harriet, 'Modern Tourism: *Eastern Life, Past and Present*', *Blackwood's Edinburgh Magazine*, August 1848, no. 64.

Mattelart, Armand, *L'invention de la communication* (1994), English translation by Susan Emanuel, *The Invention of Communication*, Minneapolis: University of Minnesota Press, 1996.

Meige, Henry, *Etudes sur certains névropathes voyageurs: le juif errant à la Salpétrière* (1893), reprinted as *Le juif errant à la Salpétrière*, Paris: Editions du Nouvel Objet, 1993.

Melton, Jeffrey A., *Mark Twain, Travel Books and Tourism: The Tide of a Great Popular Movement*, Tuscaloosa: University of Alabama Press, 2002.

Michelson, Bruce, 'Mark Twain the Tourist: The Form of the Innocents

Abroad', *American Literature*, vol. 49, no. 3, November 1977.

Moller, Susan Okin with respondents (Joshua Cohen, Matthew Howard, Martha C. Nussbaum, eds), *Is Multiculturalism Bad for Women?* Princeton, New Jersey: Princeton University Press, 1999.

de Montaigne, Michel, *Les Essais* (1588), English translation by Charles Cotton *The Essays of Michel de Montaigne* (1877), available at gutenberg.org.

Moretti, Franco, *The Bourgeois: Between History and Literature*, London and New York: Verso, 2013.

Moskowitz, Marina, 'Zoning the Industrial City: Planners, Commissioners, and Boosters in the 1920s, *Business and Economic History*, vol. 27, no. 2, Winter 1998.

Murphy, Peter E., 'Urban Tourism and Visitor Behaviour', *American Behavioral Scientist*, vol. 36, no. 2, November 1992.

Neumann, Mark, 'Making the Scene: The Poetics and Performances of Displacement at the Grand Canyon', in Simon Coleman, Mike Crang (eds), *Tourism: Between Place and Performance*, New York: Berghahn, 2002.

OECD, *Food and the Tourist Experience*, OECD-Korea Workshop, 2012.

Park, Robert E., Ernest W. Burgess, Roderick D. McKenzie, *The City* (1925), Chicago: University of Chicago Press, 1967.

Pauwels, Louis, Jacques Bergier, *Le matin des magiciens* (1960), English translation by Rollo Myers, *The Morning of the Magicians*, New York: Avon, 1968.

Percy, Walker, *The Message in the Bottle: How Queer Man Is, How Queer Language Is, and What One Has to Do With the Other*, New York: Farrar Strauss, 1975.

Picascia, Stefano, Antonello Romano and Michela Teobaldi, 'The airification of cities: Making sense of the impact of peer to peer short term letting on urban functions and economy', *Proceedings of the Annual Congress of the Association of European Schools of Planning*, Lisbon, 11–14 July 2017.

Pickett, Brent L., 'Multiculturalism, Liberalism and Philosophy', *Polity*, vol. 38, no. 1, January 2006.

Pike, David L., *Subterranean Cities: The World Beneath Paris and London, 1800–1945*, Ithaca, New York: Cornell University Press, 2005.

Plattner, Stuart, 'A Most Ingenious Paradox: The Market for Contemporary Fine Art', *American Anthropologist*, vol. 100, no. 2, 1998.

Pollitt, Katha, 'Whose Culture?' in Susan Moller Okin with respondents (Joshua Cohen, Matthew Howard and Martha C. Nussbaum, eds), *Is Multiculturalism Bad for Women?*, Princeton, New Jersey: Princeton University Press, 1999.

Pomian, Krzysztof, *Des saintes reliques à l'art modern: Venise-Chicago XIIIe–XXe siècle*, Paris: Gallimard, 2003.

Read, Geoffrey, Katrinka Ebbe, 'Post-Earthquake Reconstruction and Urban Heritage Conservation in Lijiang', in Ismail Serageldin, Ephim

Shluger, Joan Martin-Brown (eds), *Historic Cities and Sacred Sites: Cultural Roots for Urban Futures*, Washington: World Bank, 2000.

Richez, Jean-Claude, Léon Strauss, 'Un tempo nuovo per gli operai: le ferie pagate (1930–1960)', in Alain Corbin (ed.), *L'invenzione del tempo libero (1850–1960)*, Bari-Roma: Laterza, 1996.

Ricoeur, Paul, 'Alienation', in *Encyclopædia Universalis*, vol. 1, Paris 1969.

Rimbaud, Arthur, *Poésies* (1869–1873), Paris: Garnier, 1960.

Rousseau, Jean-Jacques, *Du contrat social* (1762), English translation by Quintin Hoare, *Of the Social Contract and Other Political Writings*, London: Penguin, 2012.

Rushdie, Salman, *Imaginary Homelands: Essays and Criticism 1981–1991*, London: Granta Books, 1991.

Ruskin, John, *The Seven Lamps of Architecture* (1849), Boston: Dana Estes & Co, (no date), available at gutenberg.org.

Sacks, Oliver, 'An Anthropologist on Mars', *New Yorker*, 27 December 1993; reprinted in Oliver Sacks, *An Anthropologist on Mars: Seven Paradoxical Tales*, New York: Knopf, 1995.

Sartre, Jean-Paul, *L'être et le néant: Essai d'ontologie phénoménologique* (1943), English translation by Hazel E. Barnes, *Being and Nothingness: An Essay on Phenomenological Ontology*, New York: Washington Square Press, 1956.

Scheper-Hughes, Nancy, 'The Global Traffic in Human Organs', *Current Anthropology*, vol. 41, no. 2, 2000.

Scheper-Hughes, Nancy, Loïc Wacquant (eds), *Commodifying Bodies*, London: Sage, 2002.

Schivelbusch, Wolfgang, *Geschichte der Eisenbahnreisen* (1977), English translation *The Railway Journey: The Industrialization and Perception of Time and Space*, Berkeley: University of California Press, 1986.

Schwartz, Richard B., *Samuel Johnson and the New Science*, Madison, Wisconsin: University of Wisconsin Press, 1971.

Sen, Amartya, 'The Uses and Abuses of Multiculturalism: Chili and Liberty', *The New Republic*, 27 February 2006.

Simmel, Georg, *Die Großstädte und das Geistesleben* (1903), available in English translation, *The Metropolis and Mental Life*, at hu-berlin.de, (unpaginated), adapted by D. Weinstein from Kurt Wolff (trans.) *The Sociology of Georg Simmel*, New York: Free Press, 1950.

Smith, Adam, *An Inquiry into the Nature and Causes of the Wealth of Nations* (1776), London: Methuen & Co. Ltd, 1961.

Smith, Valene L. (ed), *Hosts and Guests: The Anthropology of Tourism* (1977), Philadelphia: University of Pennsylvania Press, 1989.

Smollett, Tobias, *The Expedition of Humphrey Clinker* (1771), available at gutenberg.org.

Sontag, Susan, *On Photography*, New York: Farrar, Straus and Giroux, 1977.

Spirad, Norman, 'Quand la guerre des étoiles devient réalité', *Le Monde diplomatique*, July 1989.

Bibliography

Stendhal, *Rome, Naples et Florence* (1818), English translation, *Rome, Naples and Florence in 1817: Sketches of the present state of society, manners, art, literature, &c. in these celebrated cities*, London: Henry Colburn, 1818.

Stine, G. Harry, 'Travel and Tourism', *Analog Science Fiction/Science Fact*, vol. 111, nos 1–2, January 1991.

Stoczkowski, Wiktor, *Des hommes, des dieux et des extraterrestres: Ethnologie d'une croyance moderne*, Paris: Flammarion, 1999.

Sumption, Jonathan, *Pilgrimage: An Image of Medieval Religion*, Totowa, New Jersey: Bowman & Littlefield, 1975.

Thurot, Jean-Maurice, Gaétane Thurot, 'The ideology of class and tourism. Confronting the discourse of advertising', *Annals of Tourism Research*, no. 10, 1983.

Tuckerman, Henry T., 'Philosophy of Travel', *The United States Democratic Review*, no. 41, 1844.

———, 'Going Abroad', *Putnam's Monthly Magazine*, vol. 11. May 1868.

Tuori, Salla, 'Cooking Nation: Gender Equality and Multiculturalism as Nation-Building Discourses', *European Journal of Women's Studies*, vol. 14, no. 1, February 2007.

Turner, Victor, Edith Turner, *Image and Pilgrimage in Christian Culture: Anthropological Perspectives*, New York: Columbia University Press, 1978.

Twain, Mark, *Innocents Abroad, or The New Pilgrims' Progress* (1869), Ware, Hertfordshire: Wordsworth Classics, 2010.

Unesco, 'WHC-ICOMOS Reactive Monitoring Mission to the Old Town of Lijiang (China), 10–19 January 2008', report presented in Paris on 19 May 2008, available at whc.unesco.org/document/10058.

Urry, John, *The Tourist Gaze* (1990), London: Sage, 2002.

———, 'The Tourist Gaze "Revisited"', *American Behavioral Scientist*, vol. 36, no. 2, November 1992.

———, *Consuming Places*, London: Routledge, 1995.

Vanderbilt, Tom, 'Inside the Mad, Mad World of TripAdvisor', *Outside*, www.outsidconline.com, 13 March 2015.

Venturi, Robert, Denise Scott Brown, Steven Izenour, *Learning From Las Vegas: The Forgotten Symbolism of Architectural Form* (1972), Cambridge, MA: MIT Press, 1977.

Veuillot, Louis, *Les odeurs de Paris*, Paris: Palmé, 1867, available in French at gallica.bnf.fr.

Viollet-le-Duc, Eugène-Emmanuel, 'Restauration', in *Dictionnaire raisonné de l'architecture française du XIe au XVIe siècle*, 10 vol., Paris: Morel et Co., 1854–1868, vol. 8; available at fr.wikisource.org.

Voltaire, *De l'horrible danger de la lecture* (1765), Paris: Folio, 2015, English translation, *On the Horrible Danger of Reading*, available at openedition.org.

Waldron, Arthur, *The Great Wall of China. From History to Myth*, Cambridge: Cambridge University Press, 1990.

Weber, Max, 'Begriff und Kategorien der Stadt' in *Wirtschaft und Gesellschaft. Grundriß der verstehenden Soziologie* (1922), Chapter 9: 'Soziologie der Herrschaft', section 7. For an English version, see Max Weber, *Economy and Society*, Cambridge, MA: Harvard University Press, 2019.

Zhu, Yujie, 'When the Global Meets the Local in Tourism – Cultural Performances in Lijiang as Case Studies', *Journal of China Tourism Research*, vol. 8, no. 3, 2012.

Su, Xiaobo, 'Tourism, Migration and the Politics of Built Heritage in Lijiang China', in Tami Blumenfield, Helaine Silverman (eds), *Cultural Heritage Politics in China*, New York: Springer Science, 2013.

Su, Xiaobo, Peggy Teo, *The Politics of Heritage Tourism in China: A View From Lijiang*, London and New York: Routledge, 2011.

Žižek, Slavoj, 'Multiculturalism, or the Cultural Logic of Multinational Capitalism', *New Left Review*, no. 225, September–October 1997.

Index

abortion travel 60–1
Adams, Douglas 179
Adorno, Theodor 38–9, 43, 57, 142, 168, 173
The Adventures of Tom Sawyer (Twain) 27
Airbnb 79–80, 80n
Aldrin, Buzz 182
d'Alembert, Jean-Baptiste Le Rond 118
alienation 38–9, 40, 143, 167, 171–3, 176, 177, 190; mental 172–3; synonym of modernity 173; good 174–6, 197; and Third Worldism 173
Alps 59, 65; Alpine Club 72; alpinism 72; Club Alpin Français 72; Club Alpino Italiano 72
Amiens (France), cathedral 131; paté d' 205
Andalusia (Spain) 4, 151
Anderson, Benedict 198, 215, 241
Anderson, Perry 98, 241
Angkor Wat (Cambodia) 46, 119, 122
Ancient Astronauts, theory of 184–7
Antonioni, Michelangelo 173
Appadurai, Arjun 209–10, 210n, 216–7, 217n
Arabs, 'picturesque' 46–7
Aristotle 100, 143, 143n, 147
Arizona (US) 32, 59, 128
art as commodity 163–6
Art Basel 166
Ashworth, Gregory John 100, 109
Asia 53, 152, 212; Central 150; Southeast 57, 150; West 220
Athens 28, 56, 65, 67, 120; Acropolis of 2, 56, 93, 133
Augé, Marc 91

aura 44–5, 103, 117; of authenticity 127; commodification of the 163
Austin, John Langshaw 103–4
Australia 69, 199, 212, 233
authentic, the 44, 44n, 116, 126, 127, 170; conceptions of 124; impossible search for 45, 167; market of 102; meaning of 116–7; nostalgia for 74, 169
authenticity 40, 44–5, 102, 116, 119, 124, 167–8, 209–10, 210n; acquired 44; invention of 111; staged 84, 87, 97, 210–11; search for 87, 127, 189; urban 116–17; and the inauthentic 44–5, 117, 127
automobiles 11, 18, 19, 73, 83, 206, 240; city of 78, 135, 136, 154; diffusion of 226, 226n; future of 226

Baartman, Sartjie 25–6
Bacon, Francis 165
Bacon, Francis, Lord Verulam 12–3, 24, 30
Baedeker, Karl 9, 15
Bali, terror attack 6
Bamiyan, Buddha di (Afghanistan), destruction of 7
Bangkok (Thailand) 58, 216
Baraqish (Yemen), damaged citadel 7
Barcelona (Spain) 1, 78; Airbnb effect on 80, 80n; Las Ramblas 80; terror attack (2017) 6–7n
Barthes, Roland 36, 40, 89, 126, 178–9, 241
Bath (England) 58–9, 96, 96n; festival 96
Baudelaire, Charles 49
Baudelot de Dairval, Charles César 15